# EVERY NOSE COUNTS
## Using Metrics in Animal Shelters

J.M. Scarlett, DVM, MPH, PhD

M. Greenberg, DVM

T. Hoshizaki, BVSc

A Maddie's® Guide

Maddie's Fund

# PREFACE

JANET M. SCARLETT: When I mentioned to friends and relatives that I was co-writing a guidebook to help shelters make better use of their data, they got quiet, and the brave ones asked "couldn't you find something (anything) more interesting to write about?" Even shelter people expressed disbelief. After all, shelters already count animals entering, those euthanized and those saved, so what could a whole guidebook to data be about? So, if it seemed so weird to people, what was my motivation?

The answer for me lies in my love of animals, numbers and shelter medicine. My love of animals led me to veterinary medicine; my love of numbers led me to get a graduate degree in epidemiology and work with the National Council on Pet Population and Policy in the mid 1990's; and my love of shelter medicine led me to found the Maddie's® Shelter Medicine Program at Cornell. For those unfamiliar with the discipline of epidemiology, it is the study of events (e.g., diseases, injuries, intakes) that occur in populations and factors associated with those events that may describe, enhance or prevent their occurrence. Epidemiologists examine the frequency (e.g., incidence) and patterns (e.g., age distribution) of these events in order to understand where, when and ultimately, why they occur as they do. With enough understanding, preventive or control measures can be developed.

Numbers are essential to the study of the frequency and patterns of events occurring in populations (e.g., cat or dog populations in shelters). For example, animals that are euthanized must be counted in order to discuss the frequency of euthanasia. Counts alone fail to tell the whole story, however, as they fail to put the number of euthanized animals in the context of all animals entering shelters. To accomplish the latter, counts of both those euthanized and those that could be euthanized must be made to calculate rates. So epidemiologists use numbers and think about them a lot. We also spend time thinking about how numbers can be best used (not misused) for specific purposes.

Since the ultimate goal of epidemiology is to develop sufficient understanding of events so as to diminish the undesirable ones (e.g., disease, euthanasia) or increase the desirable ones (e.g., spay / neuter surgeries, adoptions), epidemiologists think frequently about goals (e.g., decreasing shelter intake), and assessing whether progress towards those goals is being made. As the former Director of the Maddie's® Shelter Medicine Program at Cornell University, my colleagues and I spent time in shelters making recommendations and helping to establish goals and evaluate progress towards them. This time spent in shelters was the ultimate motivation for writing this guidebook, as I began to understand how shelters use their data, and the ways in which they could benefit from using them.

For example, we were often asked for recommendations to diminish the incidence of upper respiratory tract disease (URTD) in shelter cats. When we asked how many and what proportion of cats in the shelter were getting sick, the most frequent answer was "too many." No shelter could provide a data-based quantitative answer (e.g., 30%, 24%, 10%). Without knowing - quantitatively - how much disease was present before recommendations were made, it was impossible to assess whether those recommendations diminished the frequency of disease. Theoretically they should have - but apart from subjective comments such as "there seems to be less disease" or "yes, they were helpful" based on subjective impressions or wishful thinking - without data, we weren't sure if our recommendations worked. We certainly couldn't tell by how much (e.g., a 20% reduction? 50%?).

While many shelters use data to assess progress towards goals, some use inappropriate data to answer their questions. For example, when calculating the return-to-owner rate for stray animals, shelters often use all animals entering the shelter as the denominator, not just the strays. If stray animals are the animals that are eligible to be returned to their owner, why are owner-surrendered or animals in other intake categories included in the denominator of a return-to-owner rate? If all animals entering a shelter are included in the denominator, return-to-owner rate calculations underestimate the effectiveness of a shelter's efforts to reunite strays with their owners. Experiences like those above suggested to me that shelter personnel needed a better understanding of the metrics they were using, and those that they might use.

At the same time that we were pondering writing this guide, increasing numbers of shelters were acquiring software and collecting more data than ever before. Hurley and Newbury (2013) were suggesting innovative strategies to reduce the length of residence of shelter animals and monitor a shelter's capacity for care, both requiring metrics to judge their success. The ASPCA (in light of their belief that data help improve shelter operations and the welfare of animals) created a Shelter Research and Development Department to conduct research. The goal of this research was (and continues to be) to decrease shelter intake, increase the proportion of animals released alive, and improve the welfare of at-risk animals. Peter Marsh (2010) published his book Replacing Myth with Math, in which he emphasized the importance of quality data to dispel myths and underpin decision-making in humane organizations and shelters. More recently (2012), he published another book, Getting to Zero: A Roadmap to Ending Animal Shelter Overpopulation in the United States, in which he emphasized that data play a vital role in ending pet homelessness.

National humane organizations began to facilitate data collection at the national level. For example, The National Federation of Humane Societies, working with a variety of organizations (e.g., HSUS, PetSmart Charities, ASPCA, Maddie's Fund®) and the Asilomar working group developed a Basic Data Matrix to facilitate and standardize the basic data that all shelters should collect. In 2011 discussions began that lead to the creation of Shelter Animals Count (shelteranimalscount.org), a not-for-profit organization, dedicated to creating a national database for shelters and rescue groups. This new tool will be used to monitor national progress towards improving companion animal welfare and to enable shelters to benchmark their progress against other organizations in their state, region and country. The Maddie's Fund also created a searchable database of Community Statistics on their website (Maddie's Fund, 2013), and provides annual and monthly data reporting forms online for shelters to download. Dr. Andrew Rowan, a long-time proponent of high quality data collection (Rowan, 1992), continues to encourage data collection and interpret national trends. These are but a few of the initiatives recognizing the importance of quality data and encouraging shelters to collect and analyze them.

We saw an opportunity to augment these efforts by writing this guide. We believe, as others do, that shelters can improve their operations and enhance the welfare of their animals if they collect, summarize and interpret data wisely. While we strongly support the need for collection of standardized data at the national level, this is not the primary objective of this guide. Rather the intent of this guidebook is to encourage your shelter to collect data regarding your operations, to summarize that data to better understand your animal populations, and to monitor your shelter's progress over time towards improving the welfare of your animals. We sincerely hope that our efforts will be helpful to you.

MICHAEL GREENBERG: My first job as a veterinarian took me to rural upstate New York where

I spent most of my days working on dairy farms treating individual cows and tending to the health of dairy herds. During that first year, my commute took me past a very small animal shelter, the operations of which had just been taken over by a dynamic and energetic group of volunteers. Inspired and humbled by their passion for the homeless dogs and cats in their community, I started to volunteer – stopping on my way home to give vaccines and examine sick animals. Soon, I was working with the shelter director to make modest environmental and programmatic changes to address the health of the whole shelter population. It was not terribly different from my "day job" on the farms – with one exception: with the herds of cows, I could typically ask farmers for a set of numbers, metrics, to get quantitative answers to questions that addressed, "How's the whole farm doing?" This was not the case at the shelter. Sure, we could see how many animals were coming in and how many were leaving alive, but it just seemed there must be a more to the picture. A desire to delve more deeply into these questions ultimately brought me to a Maddie's® Shelter Medicine Program's internship at Cornell University.

During my internship, I spent as much time with scalpel blades and behavior assessments as with spreadsheets and bar graphs: How many foster homes should we recruit for this summer? Should we open a satellite adoption location? – The questions that arose affirmed the need for numbers, so when Dr. Scarlett approached me about writing a guidebook about the use of data in animal shelters, I knew it would be a challenge, but I also knew there was a growing need for one.

I completed my training at Cornell in 2011. Since that time, I have worked clinically and as a consultant for multiple public and private animal shelters throughout the United States. Currently, I serve as the medical director for Pet Community Center in Nashville, TN and collaborate with Nashville's municipal shelter, Metro Animal Care and Control. I enjoy consulting with shelters and rescues of all sizes, and I have a particular interest in helping shelters and low-cost clinics find inexpensive ways to use data and technology to help improve their ef-

ficiency and target their efforts more effectively. No two shelters are the same, and I have been as much a student as a teacher; I have learned from shelter staff and personnel around the country about the ways in which they are already using their data, and I like helping them to find quantitative answers to important questions that remain.

Some people – both in the sheltering world and outside of it – have expressed concern to me that our use of numbers and equations to help manage populations of animals puts us at risk of forgetting that behind these numbers there are real animals with individual personalities, and lives. I have to say, that despite my inclination toward numbers, I also shared that concern when I first started working on this guide. However, over and over, working with shelters that have adopted a data-driven approach, it has been heartening to see that people do keep sight of the fact that these are not just numbers we are talking about; they're pets, loved-ones, lives. With that in mind, we want to make sure that everyone reading this guide also remembers this. A friend of mine has a tattoo that reads, "Every Number is a Wet Nose," – and our book title was influenced by it. My hope is that as you read the pages that follow, you begin (or continue) to develop an appreciation for the value of using data to guide decisions in your shelter. Never forget, however, to take that goofy brindle dog in kennel #12A for a walk and give a much-deserved chin scratch to the purring tuxedo cat in kennel #48B.

Thank you for all you do for the animals that pass through your doors each day, each month, each year. We know from experience, that working in the shelter is emotionally and physically demanding, to say the least. Hopefully this book provides you with a set of tools to help strengthen your efforts to save lives.

TIVA HOSHIZAKI: People become veterinarians for various reasons—I became interested in veterinary medicine because I was a hoarder. Taking care of my colony of approximately 50 rats made me develop a strong interest in infectious diseases, animal husbandry, and animal welfare. Years later, after attending a veterinary college focused on production animals in New Zealand, I realized that what I actually wanted to do was to be a shelter veterinarian.

Returning to the United States, I had to reconcile my imagined version of shelter medicine with the reality: under-resourced facilities, a lack of standard metrics, and rudimentary technology. Luckily, I spent 3 years at Cornell University working with multiple organizations, big and small, to see the scope of sheltering within the United States. My interest in shelter software and herd health was complimented by additional training with Dr. Jan Scarlett–for which I am eternally grateful. Now, I am very fortunate to be able to combine my love of shelter medicine, metrics, and technology.

I hope that this book serves as version 1.0 and that it is one piece of a larger puzzle. As the animal welfare movement in the United States evolves, we must use appropriate population-level metrics in order to make informed decisions. Transparency and honesty within our own organizations and communities are the only way to progress nationally. If shelters and researchers are able to tap into even a small portion of this knowledge, then I believe sheltering is moving towards a very bright future.

# ABOUT THE AUTHORS

**JANET M. SCARLETT, DVM, MPH, PHD**

Dr. Scarlett is a Professor Emerita of Epidemiology, founder and former Director of the Maddie's® Shelter Medicine Program at Cornell University. She received her D.V.M. at Michigan State University, and her M.P.H. and Ph.D. in Epidemiology from the University of Minnesota. During her career she focused on problems of companion animals. In the mid 1990's she became interested in the health and welfare of homeless animals, particularly those in or at risk of being placed in animal shelters. She has worked on shelter-related projects including those involving infectious disease, reasons for relinquishment, effectiveness of spay/neuter programs, and the use of metrics to improve shelter animal welfare. She continues her interest in the use of shelter metrics to improve animal welfare.

**MICHAEL GREENBERG, DVM**

Dr. Greenberg completed his training in shelter medicine with the Maddie's® Shelter Medicine Program at Cornell's College of Veterinary Medicine in 2011.

Since that time, he has worked clinically and as a consultant for multiple public and private animal shelters throughout the United States. Currently, he is the medical director for Pet Community Center in Nashville, TN and collaborates with Nashville's municipal shelter, Metro Animal Care and Control. He enjoys consulting with shelters and rescues of all sizes, and has a particular interest in helping shelters and low-cost clinics find inexpensive ways to use data and technology to help improve their efficiency and more effectively target their efforts. When not in Nashville, he enjoys volunteering with several international organizations participating in spay-neuter and large-scale vaccination campaigns throughout the world.

**TIVA HOSHIZAKI, BVSC**

Dr. Hoshizaki is a 2012 graduate from Massey University, New Zealand. In 2016, she completed three years of advanced training in shelter medicine with the Maddie's® Shelter Medicine Program at Cornell University. She has also completed the Maddie's® Graduate Certificate in Shelter Medicine through the University of Florida. Dr. Hoshizaki's passion lies in the application of technology to improve the welfare of companion animal populations. She currently works as a consultant and outreach veterinarian.

Maddie's Fund

# THANK YOU TO MADDIE'S FUND®

Founded in 1994, Maddie's Fund (www.Maddies-Fund.org) is a family foundation whose mission is to revolutionize the status and well-being of companion animals. Its founders, Workday co-founder Dave Duffield and his wife, Cheryl, have endowed the Foundation with more than $300 million. Through fiscal year 2015-16, the Foundation has awarded more than $187.8 million in grants toward increased community lifesaving, shelter medicine education and pet adoptions across the U.S. The Duffields named Maddie's Fund after their Miniature Schnauzer, Maddie.

Maddie's Fund is the fulfillment of a promise to an inspirational dog, investing its resources to create a no-kill nation where every dog and cat is guaranteed a healthy home or habitat.

# THANKS TO MADDIE

Maddie was a beloved Miniature Schnauzer whose unconditional love, devotion, loyalty and spirit inspired her guardians, Dave and Cheryl Duffield, to start a charitable foundation, Maddie's Fund, in her name.

Dave and Cheryl Duffield founded Maddie's Fund to honor their sweet yet feisty and spirited dog. The fulfillment of a promise made to Maddie while playing together on the living room rug: that if they ever had any money, they would give back to her and her kind so other families could experience the immense joy they have with her. And the rest, as they say, is history, #ThanksToMaddie.

# SPECIAL THANKS FOR FUNDING THIS PROJECT

This project has been a long time in the making. A special thanks to Dr. Laurie Peek and everyone at Maddie's Fund for their patience as we took the long, bumpy road to this book's completion. We hope that the book's contents will help further the mission of Maddie's Fund and help improve the lives of shelter animals.

# ACKNOWLEDGEMENTS

We have skipped over reading the Acknowledgements in books many times in the past. Our experience with this book, however, has given us a deep appreciation of how important the contributions of so many can be to the completion of a project like this.

We extend our sincere thanks to the numerous Executive Directors of Animal Shelters, shelter veterinarians and other shelter colleagues who so graciously gave of their time to read and offer suggestions to parts of this Guide. They include Elizabeth Berliner, Danielle Boes, Pam Burns, Barbara Carr, Kate Hurley, Linda Jacobson, Pam Levin, Anne Marie McPartlin, Christine Petersen, Holly Putnam, Bob Rohde, Margaret Slater, Karen Ward, Emily Weiss, and Matt Witte.

We are indebted to Sue Honig, Jack Robbins and Frohman Lee for their invaluable assistance in extracting data from shelter software and creating initial graphs to display the data.

We are grateful to Dr. Suzanne Nelson for her critical comments and diligent editing as we began this project. Our special thanks are extended to Ms. Karen Fleming for her superb editing of everything at the end.

We cannot thank Ms. Christa Schoenbrodt of Studio Haus enough for her creativity in presenting the information in this book. Thank you for your infinite patience with revisions, new suggestions, and your commitment to seeing this through.

Our special gratitude goes to the animal shelters who graciously agreed to allow us to use their data as examples, and without which this book would not have been possible.

We extend a heartfelt thank you to Dr. Laurie Peek for her encouragement, patience, and advocacy with the Maddie's Fund for the funds that supported the preparation and distribution of this book. We are in your debt and that of everyone at Maddie's Fund.

Lastly, thank you to our families who have endured many tele-discussions and given freely of our time with them to this project. We love you all!

If we have forgotten anyone, please forgive our poor memories. We appreciate all those who helped us along the way.

# TABLE OF CONTENTS

# BEFORE YOU BEGIN

*The overall goal of this guide is to encourage animal shelters to make greater use of the data they already collect to improve the welfare of shelter and community animals.*

As frontline humane organizations in communities, animal shelters should model good animal welfare. Good welfare is achieved through a broad range of strategies, including the collection and analysis of quality data as described in the Association of Shelter Veterinarians' *"Guidelines for Standards of Care in Animal Shelters"* (ASV, 2010), as well as in publications by humane and other organizations (e.g., Clancy & Rowan, 2003), websites (ASPCA Professional 2015a; Maddie's Fund, 2015); webinars (Scarlett, 2012), and articles in the scientific literature (Rowan, 1992; Rowan & Williams, 1987; Wenstrup & Dowidchuk, 1999; Zawistowski et al, 1998).

Many shelters not only provide for the welfare of animals in their care, but also proactively seek to enhance the welfare of community animals through education, subsidized spay / neuter surgery, free-roaming cat TNR, and a myriad of other programs (e.g., behavior hotlines). Collection and regular analyses of quality data are essential to assessing the effectiveness of these community-centered initiatives that cost humane organizations millions of dollars annually across North America (Marsh, 2010). Without good information, it is difficult, if not impossible, to judge whether these monies are being spent wisely or whether programs should be redesigned to enhance their effectiveness.

We refer to summarized data that shelters use to measure how they are doing as **"metrics"**. The word metrics is also used to refer to a standard of measurement or a benchmark. Our use of the terminology will sometimes refer only to summarized data as a measure of what a shelter is doing (e.g., the shelter is accepting 32% of cats that have already been neutered), and at other times as a measure of how a shelter is progressing (e.g., benchmarking its progress over time towards meeting its goals). We have avoided using the terminology "statistics", although in many instances we are reporting statistics (e.g., average length of residence in a shelter). Unfortunately, the word "statistics" makes many people apprehensive because they fear they won't understand the data or comparisons to which it is referring. Or, they confuse the use of the word "statistics" that refers to pieces of summary information with its use to describe a discipline of study (of the techniques used to analyze data). **We want our readers to think of metrics as numbers that enable shelters to measure important**

Photo Credit: Pamela Parton Photography

**information, track that information over time to assess progress and inform decisions.**

The collection of data in shelters has increased dramatically over the past 15 years (as has been true for many organizations throughout the world). In particular, affordable, shelter-dedicated products have become readily available, making data entry and retrieval easier than ever before. Shelters can now choose from a smorgasbord of programs, and thousands of shelters utilize shelter-dedicated software as a result. Petfinder maintains a list of software providers on their website (https://pro.petfinder.com/shelter-software-guide/) with links to each company's website. Shelters seeking to computerize their data must carefully research current choices and choose the provider that best meets their needs and budget.

Data collection and analysis requires use of resources – funds for software, computers, computer maintenance, staff training, data entry and analysis. Despite a significant investment of time and money, however, most shelters underutilize the information they collect. Underutilization occurs for numerous reasons such as lack of time, lack of expertise, difficulty in accessing the necessary information, difficulty in identifying the most pertinent questions to ask, and failing to understand the impact that data and data analysis could have on shelter operations.

# TIE YOUR QUESTIONS TO SHELTER GOALS

This guide was written to encourage shelters to utilize their data more extensively by linking data collection and analysis to the achievement of their Mission and related animal welfare goals. Shelters invest many resources toward collecting and storing information and this investment should maximally benefit each shelter. Therefore, we strongly encourage shelters to use their data to assist in setting goals and evaluating progress towards their achievement.

# APPROACH USED IN THIS GUIDE

We generated a list of objectives and goals common to many shelters before writing this guide. The goals described in each chapter are somewhat arbitrarily grouped and the questions posed could often be posed in multiple sections. We identified questions that we think are of interest to most shelters, recognizing that others in the humane and shelter medicine communities may have different opinions. It is not our intention to impose our thoughts on others, but rather to *share our thoughts* in hopes of stimulating interest in the collection, management, analyses and interpretation of data in shelters that will improve the welfare of the animals about whom we all care.

We use summary data from real shelters to answer those questions, present that information in tables and graphs, and offer our interpretations of the data. This approach is followed throughout the book in an attempt to provide clear examples for data use in your shelter. We categorized our questions into three groups: *Strongly Recommended, Recommended*, and *For Your Consideration*. For us, *Strongly Recommended* questions are those that relate to metrics that (in our opinion) all shelters should be tracking. *Recommended* questions focus more on specific information and subtleties that may or may not be a priority for your shelter at this time. The questions *For Your Consideration* include metrics we find helpful, and they are offered as ideas for you to consider. We categorized questions based on our experience, but our questions may not be of interest to all shelters and our list is not exhaustive. **Ask questions of your shelter's data and utilize that information in ways that are most helpful to your shelter!**

This guide is divided into three general areas: 1) intakes, 2) animal management and health within the shelter, and 3) outcomes (Figure 1.1). Shelters generally have objectives relating to each of these areas: they want to reduce intake of homeless animals from their community, provide for the best animal welfare possible while in the shelter, and

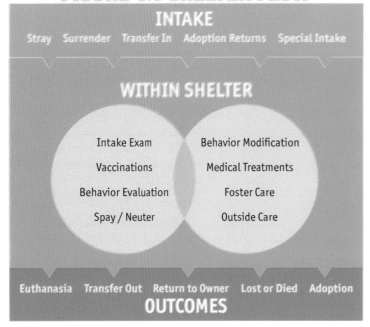

## FIGURE 1.1 SHELTER FLOW

**INTAKE**

Stray    Surrender    Transfer In    Adoption Returns    Special Intake

**WITHIN SHELTER**

Intake Exam      Behavior Modification

Vaccinations      Medical Treatments

Behavior Evaluation      Foster Care

Spay / Neuter      Outside Care

Euthanasia    Transfer Out    Return to Owner    Lost or Died    Adoption

**OUTCOMES**

Shelters can enhance communication with their constituencies and granting agencies using quality data. Data, appropriately analyzed and presented, can be a persuasive element in requests for program funding from Boards of Directors, prospective donors, and granting agencies. Demonstrating need through numbers is a time-tested strategy to attract funding. Numbers can also help improve communication with your community, documenting the breadth and depth of your efforts to enhance animal well-being in the community. They are also critical to monitoring the success of shelter programs designed to achieve welfare-related goals (e.g., reducing the intake of kittens or increasing returns-to-owners). Accurate and timely data can suggest new goals when problems are documented and brought to light. Good data sometimes serve to dispel commonly accepted dogma (e.g., colony housing of cats results in a higher incidence of upper respiratory tract disease compared to individual housing), or uncover circumstances where commonly accepted practices do not work as predicted.

Good animal welfare cannot be achieved without physical and mental (or behavioral) health. These cannot be achieved in shelters without a sound, comprehensive population health program that actively promotes individual and population-level health. Collection, maintenance, periodic analysis and dissemination of health-related data are essential components of a comprehensive population health program. Without data, population health can, at best, be described with vague words (e.g., excellent, good, fair) based on subjective impressions that are difficult to define and compare across populations or over time. Reviews of the components of good population health programs can be found in a wide variety of sources (Hurley, 2004, Newbury & Hurley, 2013, Cannas da Silva et al, 2006).

strive to release alive as many animals as possible. In the coming chapters we will return to Figure 1.1, focusing on each of these areas, their objectives, and some common specific goals.

# WHY IS DATA COLLECTION AND ANALYSIS OF DATA IMPORTANT TO ANIMAL SHELTERS?

We cannot overstate the value of quality data collection and analysis. Metrics can help your shelter address a variety of issues, including those related to goal-setting, program evaluation, enhanced communication with constituencies, grant writing, assessment of the effectiveness of protocols, enhancement of animal welfare, financial accountability, and the assessment of return on investment.

Good animal welfare is also good for the business of animal sheltering. Regardless of whether shelters view themselves as such, they are a type of business. Animal sheltering requires staff, facilities, managers, management of inventory, budgets, fiscal responsibility, and other attributes of any business. As a business, shelters need to collect and utilize data to manage their resources wisely and improve their operations while adhering to their humane mission. Shelters have inventory (e.g., animals) to market and place, customers to attract, and other sources of pets to compete with, all while modeling good animal welfare. They must, therefore, be able to track their animals, assess their health, evaluate their programs, and advertise their successes. To do these well, quality information and data analyses are required.

# FOCUS OF THIS GUIDE

Shelters can and do collect data regarding a myriad of issues (e.g., revenue, expenditures, number of grants received). **This guide focuses on data relating directly to animals, including traditional intake and outcome numbers, information impacting utilization of housing space, animal movement within the shelter and the physical health of shelter animals.** You may notice that we did not include chapters on behavioral health, animal control operations, or the economics of preventive programs and animal care. These issues were omitted, not because we don't recognize their importance, but because we lacked real data to illustrate their use and / or we felt unqualified to address them. We have also limited our examples to those pertaining to dogs and cats because they are the most common species in shelters and because many of the questions and analyses suggested can be applied to other species in shelters as well.

The objective of this guide is to help individual shelters use their data more effectively to improve the health and welfare of their animals. The objective is *not* to standardize data collection across North American shelters or to develop a national database that tracks progress towards diminishing national intake and euthanasia. Other organizations (e.g., Shelter Animals Count, Maddie's Fund) are working towards these goals and we support their efforts.

# HISTORICAL USE OF SHELTER DATA

Several seminal articles in the 1970's and 1980's (Gavin, 1989; Rowan & Williams, 1987; Rowan, 1992) bemoaned the lack of information regarding pet population dynamics and, in particular, data pertaining to homeless animal populations and euthanasia of animals within them. These authors questioned the expenditure of millions of dollars on shelter programs (e.g., spay / neuter surgery) with few, if any, evaluations of the effectiveness of those programs. They uniformly called for more data collection and analysis such that the sheltering community could gauge its progress in reducing pet homelessness and euthanasia, and direct the use of its resources more wisely.

Some animal shelters have collected data and used them to evaluate their programs for many years. Zawistowski et al (1998) published summarized data from the American Society for the Prevention of Cruelty to Animals (ASPCA) tracking the numbers of euthanasias performed in the largest shelters in New York City between 1895 and 1994, the year when the ASPCA ceased managing these organizations. Barbara Carr, former Executive Director of the Erie County SPCA, had staff bring appropriate metrics to staff meetings and frequently searched for answers to questions relating to the shelter (e.g., where should the shelter focus its spay / neuter efforts?) by looking at her data. Bob Rhode and his colleagues at the Denver Dumb Friend's League have long used data to enhance management of their animals and to reduce community animal homelessness.

Many shelters have collected basic information (e.g., relating to intake and outcomes) for years, but only recently expanded their data collection to include a myriad of other pieces of information with

## TABLE 1.1 DATA FREQUENTLY USED

### TYPE OF DATA: INTAKE

#### USES

Monitoring the number and percentage of entering animals
> *By species, breed, age, etc.*

Characterizing animals
> *By source (e.g., stray, owner surrender, cruelty case)*
> *By program (e.g., TNR, public spay/neuter)*
> *By jurisdiction (e.g., address)*
> *By Asilomar or medical status*

Reuniting lost animals with their owners

Grant writing

### TYPE OF DATA: WITHIN SHELTER

#### USES

Characterizing animals
> *By location in the organization (e.g., ward, offsite location, foster care)*

Helping prospective adopters find an animal

Counting spay/neuter surgeries

Monitoring daily census and length of stay

### TYPE OF DATA: OUTCOME

#### USES

Monitoring the number and rates of euthanasia, live releases, adoptions, etc. over time

Tallying dispositions
> *By Asilomar or medical status*

the enhanced availability of affordable computer software programs. Some of these shelters collect, but never use much of the new data. Still others don't collect or analyze any data routinely.

# EXPANDING THE DATA YOU USE

In our experience, shelters commonly use their animal-related data for many of the reasons listed in Table 1.1.

These analyses are useful and necessary, but represent a small percentage of data uses that could benefit shelters. Some of the data in Table 1.1 are used to track trends over time (e.g., intake, number of euthanasias or spay/neuter surgeries), while others relate to finding and managing individual animals (e.g., locating the young border collie admitted 2 days ago, accepting a returned adoption). We make suggestions for other uses of data in Table 1.2.

Obviously, this list is not exhaustive, and many shelters already evaluate metrics relating to these suggestions. We encourage each shelter to carefully consider its objectives and goals as a first step (see Chapter 2 for more details). **Once clear goals have been set, consider the metrics your shelter needs to evaluate progress towards its goals and ensure that those data are being collected and monitored.**

# SHELTER METRICS, BIOLOGY AND PARTITIONING SHELTER DATA

Analyzing data for all species combined is rarely helpful and is often misleading. Most questions are better posed separately for dogs, cats, and other species since species differ widely on a myriad of important needs and characteristics. Lumping information about all species together can mask the many differences and provide nonsensical answers.

Animal characteristics (e.g., age, neuter status at entry, breed), environmental factors that influence exposures (e.g., colony vs. non-colony housing) and time (e.g., season) can also profoundly affect the answers to common goal-related questions and their interpretation. In this book, we frequently suggest separating data *by* these types of factors and evaluating them separately. We use terminology such as assess the "annual intake *by* species". This means examine the annual intake numbers for dogs, cats, and other species separately. Most commonly, we recommend grouping data *by* species, age group, intake-type (e.g., stray, owner-surrender), and time-frame (e.g. by month). Whenever you are looking at metrics, get into the habit of grouping data, as it will usually provide more refined and accurate answers to questions of interest.

**COLLECTING AND RECORDING ANIMAL AGE** The age of animals is one of the most important descriptors of shelter animals for many reasons, including medical management and husbandry, marketing, and disease risk. We use age categories rather than age (e.g., 4, 5) for most of our calculations (and graphs) because actual ages are difficult to establish for the majority of shelter animals. It is usually easier (and more accurate) to estimate the age group to which an animal belongs than to accurately assess his precise age. Also, in our experience the variable "age", captured as one number in shelter databases, is usually associated with a high proportion of missing data. A disadvantage of using the variable "age group" for some questions, however, is that it is usually "fixed" at the age group of the animal when she enters the shelter. At least one software package allows the entry of birthdate or assigns a birthdate if a specific age (e.g., 4 years old) is known and entered. Once a date is assigned, the program uses that birthdate to calculate the animal's age for subsequent "events" (e.g., neuter, adoption) experienced by the animal over time. When the initial age is estimated (or known) within approximately one year, assigning an arbitrary date of birth is not unreasonable. When the estimate of age could be off by several years, then assigning an age group is

# TABLE 1.2 SUGGESTIONS FOR OTHER USES OF DATA

## TYPE OF DATA: INTAKE

### USES

Tracking the origin of entering animals (e.g. by zip code and GPS coordinates)

Monitoring the prevalance of specific diseases at intake (e.g., heartworm infection, FeLV, FIV)

Characterizing animals at entry

| | |
|---|---|
| *By their neuter status* | *By their behaviorial status* |
| *By their medical status* | *By those wearing identification* |

## TYPE OF DATA: WITHIN SHELTER

### USES

Calculating average time to final dispositions

Calculating time from intake to common "events"(e.g., time to vaccination, first examination)

Tracking shelter capacity (animal and staff) overall and by area

Monitoring disease rates (e.g., URI, kennel cough)

Monitoring trends in all of the above over time

Assessing the effectiveness of changes in protocols for reducing disease

Characterizing and monitoring surgical complication rates

Scheduling recurring events (e.g., dewormings, vaccinations)

## TYPE OF DATA: OUTCOMES

### USES

Calculating probabilities of experiencing various dispositions for animals entering the shelter  (e.g., euthanasia, death, adoption)

Monitoring numbers (and proportions) of euthanasias

*By reasons, age group, source of animals*

more accurate. At least one software provider plans to allow the variable "age group" to be updated as the animal ages in the shelter which will facilitate the use of this variable for events happening subsequent to entry.

Using updated ages or age groupings for animals is important when planning for appropriate housing and staffing over time and for other considerations discussed later in the book. Always record age-related data as accurately and completely as possible and understand how your software provider manages those pieces of information in your database (if you use software). If you don't use software, think carefully about the age information in your records when you use that data.

## QUALITY OF DATA

The old adage of "garbage in / garbage out" applies to any information that shelters collect and plan to use to answer important questions. What sense does it make to collect poor quality data? It wastes precious resources. We believe that shelters should collect quality information relating to those questions that are of interest to them or that facilitate their operations. Data collection should not be busy work. Either collect quality data that are helpful to your organization and make use of them, or don't bother collecting that type of data at all. It is better to collect a small amount of high quality data than a lot of suspicious or mediocre data. Collect what you need and do it well (and convey that importance to your staff).

## HOW CAN SHELTERS IMPROVE THE QUALITY OF THEIR DATA?

| STRATEGIES TO COLLECT QUALITY DATA |
| --- |
| *Standardize the definitions of commonly used variables (e.g., age, source)* |
| *Have the most knowledgeable person assess and enter variables whenever possible* |
| *Record the information at the time of the assessment* |
| *Train staff and hold them accountable for quality data and their entry* |
| *Reward excellent data collection* |
| *Address errors in data collection and entry promptly* |
| *Monitor data regularly and provide constituents with regular feedback* |

**STANDARDIZE THE DEFINITIONS OF COMMONLY USED VARIABLES** Commonly used variables (e.g., age, health status) should be clearly defined. For example, the categories for "age group" are determined by individual shelters and many use general terms such as "unweaned," "juvenile," "young adult," or "senior'. If your shelter uses terms like these, we strongly recommend that they be changed to more specific categories. For example, "unweaned" kittens might be redefined as " ≤ 4 weeks old" and other age groups also defined with quantitative age boundaries. Also, the age groups should not be overlapping as staff will be confused as to where to put an animal whose age appears in two categories. For example, where should an 8 year old dog be put if the age groupings are 2-8 years and 8-12 years? By specifying unique age ranges for each category, the guesswork of staff members is reduced and the clarity of communicating age-related data is enhanced. Everyone assessing or recording variables should understand the definitions of each variable category used by their shelter. If a shelter is using software, these definitions are ideally defined in drop-down menus.

Another consideration for "age group" categories is using the fewest number of categories that still meet the shelter's needs. In the Medical chapter we discuss disease-related metrics that rely heavily on age groups, so it is important to have biologically relevant age categories. If you choose to change your current age categories, try to lump ones you have, rather than beginning with a whole new set. However, if your categories are overlapping or do not meet your needs, then it is better to re-categorize now than to continue to use dysfunctional categories into the future.

Whether the descriptor is age or some other potentially subjective variable (e.g., disease is mild, moderate, severe), the categories used should be defined to assist staff members recording the information, help standardize the use of the terms, and facilitate interpretation of the data.

**HAVE THE MOST KNOWLEDGEABLE PERSON ASSESS VARIABLES WHENEVER POSSIBLE** Going back to the example of age: for most animals, the most trustworthy source of age assessment will be the person physically examining that animal (e.g., veterinarian, veterinary technician, trained examiner). If the trained examiner disagrees with owner-supplied information, then previous age information should be corrected and the examiner's age assessment should be entered (with the possible exception of the owner who provides a birthdate or is sure of the age).

**RECORD THE INFORMATION AT THE TIME OF ASSESSMENT** Ideally the person assessing information should also be the person to record the data at the time of assessment. This generally reduces the likelihood of a data entry error because of illegible writing, entry in the midst of many entries, or failure of memory. Entry by the assessor, particularly at the time an animal is being examined or treated, is often difficult. Some shelters have invested in technology to facilitate data entry at the point-of-care. As technology advances and becomes available at a reasonable cost, point-of-care entry will become commonplace.

**TRAIN STAFF AND HOLD THEM ACCOUNTABLE FOR QUALITY DATA** If a shelter wants quality information, staff members must be trained and held accountable for entering complete and accurate data. Collection of quality data should be part of the job description for any staff member (or volunteer) that is expected to record data for the shelter. Even experienced people can drift away from ideal practices. This is not deliberate. People often identify shortcuts and time-savers and forget in the process the rationale for some of the original safeguards. Regularly scheduled re-training is important for all aspects of staff jobs, including data collection and recording.

**REWARD EXCELLENT DATA COLLECTION** Periodic performance reviews must include a discussion of the diligence with which a staff member approaches data collection. Most people respond favorably to tangible rewards for work well done. If the shelter values and uses data, the importance of quality must be transmitted to staff members and they must be rewarded when they comply.

**ADDRESS ERRORS IN DATA COLLECTION AND ENTRY PROMPTLY** When data are used routinely, errors in data collection and entry are more likely to become apparent. These errors must be shared with those collecting the data, not to penalize them, but rather to address the situation that led to the error. Data errors are often mistakes, but can also reflect a misconception or inattention to detail. Also, the data should be corrected in the medical record, software or within other means of tracking (e.g., spreadsheet) at the time errors are detected.

**MONITOR DATA REGULARLY AND PROVIDE CONSTITUENTS WITH REGULAR FEEDBACK** Much of the data collected by shelters is time sensitive, and therefore should be summarized and presented to staff in a timely manner. For example, data regarding the incidence of upper respiratory tract infections should be tracked frequently and regularly if the shelter hopes to detect an outbreak early in its course and take timely control actions. Similarly, if a shelter switches to a new disinfectant, feedback as to whether it is lowering disease rates or (heaven forbid) raising them, should be known quickly, not six months later.

If data evaluation becomes routine, reporting the results to animal care staff should also become routine. If disease rates fall, then staff should be rewarded and encouraged to maintain their good work. If disease rates rise, then the reason(s) must be found quickly in order to address the problem(s) leading to the increase. *Prompt feedback to staff has the added benefit of reinforcing the need for quality data.*

**NOTE:** We have encountered staff members that resist collecting data by arguing that it contains errors. Almost all data are imperfect – including data from the U.S. Census Bureau, Department of Motor Vehicles, forensic databases, or our Christmas lists – but they are incredibly useful in our society. The same is true for animal shelters. While all of the suggestions listed above will help to maximize data quality, data need not be perfect to be useful.

# WHO SHOULD MONITOR THE DATA?

Too often only the executive director or shelter manager reviews data. The people whose area or animals will be most profoundly affected by particular data can be taught to monitor that data. They can most quickly detect data quality issues and track changes,

address them (when possible) and alert the administration. This can encourage good data collection habits, and engender excitement for the benefits of data collection among all staff members. It also spreads out the work, such that one or two people are not left with the whole task of data analysis.

# FORMULATING AND CLARIFYING QUESTIONS:
## IT'S ALL ABOUT THE QUESTION(S) YOU WANT TO ANSWER

Using data effectively begins with asking the "right" questions. By "right" we mean the specific questions your shelter would like to answer. This sounds obvious, but specifying the questions of interest to your shelter is often challenging - which is why we have made suggestions throughout the book.

For example, if your shelter wants to know whether cat intake is declining in your county as a consequence of its community-based spay / neuter surgery program, the questions asked must specify the intake groups and time periods relevant to the question. For example, a question might ask "Is the intake of owner-surrendered and stray cats from the community decreasing?", (excluding cats surrendered from out-of-county or transferred -in). Similarly, if a shelter wants to assess the impact of its new S/N program, the question posed must pertain to a period of time that could reasonably be influenced by the program. The question might be "Is the intake of owner-surrendered and stray cats from the community beginning to decrease during the 6 year period following initiation of the program?" giving the program (depending on its magnitude) an opportunity to affect sufficient numbers of cats such that an effect on intake can be detected. Notice also that it will be important to assess intake for a period (e.g., 5 year period) preceding the S/N program in order to assess the usual variability in intake numbers and detect intake trends that might not reflect the effectiveness of the program.

We cannot overemphasize the importance of framing your questions clearly and specifying precisely the nature of groups (e.g., age, geographic, source) and time frames that are pertinent to each question. This process, in our experience, is dependent on the time and effort your shelter devotes to thinking about its questions, staff understanding of the nature of your data, and sometimes on how your software processes or reports them. As with most human endeavors, your shelter will get better at posing good questions with practice.

# WHO COULD BENEFIT FROM THIS GUIDE?

The metrics discussed in this Guide pertain principally to brick and mortar organizations that provide care for homeless animals and have programs to reduce homelessness in their community. The principles and many of the metrics, however, have application to rescue groups, spay/neuter clinics of all types, pet shops, and breeders caring for large numbers of companion animals. Even the brick and mortar organizations vary

considerably in their missions and specific goals, and the data collected by each should be tailored to address questions specific to each of them.

# THE CHALLENGES OF WRITING A GUIDE BOOK ABOUT THE USE OF METRICS

**HOW TO ACCESS DATA** *The biggest challenge we faced as authors of this book was recognizing that we were advocating for the use of data and metrics that may not be readily available/accessible to many shelters today.* We imagine that this will be as frustrating to you as it was to us. If your shelter does not currently collect some of the data we suggest, we hope that this book will assist you in arguing that it should. If your shelter collects the data you need, but cannot currently access them easily (e.g., they are in individual paper records), we encourage you to use the book to argue that the data be computerized in a manner that enables them to be summarized and used. If your shelter uses software, we encourage you to request that your software provider make the data you need easily available to you from their software.

Since numerous companies produce shelter software programs that vary in their capabilities to collect and retrieve data, we have outlined the nature of the data needed to address the questions we suggest. We leave the means of collection and retrieval to individual software companies. Also, some software packages currently have the capability of generating charts that we believe enhance people's ability to understand their data. If your software does not have this capability, we strongly recommend that you request that their software company incorporate it.

**DISPLAYING YOUR DATA** We recognize that the means by which people choose to display their summarized data can vary. The graphs and tables that we present are not the only means to display information, and we encourage you to choose display methods that best suit your shelter's needs. We do believe strongly that simplicity and clarity of understanding should always take precedence over "flashy", but confusing or unintelligible presentations. In Appendix 2 we discuss considerations for the generation of tables and charts and provide references that you can consult when making decisions about data display.

The data and the majority of examples used in this manual were taken from real shelters. In some instances we modified the data somewhat to preserve the anonymity of the contributing shelters. Rarely, we manufactured data because our contributing shelters didn't collect that data, or we couldn't retrieve them. We believe that everything we suggest is possible if shelters see the value in collecting the data and software companies are willing to assist shelters to retrieve the information in a form that is most useful to them. The charts in this guide were initially generated in a spread sheet after importing data from a dedicated shelter software company. They were then stylized for publication. Hand-entered data can also be graphed using a spread sheet or graphed using dedicated graphing programs.

# SUMMARY

**Our motivation in writing this manual is to create a widely accessible reference that helps shelter staff members understand, analyze, and convey the meaning of their data.** We encourage your organization to identify explicit shelter goals using this Guide as a resource. Write down those goals, prioritize them, identify and regularly analyze the data needed to track progress toward their achievement. Make plans to collect and retrieve the data you need (if you don't already), and after their analysis, disseminate the results to relevant constituents.

This Guide is a work in progress, and we recognize that some sections may be controversial. We welcome your feedback and suspect that the discussion that ensues may change our recommendations in the future. We believe strongly that data collection, analysis and regular presentation should form an integral and routine part of shelter operations. Many shelters already collect large amounts of data and our goal is to help them put that data to greater use. We believe that by collecting quality data and performing appropriate analyses, your shelter will improve its operations, as well as enhance the welfare of shelter and community animals. We hope that this Guide meets these goals and serves you well.

# GOALS AND METRICS

*"If you don't know where you are going, any road will get you there." – Lewis Carroll*, Alice in Wonderland

## VALUE OF GOALS

Much has been written about the value of organizational goals (Conrad, 2012; Davis, n.d.; Cothran & Wysocki, n.d.; Haughey, 2012; Locke et al, 1990) and this chapter is based on these references. Successful for-profit and not-for-profit organizations set goals, both to increase profits and services offered, but also to assure progress consistent with the Mission and to increase consumer confidence. When shelters have specific goals, numerous benefits accrue. Goals provide direction, focus resources, clarify decision-making, motivate staff, and help to reinforce the importance of the Mission of the organization. Even the process of setting goals forces staff to stop and take time-out from daily duties, think, discuss, and plan to reach the priorities of the shelter. Once goals are formulated, the use of metrics is one means of measuring whether the goals have been reached (which is why we have included the topic of Goals in this guidebook).

Shelters have always set goals, particularly relating to fund-raising, capital campaigns, staff hiring and shelter maintenance. Fewer have explicit goals relating to continued improvement of animal health and welfare (which is our focus). Shelters today are operating in a rapidly changing environment. With the ever-increasing availability of information and ideas to enhance animal health and welfare, shelters must consciously select and prioritize those ideas that they will implement. Reserving time to engage staff in planning, implementation and evaluation of changes that lead to improved animal health and welfare is critical to the Mission of shelters.

The intent of this chapter is to emphasize the value of goal-setting and planning in the shelter environment, to encourage shelters to set explicit goals for animal health and welfare, and when appropriate, to use their data to monitor progress towards achievement of those goals.

## TERMINOLOGY

Before proceeding, several terms require clarification to enhance communication. We use the following words and definitions in this chapter, recognizing that other resources may use these terms differently (Davis, 1996).

**SHELTER MISSION:** The Mission statement of a shelter describes why it exists. It describes what the shelter is working to accomplish, how it hopes to achieve it, and the core values by which the organization will operate. Reviewing the Mission should precede goal writing to ensure that goals are in-line with the shelter's Mission.

**OBJECTIVES:** Objectives usually flow from the Mission statement and state in broad terms what a shelter wishes to accomplish. Objectives generally are lofty aspirations that may take many years to accomplish or may never be completely achieved. For example, a shelter might have an objective of eliminating animal intake from the community, realizing that this might take years or never be achieved. Many shelters develop a few broad objectives accompanied by many sub-objectives.

**STRATEGIES:** Strategies describe in general terms how the objectives will be achieved. They often precede the formulation of specific goals. For example, strategies for reducing shelter intake from the community might include a spay/neuter program for low-income residents, a TNR program for free-roaming cats, and a behavior hotline to assist residents with behavioral issues that might lead to relinquishment. Multiple strategies are usually associated with any objective.

**GOALS:** Goals, on the other hand, are very specific, actionable steps tied to an objective that are designed to make progress towards achievement of that objective. For example, a goal related to the strategy of performing S/N surgeries in the community to reduce shelter cat intake might be "the shelter will double the number of owned cat surgeries in two trailer parks (from which multiple cats come annually) over the next 6 months." **Goals are the steps associated with achieving an objective.**

Photo Credit: Penny Adams

**ACTION PLANS:** Action plans describe in detail how the goal will be achieved. Such plans are most effective if they include a prioritized checklist of how the goal will be achieved. The action plan serves as a roadmap to the achievement of the goal.

Each of these components can have subcomponents and are open to revision if the original goals or plans fail to work as predicted.

# GUIDELINES FOR SETTING GOALS

Many organizations use the pneumonic acronym S.M.A.R.T. to remind them that goals should be specific, measureable, attainable, relevant and time-bounded (Locke et al, 1990; Haughey, 2014). Variations on the meaning of the last three letters in the acronym exist in the literature, and some authors have added additional concepts. Regardless of which interpretation you use, the concepts are helpful.

**SPECIFIC:** When writing a goal, always include what is to be achieved, by whom, where and by when the goal is to be reached. Sometimes "why" the goal is important is added. A specific goal could be "The shelter's live release rate for cats will be increased by staff and volunteers by at least 5% during the next calendar year" or "Daily shelter rounds will be implemented by management and the medical staff by 1 week from today."

**MEASURABLE:** A goal must lend itself to some means of assessment as to whether it was achieved. Achievement of some goals can be measured quantitatively while others can be qualitatively assessed. Both of the goals mentioned above have measureable outcomes – one can be measured with metrics (e.g., % increase in Live Release) and the other can be observed to have happened or not.

**ATTAINABLE (OR ACHIEVABLE):** This may seem obvious, but shelters should not set goals that are not possible to achieve in a finite time period. For example, as much as a shelter may want to drop its intake of strays to zero in the next year, this is not realistic. Also, those that will implement the plan to achieve a goal must believe that it is possible, or they are unlikely to take it seriously. That said, goals should not be too easily achieved, as goals that are perceived to be trivial are also often not taken seriously by staff. More arduous goals are frequently associated with greater progress by the organization.

**RELEVANT:** Every goal should relate in some way to the objectives of the shelter. It is tempting to write a goal that will be popular and easy to achieve to guarantee its success. If it does not relate to what the shelter is striving to accomplish, however, it is distracting and retards progress towards the true objectives. For example, the goals mentioned above are relevant to the shelter's objectives of saving lives and of providing for the best welfare for the animals in their care.

**TIME-BASED (OR TIME BOUNDED):** Always put a realistic time deadline on a goal. A deadline helps to ensure that staff members do not procrastinate, and that there is a point at which the shelter will assess progress made towards fulfilling the goal. Goals should be crafted such that they can be achieved in a relatively short time frame. It is usually easier to achieve goals that have an end point in the near future than those that may take years to attain. As a guideline, most goals should take a year or less. A relatively short time period pushes a shelter to assess progress towards attainment of a goal frequently.

# WRITING GOALS

Goals must be put in written form to preserve their content, enhance clarity and communication, and minimize conflict. It is imperative that the goal be clearly understood by everyone involved throughout the period allocated for its achievement (Conrad, 2012). In a constantly changing and challenging environment (such as is found in animal shelters), people can forget the goal's original intent or the goal may get modified over time. If a goal is modified, the change and reasons for the change must also be recorded and shared with those involved.

# WHO SETS THE GOALS?

Management staff and others that will be involved in the implementation of plans should be involved in the process of formulating specific goals (Table 2.1). When people provide input and understand the process by which a goal was crafted, they are more likely to understand and be motivated to help achieve it.

In order to facilitate this process, time must be set aside for discussions by all involved. These discussions must be conducted in a manner that ensures everyone has an opportunity for input, and understands the process by which the goal will be finalized. Laying out the process for goal setting (e.g., how input will be solicited, who makes the final decision) must be clear from the outset of discussions.

Photo Credit: Penny Adams

# PROCESS OF GOAL-SETTING

## TABLE 2.1 STEPS TO GOAL-SETTING

Setting and prioritizing goals takes time. The process of setting goals, developing action plans, and reviewing progress made towards goals should be ongoing (during regularly scheduled meetings). The list below is provided to help initiate the process. Once staff members understand and become accustomed to the process, it becomes second nature. With time, a list of successfully achieved goals will accumulate that have benefited the organization, further motivating the staff to repeat the process (Davis, 1996, Conrad 2014).

**1** *Brainstorm and record objectives relating to animal health and welfare that flow from the Mission statement of your shelter. This initial list should be fairly general and encompass as many objectives relating to animal health and welfare as possible.*

**2** *Once a list is created and agreed upon, prioritize the list, understanding that you may choose to work on several objectives simultaneously.*

**3** *Think carefully about specific goals (that are SMART) associated with each of the prioritized objectives. Prioritize these goals.*

**4** *Begin work on explicitly drafting those goals that have high priority and that meet the litmus test of being SMART.*

**5** *Develop action plans for the goals that are of highest priority. Don't try to tackle too many goals at one time. It is far better to sequentially formulate and achieve goals than to attempt too many goals simultaneously and fail to achieve them. Success will breed success as staff members recognize progress to which they have made a contribution.*

# TABLE 2.2 STEPS TO WRITING A SPECIFIC ACTION PLAN

Writing a specific action plan takes time and patience. Suggested steps (Hines, 2014) are outlined in Table 2.

**1** *Write the specific goal at the top of the action plan. It is critical that the steps in the plan have a specific and clear outcome to be achieved.*

**2** *Identify the resources (e.g., people, funds, materials) that will be necessary.*

**3** *Solicit the resources if they are not readily available.*

**4** *Define explicitly what each step requires to achieve the goal within a projected time frame. (This often takes the form of a time-ordered check list.)*

**5** *Assign a person to be responsible for the completion of each step in the plan. More than one person may work on a step, but the responsible person will ensure that the step is completed and report progress at regular intervals.*

**6** *Set a deadline for completion of the goal.*

**7** *Schedule regular time points at which progress will be assessed and reported.*

**8** *Develop a set of criteria (e.g., metrics, completion of tasks) by which you will assess whether progress is being made.*

**9** *Define how achievement of the goal will be measured.*

**10** *Brainstorm possible impediments to achieving your goal. By anticipating what may go wrong, alternate plans can be drafted to overcome those impediments if they occur.*

Recognize that the steps need not be accomplished in the order they are listed in Table 2.2. It is common to encounter snags in the completion of some tasks leading to the ultimate outcome. Do not give up on the process too quickly. Persevere. If you have diligently developed a SMART goal, rethink the plan before abandoning the goal. Shelters too often "give up" on a goal when things don't go according to their first plan. Make the assumption up front that your original plan may go awry and be comfortable with investigating why it did so and devising strategies for overcoming obstacles and re-formulating the plan if necessary.

# ACTION PLAN IDEAS
## OBJECTIVES, SUB-OBJECTIVES, GOALS & THE CONTENT OF SHELTER-RELATED ACTION PLANS RELATING TO SHELTER ANIMAL HEALTH AND WELFARE

The beginnings of 2 example action plans (related to objectives and goals) are provided in Tables 2.3 and 2.4.

## TABLE 2.3 EXAMPLE 1
## DECREASING INCIDENCE OF INFECTIOUS DISEASE

### OBJECTIVE: REDUCE THE INCIDENCE OF INFECTIOUS DISEASE AMONG CATS IN THE SHELTER

### SUB-OBJECTIVE: REDUCE THE INCIDENCE OF UPPER RESPIRATORY TRACT DISEASE (URTD) IN CATS

GOAL: Reduce the incidence of URTD in shelter cats by 5% in the next year.

ACTION PLAN: (depending on what the shelter already does)

*Calculate the current annual incidence of URTD and what will constitute a 5% decrease.*

*Reduce stress in cats by placing towels over the front of cages of all newly admitted cats for at least 48 hours; insure that cats are handled appropriately by staff; provide enrichment for all cats.*

*Place portals in cages not meeting minimal space requirements to reduce stress and enhance the welfare of the cats. Spot clean cat cages except if heavily soiled or if a cat is permanently moved out of the cage. Vaccinate all cats within 24 hours of entry into the shelter.*

*Detect and isolate cats displaying signs of URTD within 12-14 hours of onset of signs.*

*AND any other steps that will help reduce URTD in this particular shelter.*

*Assess progress*

*For placement of towels on the cages of incoming cats at weekly staff meetings with a report by the "responsible" person.*

*For placing portals in cages at monthly staff meetings.*

*ETC : [the timing and frequency of assessing progress for the various steps may vary depending on the nature of the step].*

## TABLE 2.4 EXAMPLE 2
## DECREASING THE AVERAGE LENGTH OF STAY

### OBJECTIVE: DECREASE THE AVERAGE LENGTH OF STAY OF DOGS WITHIN THE SHELTER

### SUB-OBJECTIVE: REDUCE THE AVERAGE TIME TO COMPLETION OF TEMPERAMENT EXAMS

GOAL: Reduce the average time to completion of temperament exams by the behavior staff by 1.5 days within the next 6 months.

ACTION PLAN:

*Calculate the average time to completion of temperament exams for dogs over the last 6 months.*

*Hire a full-time animal behaviorist.*

*Schedule a dedicated staff member to assist the behaviorist when exams are conducted.*

*Schedule a time for behavior evaluations and make sure that everyone is aware of the time frame.*

*Insure that the room used for behavior evaluations is uncluttered and open for use during scheduled times.*

*Add the behaviorist to the team conducting daily dog rounds.*

*ETC. And any other steps that will help reduce the time to behavioral evaluation in this particular shelter.*

*Set the frequency and timing of assessments of progress.*

Photo Credit: Penny Adams

# SUMMARY

Questions throughout this Guide are tied to metrics that might be used to measure progress towards completion of goals common in many shelters. Obviously, the achievement of all goals need not be measured using metrics, but since this Guide relates to metrics, the goals we use have outcomes that can be measured with metrics. We believe strongly that improvements in the health and welfare of shelter animals can be enhanced by using metrics (both to set goals and to evaluate whether they have been achieved). As is true for setting and evaluating fund-raising targets, goals to improve animal health and welfare provide direction for the organization, focus resources, clarify decision-making, motivate staff, and reinforce the importance of contantly improving animal lives in our shelters and communities.

# 3

# INTAKE

The shelter is a dynamic environment. Animals not only enter and exit regularly, but move through the shelter. While the paths that individual animals take through the shelter vary, all begin at intake. Intake metrics enumerate animals entering the shelter so we'll start there (Figure 3.1). We define "intake" broadly because shelter software packages often include all animals entering the shelter system in their major intake categories or intake subtypes (and therefore, in their intake reports). Since animals may enter the shelter's metrics through numerous avenues depending on the mission and resources of the shelter, intake is usually subdivided by the source from which animals originate. The largest sources of animals for most shelters are owner-surrendered and / or stray animals, and as such, preventive programs are often developed to reduce intake of animals from these categories. Other sources may include: returned adoptions, transfers-in (that can be sizeable in some shelters), animals born in the shelter's care, legally held animals (e.g., seized and health department holds for rabies observation), animals boarding, in special programs (e.g., domestic violence housing for pets), dead on arrival (DOA), animals euthanized at the owner's request, privately-owned animals entering to be sterilized, or community cats sterilized and returned to the community or a colony. Different shelters include different categories when reporting their overall metrics,

**FIGURE 3.1 SHELTER FLOW**

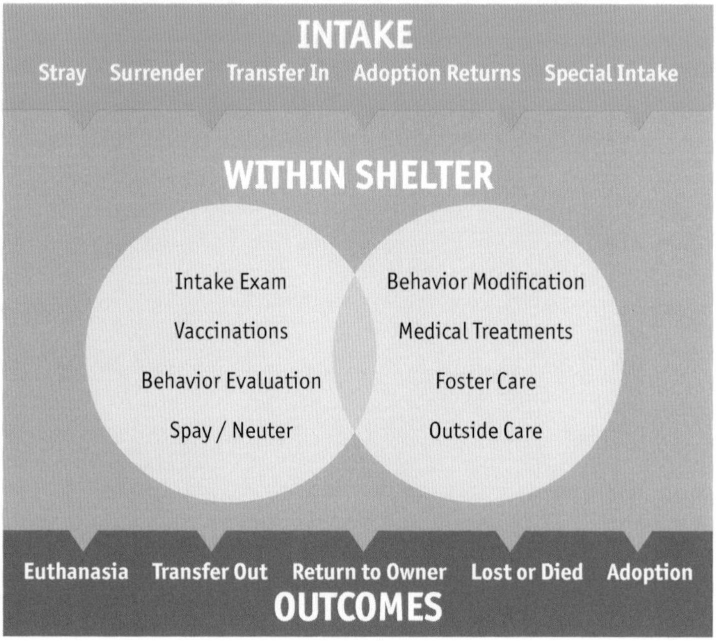

**INTAKE**

Stray　Surrender　Transfer In　Adoption Returns　Special Intake

**WITHIN SHELTER**

Intake Exam
Vaccinations
Behavior Evaluation
Spay / Neuter

Behavior Modification
Medical Treatments
Foster Care
Outside Care

Euthanasia　Transfer Out　Return to Owner　Lost or Died　Adoption
**OUTCOMES**

and shelters may have more or fewer of these categories. Understanding the numbers and sources of entering animals, particularly as they are reflected in your shelter's metrics, is important for many reasons which we will discuss in this and other chapters.

# OBJECTIVES, GOALS, AND QUESTIONS

**INTAKE REDUCTION** While no two shelters share exactly the same objectives, reducing homeless animal intake from the community is one that is common to most, if not all, shelters. A reduction in owner-surrendered and stray animal intake can be one indicator of fewer unwanted companion animals in a community. Many shelters have programs aimed at intake reduction, such as spay-neuter (S/N) programs, behavior "hotlines," obedience classes, and pet food banks. Determining the effectiveness of such programs requires an examination of intake data over time. Throughout this section, we refer to intake reduction of homeless community animals as a central shelter objective.

**MAKE YOUR QUESTIONS SPECIFIC** While we focus heavily on intake reduction, shelters may have other intake-related objectives. The success of these other objectives might actually increase intake in some categories. For example, enhanced surveillance and reporting of cruelty cases might result in an increase in seizures; transport programs bringing animals from areas where they are at higher risk of euthanasia would also increase overall intake numbers. Similarly, special programs aimed at spaying and neutering privately-owned animals might grow over time, increasing the number of animals entering through these programs. If your shelter has these types of programs (and animals in them are included in your overall intake metrics), an increase in overall shelter intake (as reflected in software reports) may reflect the success of these programs, not an excess of homeless animals in the community. For these reasons, it is important that shelters avoid reviewing and reporting their intake statistics as one summary number by species without at least **specifying which categories are encompassed in their numbers**. We prefer that shelters report their summary intake data by various groupings described below.

Also, when asking specific questions about intake, think carefully about which intake categories are pertinent to each question. For example, when evaluating the effectiveness of community-based programs to reduce intake of homeless animals in your community, exclude those from outside of the community, seizures, owner-intended euthanasias, transfers-in, those dead on arrival, those in special programs (e.g., cats in TNR

returned to colonies, S/N of public animals) and any other non-pertinent categories. **Always be attentive to whether the numbers you use are applicable to the question your shelter is asking.**

**REPORTING ON INTAKE CATEGORIES** Since we encourage shelters to view their data in the context of their objectives, we recommend that shelters generate several intake reports for their constituencies. For example, a shelter might have intake reports relating to the objectives for: homeless community animals, seized animals, spay / neuter and TNR programs, and other special service programs (e.g., health department holds, boarding for victims of domestic violence). Since most shelters have the objective of reducing the number of homeless animals in their communities, most of the following questions deal with stray and owner-surrendered animals. We have also included animals that are transferred-in for some reports because they represent a significant number of animals for some shelters and these animals are of great interest to many shelter constituencies (e.g., board members, the public).

Accurate and complete intake data are important for many reasons discussed below. Also, as discussed in a 2015 webinar (Haston, 2015), good intake data is critical to constructing valid prediction models that assist shelters in their decision-making at the community level.

# STRONGLY RECOMMENDED QUESTIONS

**1** *How would you describe your annual shelter intake in a sound bite?*

**WHAT AND WHY?** Annual intake provides a broad measure of the number of animals entering a shelter's care each year. It is typically calculated over 12 months, from January 1st through December 31st, but any 12 month period of importance to your shelter could be used. We recommend that every shelter creates an annual **Intake Profile** that can be shared with stakeholders to provide a "snapshot" of annual intake.

The **Intake Profile** reports summary intake data that serve as a baseline for comparisons over time and to establish a context within which to interpret other metrics (e.g., incidence of disease). While no two shelters are the same, a shelter's Intake Profile is a starting place for informing staff and the community of the nature and magnitude of the homeless animal problem addressed by the shelter. It highlights the number of animals to which the shelter provides various services. It also provides data that serve as the basis for planning, setting and prioritizing goals, and monitoring progress towards achieving those goals.

To put the data into context, it should include a brief description of the nature of your shelter such as whether it is open or limited admission, and if, and for what areas, the shelter has animal control responsibilities. Additionally, we recommend that the report contain summary data regarding shelter intake by species, age distribution, sources of animals, and jurisdiction (if your shelter does animal control). Species and age distribution are included because they profoundly affect many aspects of sheltering, including the need for resources (e.g., financial, facility, staff and volunteer time). Source of animals and jurisdiction are important when negotiating animal control contracts and for planning preventive strategies to lower intake. Tables 3.1 and 3.2 show the annual **Intake Profiles** of two shelters.

**DATA NEEDED** Specify the time frame to which the data pertain, separate intake numbers by dog and cat, the total number of dogs (and cats) admitted to the shelter, and the number of dogs (and cats) admitted in each age, source and jurisdiction category. Also include the type of shelter (open or limited admission), whether it has animal control contracts (yes or no), or cruelty investigation authority (yes or no).

Notice that the **Intake Profile** includes both numerator data (e.g., number of strays) and denominator data (e.g., all dogs or cats that entered), and the percentages based on these numbers. If your shelter accepts many animals of other species, you may want to display these numbers and percentages as well.

**INTERPRETATION** The Intake Profiles of the two shelters in Tables 3.1 and 3.2 clearly indicate differences in the numbers of animals handled, the mission of the shelters and their definitions of intake types/subtypes. Direct comparisons of numbers between the two shelters could be misleading if the definitions of the categories were not provided. The shelter in Table 3.1 did not perform owner-intended euthanasia and included "bite holds" in their seized category. Similarly, these shelters defined their categories for source and age groups differently.

The shelter in Table 3.1 defined "service-in" animals as those born-in-care, boarding (e.g., temporary housing relating to domestic violence) and in their TNR program. The shelter in Table 3.2 defined "service-in" animals as euthanasia request, special cremation, feral cat surgery, disposal, and included several other categories of animals for which the shelter provided services. Also, the shelter in Table 3.2 defined its age categories differently. "Returned adoption" percentages were calculated using the total shelter intake in the denominator as the intent of this table was to show the distribution of animals from all sources. A shelter could also show these percentages as a proportion of *all adoptions* to emphasize the effectiveness of efforts to successfully "match" animals to long-term owners.

Shelters should think carefully about how they categorize their intake data and the characteristics of animals that will be associated with each category. The categories should facilitate answering questions important to a shelter. For example, in what category should animals "born in the shelter's care" be put? We prefer to have them categorized by the intake type (or source) of the mother (e.g., "stray," if mom was a stray). For software programs with intake subtypes, the subtype would be "born in shelter." As demonstrated by the shelter in Table 3.1, shelters vary in the manner in which they categorize animals "born in the shelter's care."

We discourage most comparisons between shel-

# TABLE 3.1  SHELTER INTAKE PROFILE (2014)

**OVERALL INTAKE = 2237**
**SHELTER DESCRIPTION: Open Admission**
**ANIMAL CONTROL CONTRACT: Yes, Towns of A, B, C and D**
**CRUELTY INVESTIGATION: Yes**

| INTAKE CATEGORY | 🐕 TOTAL = 661* | | 🐈 TOTAL = 1,576* | |
|---|---|---|---|---|
| **Source** | # | % | # | % |
| Owner-guardian surrender | 207 | 31.3 | 699 | 44.3 |
| Stray | 277 | 41.9 | 685 | 43.5 |
| Returned adoption** | 49 | 7.4 | 71 | 4.5 |
| Transfer in | 57 | 8.6 | 9 | 0.6 |
| Seized | 70 | 10.6 | 56 | 3.6 |
| Service-In*** | 1 | 0.2 | 56 | 3.6 |
| **Age Group** | # | % | # | % |
| 0- 6 months | 184 | 27.8 | 806 | 51.1 |
| 7– 23 months | 76 | 11.5 | 126 | 8.0 |
| 2- 7 yrs | 358 | 54.2 | 619 | 39.3 |
| 8 yrs & older | 43 | 6.5 | 25 | 1.6 |
| **Jurisdiction for animal control**** | # | % | # | % |
| Town A | 79 | 29.3 | | |
| Town B | 85 | 31.3 | | |
| Town C | 59 | 21.7 | | |
| Town D | 48 | 17.7 | | |

*Total intake by species.

** The percentages of returned adoptions were calculated using the total intake in the denominator as the intent of this table is to show the distribution of animals from all sources. A shelter could also show these percentages as a proportion of all adoptions to emphasize the effectiveness of efforts to successfully "match" animals to long-term owners.

***Service-In category: this shelter included animals born in the shelter, TNR cats, and animals sheltered for domestic violence cases.

**** Percentages are out of a total of 271 stray dogs with jurisdiction data from these towns.

# TABLE 3.2 SHELTER INTAKE PROFILE (2014)

**OVERALL INTAKE = 11,213**
**SHELTER DESCRIPTION: Open Admission**
**ANIMAL CONTROL CONTRACT: No**
**CRUELTY INVESTIGATION: Yes**

| INTAKE CATEGORY | 🐕 TOTAL = 3,201* | | 🐈 TOTAL = 8,012* | |
|---|---|---|---|---|
| **Source** | # | % | # | % |
| Owner-guardian surrender | 1909 | 59.6 | 6057 | 75.6 |
| Stray | 209 | 3.1 | 660 | 1.3 |
| Returned adoption** | 99 | 2.5 | 102 | 0.9 |
| Transfer in | 528 | 11.8 | 235 | 11.0 |
| Seized | 79 | 6.5 | 73 | 8.2 |
| Service-In*** | 377 | 16.5 | 885 | 2.9 |
| **Age Group** | # | % | # | % |
| 0-5 months | 428 | 13.4 | 3024 | 37.7 |
| 5-12 months | 464 | 14.5 | 905 | 11.3 |
| 1-9 years | 1576 | 49.2 | 2150 | 26.8 |
| 9 yrs and older | 436 | 13.6 | 499 | 6.2 |
| Adult | 176 | 5.5 | 745 | 9.3 |
| Unknown | 121 | 3.8 | 689 | 8.6 |

*Total intake by species.

** The percentages of returned adoptions were calculated using the total intake in the denominator as the intent of this table is to show the distribution of animals from all sources. A shelter could also show these percentages as a proportion of all adoptions to emphasize the effectiveness of efforts to successfully "match" animals to long-term owners.

***Service-In: this shelter includes owner-intended euthanasias, special cremations, feral cat surgeries, disposal and other miscellaneous reasons. Owner-intended euthanasias are those brought to the shelter by their owners with the express intent of euthanasia (Shelter Animals Count, 2016).

ters because differences in definitions, mission, and other important factors are common. *If comparisons are made, restrict them to common intake categories (e.g., owner-surrendered and stray), or mini-* *mally provide the definition of all intake categories to promote "fair" conclusions.* To reiterate, as you read through this guide, think carefully about how categories of variables (e.g., age, source) are defined by your shelter and which of those categories are appropriate for answering your specific questions.

## SUMMARIZING INTAKE DATA BY AGE GROUP

Understanding the age distribution of shelter populations is essential for planning for care, and setting and monitoring goals. Animals of different ages have different needs for such things as housing, feeding, medical care, staff time, fostering, and marketing. Additionally, in shelters with spay / neuter programs, a decline in kittens (or puppies) may precede a decline in adult animals over time if the S/N program is effective. As mentioned in Chapter 1, shelter software often allows age to be entered in several ways. When age groups are used in software, shelters usually define these groups themselves. The shelters supplying the data in Tables 3.1 and 3.2 use quite different age categories.

**HELPFUL HINTS** As discussed earlier we prefer reporting age information using clearly defined age groups rather than summarizing age with mean or median ages because the age-grouped data are likely to be more accurate for most animals. Also, since animals' ages are often difficult to establish, it is important that the aging of incoming animals be finalized by veterinary technicians, veterinarians, or specially trained staff members. If their physical examination suggests an age different from that entered at the intake desk, the animal's record should be updated immediately to reflect the more accurate estimate. Age categories should not overlap as was done by the shelter in Table 3.2. You don't want staff members to decide for themselves into which category animals with certain ages (e.g., 5 months, 1 year, 9 years in Table 3.2) should be recorded because the preferences across people will differ. This mistake in defining categories leads to inconsistency in data and clouds their interpretation. The defined age ranges should be available wherever age data are ascertained (either within the software or otherwise) to facilitate collection of standardized age data. Incorrect or incomplete age data can compromise their usefulness.

## SUMMARIZING INTAKE DATA BY SOURCE OF ANIMALS

*Sources* (or intake types) commonly include owner/guardian surrendered, stray, transfers from other organizations, legal / seizure / cruelty cases, health department holds, adoption returns, public assistance cases, animals born in the shelter, owner-intended euthanasias, and animals dead-on-arrival. These intake categories are depicted in the diagram in Figure 3.1. Your shelter may have additional categories to track privately owned or free-roaming animals entering the shelter for specific services (e.g., spay / neuter, TNR). As mentioned previously, some categories of animals should be removed from specific analyses when they are inappropriate for a particular question. Displaying data graphically as in Figure 3.2 helps emphasize the differences among intake sources, augmenting the same data in tabular form in the Intake Profile. For many shelters, strays and surrendered animals make up the majority of intake (Figure 3.2). All intake categories should be monitored even though some may not contain large numbers of animals. These other groups (e.g., seizures, transfers) can have a large effect on the shelter's capacity for care or be related to other shelter goals. For example, if your shelter is involved in legal cases, you may be required to hold animals for long periods of time. When this happens, even a small number of legal cases can lead to a large investment of time, staffing, housing space and other resources (see Chapter 5 for more information on capacity and length of stay within the shelter). Exactly how a shelter categorizes its intake data should reflect the goals a shelter has for its specific categories. Check your software as it may dictate which intake categories are fixed and which can be customized to meet individual shelter needs.

**HELPFUL HINTS** In Figure 3.2, the percentages of animals from each source are shown, but you could also graph the numbers that each category contributes to overall intake, depending on the question of interest. You can also include both the percentages and numbers on the graph or provide the overall numbers on which the percentages are based as

# FIGURE 3.2 PERCENTAGE OF ANNUAL INTAKE* (2014)

## BY SOURCE AND SPECIES

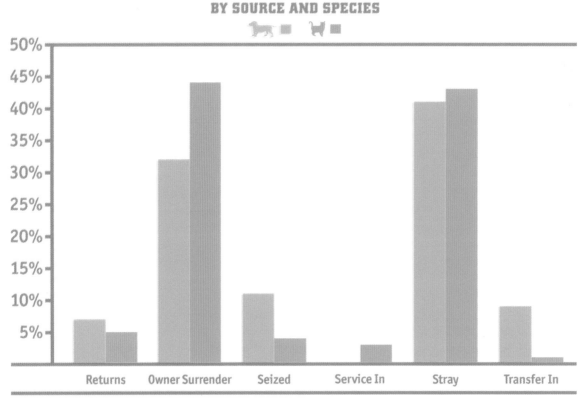

*Based on total intake (n= 661 for dogs and n=1576 for cats).

Service-in: includes born-in-shelter, TNR cats, and animals sheltered for domestic violence victims.

shown in Figure 3.2. (See Appendix 2 for more discussion.) When displaying these data to people who are not familiar with the nature of the data categories (like "service-in"), provide an explanation for the content of those categories.

## SUMMARIZING INTAKE DATA BY JURISDICTION

If your shelter provides animal control services, good data regarding the geographic origin of stray dogs (and cats if appropriate) is important. Examining stray dog intake (or stray cat if ordinances pertain) by jurisdiction can facilitate fairly and transparently assigning costs for animal control to various municipalities, towns or other political designations to which your shelter provides services. The more animals originating in an area, the more it should cost that area (e.g., municipality, town) for the shelter's services. This knowledge enables the shelter to direct services and preventive measures to those areas contributing the highest numbers of animals. The same should be done with other services (e.g., animal-related complaints) provided by the shelter under contract. In some shelters (e.g., municipal), it may be possible to track animal numbers and percentages by neighborhood or even by particular residences using **Geographic Information Systems (GIS)**. Municipally employed GIS technicians or other GIS technicians in the community may be able to help your shelter. See GIS discussion at the end of this chapter. Some shelters use zip codes to more precisely target preventive measures such as spay/neuter or educational efforts, even without GIS.

Examination of intake data by town dramatically illustrated to the shelter in Figure 3.3 the disproportionate contribution of several towns to the intake of stray dogs relative to other towns in the county. Examination of these data resulted in a redistribution of town-level costs, such that the animal control fees charged towns with low numbers of animals were reduced and those with high numbers were raised.

**HELPFUL HINTS** Animal control officers and staff members accepting stray intakes must be aware of the various animal control jurisdictions and understand their geographic boundaries. They must work to obtain addresses or other local data as precisely as possible. Some shelters keep maps at the intake desk to enable people bringing stray animals to a shelter to identify as closely as possible where the animal was found. This approach improves the quality of stray location data and helps justify costs associated with animal control to the various jurisdictions. This attention to detail can bolster the confidence of municipalities or town officials that are responsible for allocating funds for animal control.

**If your shelter is at the stage of defining your intake categories (e.g., you are considering acquiring new software), think very carefully about how you hope to use the data once they are collected.** Having categories that facilitate (rather than confuse) your ability to set and monitor progress towards goals can save you time and frustration when you use the data. Similarly, if your current

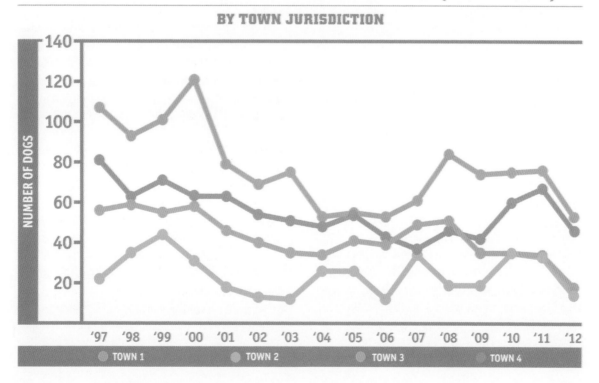

## FIGURE 3.3 ANNUAL STRAY DOG INTAKE (1997-2012)

### BY TOWN JURISDICTION

NUMBER OF DOGS

'97 '98 '99 '00 '01 '02 '03 '04 '05 '06 '07 '08 '09 '10 '11 '12

TOWN 1      TOWN 2      TOWN 3      TOWN 4

# FIGURE 3.4 ANNUAL INTAKE OF OWNER-SURRENDERED & STRAY ANIMALS (1997 – 2011)

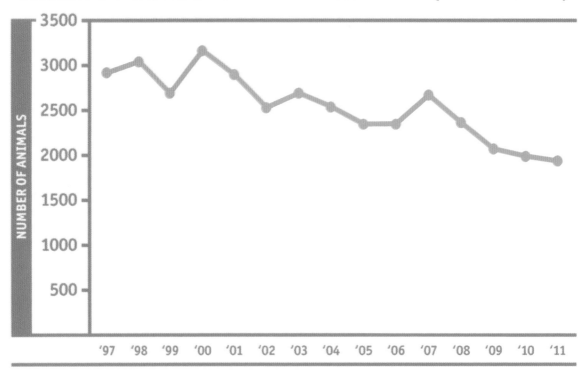

intake categories need revisions to facilitate your use of the data, we suspect that it will be "easier" to make the changes now, rather than later.

## REPORTING OF OWNER-INTENDED EUTHANASIA DATA

Some shelters include animals euthanized at the owner's request in their overall intake numbers. These animals, for example, are counted in the intake numbers of shelters using Asilomar report recommendations. We prefer tracking these animals in their own category and not lumping them into a "service-in" or "other" grouping. We also recommend that they not be included in "Live Release Rate" calculations (see Chapter 4). Having them in a separate category enables shelters to include or exclude them from the analyses of various questions they may ask of their data.

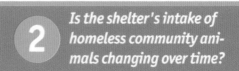

**2** *Is the shelter's intake of homeless community animals changing over time?*

**WHAT AND WHY?** Perhaps the most common goal in shelters is diminishing the intake of homeless animals from the community which is highly correlated with diminishing euthanasia numbers (Marsh, 2010). Intervention programs such as spay/neuter, behavior hotlines, SNR, and TNR seek to reduce the intake of animals from the community. Plotting annual intakes over time highlights long-term trends. The overall annual intake of owner-surrendered and stray animals from a shelter over a 15 year period is plotted in Figure 3.4. This graph suggests that the intake of homeless community dogs and cats is declining in this shelter.

**INTERPRETATION** Intake data for dogs and cats were combined in Figure 3.4, but summary data such as these can be misleading. If the data are divided by species, it is clear that the decline in dog intake masks the relatively stable intake of cats over time in this shelter (Figure 3.5). By separating the data by species, this disparity between species became clear.

Monitoring data over a long time frame also helps to identify the yearly variability that is often inherent to intake data. For this reason, snapshots of only two or three years can be misleading as demonstrated in the cat intake numbers from 2004 – 2006 (Figure 3.5). If you viewed a graph of intake data from those three years only, it would appear that intake of cats was decreasing significantly with time. The data for subsequent years show, however, that the decline between 2004 and 2006 was a fluctuation in the long-term experience of this shelter.

**HELPFUL HINTS** If Figure 3.5 had included intake categories that the shelter was deliberately increasing (e.g., transferred-in), the trends would have been difficult to interpret.

When looking at long-term trends in intake at any shelter, especially if data from intake groups are combined, it is important to keep the shelter's history in mind; and to have a timeline of important events close at hand to facilitate interpretation of the data. For example, large seizure cases, changes in hours of operation, or even changes to the mission of the shelter can have dramatic effects on intake. Be sure to include factors outside of the shelter that could influence your shelter's intake. For example, the addition or loss of other rescue groups in your area, or community-level economic changes can impact intake at your shelter dramatically and affect interpretation of your data. An example of a log of important chronological

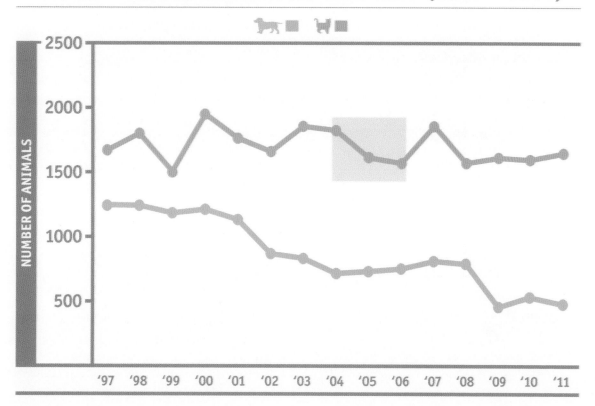

FIGURE 3.5 ANNUAL INTAKE OF STRAY & OWNER-SURRENDERED DOGS AND CATS (1997 – 2011)

# TABLE 3.3 LOG OF EVENTS AND PROTOCOL CHANGES

## 2008

**January 1:** Special annual county allocation ($30,000) for stray cat care in shelter was discontinued.

**February 14:** A seizure of 75 dogs from Margaret Able is undertaken. Dogs exceed housing capacity of the shelter. Crates set up and dogs in staff offices.

**March 28:** Grant (~$15,000) received to increase TNR efforts.

**March 30:** Shelter lost part-time veterinarian due to financial concerns.

**April 9:** Intake policy changed. Manage the nuisance feral cats by providing traps and S/N services. AC officers were trained to do prevention when on the road.

**June 10:** Shelter lost 2 full-time staff members due to budget crisis; shelter is now understaffed.

## 2009

**January 1:** Animal control contracts from towns of Jenoa, Marbeau, and Jackson are dropped. Shelter continues to accept owner-surrendered dogs from these towns. Cat impoundments are not affected.

**January 1:** The shelter management software replaces previous software.

**February 28:** Shelter begins recording Asilomar definitions for this community.

**February 28:** New offsite adoption center opens with 6 cages at a local Mall.

**May 5:** Mark Main becomes ED.

**June 1:** People hoping to surrender owned cats are asked to look for homes and hold on to animals until space in the shelter opens up. They are placed on waiting lists.

**July 22:** Seizure of 60 cats from Mrs. Cross; cat capacity is exceeded; 15 cats placed in foster care

**October 30:** Full-time staff member hired; shelter still somewhat understaffed.

# FIGURE 3.6 ANNUAL OWNER-SURRENDER & STRAY CAT INTAKE (2008 - 2013)

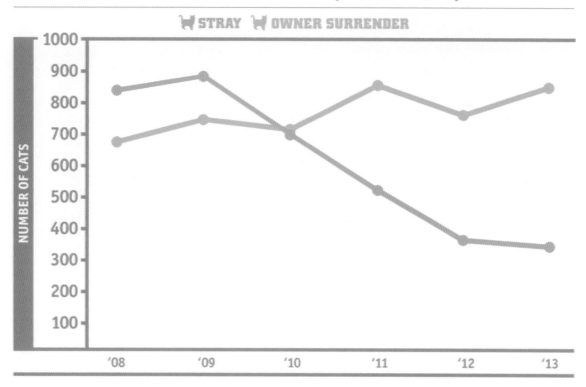

events maintained by a shelter is provided in Table 3.3. This was made in a spread sheet (changing the names of people and towns to maintain confidentiality) and is easy to update periodically. Routinely updating this log at the first staff meeting each month is one approach to keeping this log of events current.

When evaluating long-term trends consider separating the data by owner-surrendered and stray animals. Combining them may obscure the answers to questions relating to these two groups separately. The overall annual intake of stray and owner-surrendered cats from another shelter over a 6-year period is graphed in Figure 3.6.

**DATA NEEDED** Specify the time frame to which the data pertain - in this case year(s) of interest; intake numbers of stray and owner-surrendered dogs and cats (separately) by year.

**INTERPRETATION** The intake of stray cats in the shelter in Figure 3.6 decreased 60% from 2008 to 2013. Owner-surrendered cats increased 27% in the same interval. The question is: What factor(s) precipitated this change? The decline in strays in this shelter was partially explained by changes in labeling of kittens < 8 weeks of age. The shelter stopped labeling these young kittens as strays and instead categorized them as owner-surrendered. Correcting for this change, however, did not account for the total decline in stray intake. Other possible explanations included increases in the numbers of unowned cats brought in by homeowners for neutering and returned to the community (and never surrendered to the shelter); the effect of the shelter's S/N program; or possible declines in the free-roaming cat population (e.g., due to weather, disease outbreaks).

## 3
**Is the shelter's intake of kittens or already sterilized community animals changing over time?**

**WHAT AND WHY?** Other potential, measurable indicators of the effectiveness of spay/neuter programs relating to the goal of diminishing community animal intake can be explored. Such indicators might include a decreasing intake of kittens or an increasing intake of sterilized adult cats. The shelter in Figure 3.6 had not experienced an increase in the number of cats already sterilized at intake (Figure 3.7) or a decline in kitten intake during the same interval as they experienced a decline in stray cat intake. Other metrics that might reflect a measurable impact of your S/N efforts are a decrease in the number of cat-related service calls and complaints (Scarlett & Johnston, 2012).

Monitoring intake metrics in areas served by S/N programs can not only serve to evaluate the effectiveness of your programs, but enhance the success of your funding requests to continue or expand those programs. Increasingly, granting organizations are requesting data pertinent to their S/N grants.

## FIGURE 3.7 PERCENTAGE OF CATS* ALREADY NEUTERED AT INTAKE (2008 – 2011)

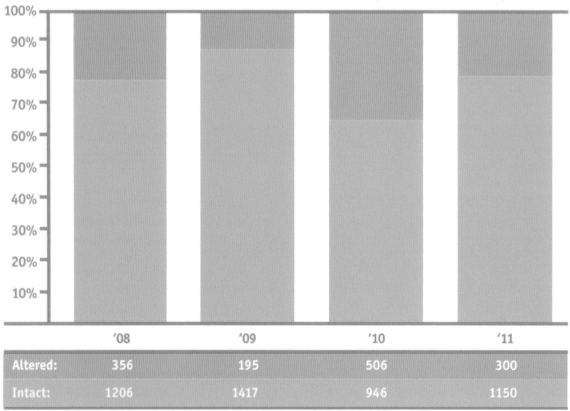

|  | '08 | '09 | '10 | '11 |
|---|---|---|---|---|
| Altered: | 356 | 195 | 506 | 300 |
| Intact: | 1206 | 1417 | 946 | 1150 |

*Includes owner-surrendered and stray cats only.

**DATA NEEDED** Specify the time frame to which the data pertain, intake numbers by gender and by sterilization status (neutered or not) *at entry* from the areas served by the preventive programs.

**HELPFUL HINTS** Monitoring and interpreting data to help assess the effectiveness of preventive programs such as S/N must be done thoughtfully. Other factors (e.g., growth in human population, changes in federal housing rules) may also impact intake and if not taken into account, lead to inappropriate conclusions regarding program effectiveness. Also, preventive programs can take years to impact shelter intake, so data should be monitored during time frames that could realistically reflect progress.

The data examined must be of high quality. Efforts must be made to capture the most accurate and complete information possible regarding the gender and sterilization status of all animals at intake. Staff at the intake desk may not have the time or expertise to determine the gender/sterilization status of animals with questionable information. When newly admitted animals are first examined, the person conducting the physical exam should update sterilization status and gender information rather than leave the data field empty or incorrect. A large percentage of missing or incorrect data regarding sterilization status or gender will hamper efforts to graph and interpret trends accurately.

Software packages usually enable collection of data regarding the spay/neuter status of each animal at entry (or that information can be tracked on paper, in a spread sheet, or by some other means). Be aware that as shelter software programs become more sophisticated in their capabilities, the sterilization status of intact animals at intake may be tracked separately from their sterilization status after surgery. *Knowing which software reports provide the data you want is critical.* Sterilization status should be evaluated by gender. Obviously, more resources must be invested in spaying females than castrating males, so understanding the numbers and percentages of males and females that the shelter must "pay" to spay or neuter (either within or outside of the shelter) is important if your shelter alters animals before adoption.

Identifying the area served by your spay / neuter program may be difficult, particularly if other shelters or S/N clinics also sterilize animals from areas overlapping with yours. Similarly, some animals in your S/N program may not originate from the area served by your shelter and, therefore, your program may influence the intake of other area shelters as well. Ideally, combining intake and spay/neuter data across organizations serving a community will provide the most accurate assessment of the combined impact of S/N programs on shelter intake in your community.

**What is the shelter's _monthly_ intake by species and age group?**

**WHAT AND WHY?** Knowing the shelter's monthly intake by age group is important because these numbers serve as denominator data for many rate calculations. It also helps your organization anticipate population fluctuations, plan housing, staffing, foster care needs, and accompanying expenses that may vary throughout the year. Also, being able to predict monthly or seasonal drops in intake can assist planning for other activities (e.g., fundraisers or facility maintenance) so as to efficiently use staff members' time.

**INTERPRETATION** For many shelters, intake fluctuates dramatically by season, a common example being "kitten season" in many parts of the country (Figure 3.8).

# FIGURE 3.8 MONTHLY INTAKE* OF KITTENS AND ADULT CATS (2009-2010)

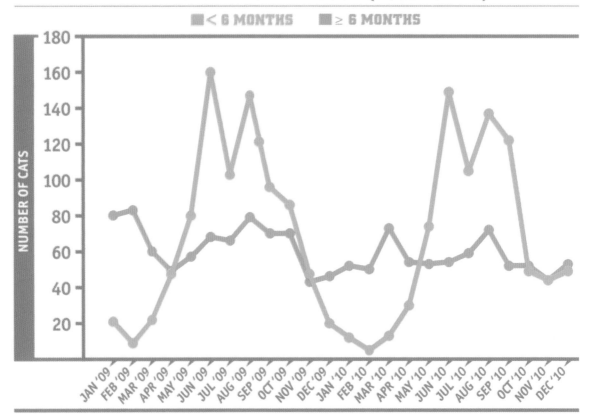

■ < 6 MONTHS     ■ ≥ 6 MONTHS

*Includes owner-surrendered and stray cats only.

In this shelter it is clear that the seasonal fluctuation in cat intake is due to the influx of kittens from April to October and that the monthly intake of adult cats is relatively stable.

**DATA NEEDED** Specify the time frame to which the data pertain, monthly *intake* numbers by species, and age group at intake (e.g., < 6 mos of age, ≥ 6 mos of age).

**HELPFUL HINTS** The shelter in Figure 3.8 looked at kitten intake with kitten defined as < 6 months of age. A similar graph could be created to look at kittens of an age to be sent to foster care (e.g., < 8 weeks of age) in order to anticipate the number of foster care providers needed in high intake periods (if young kittens are not kept in the shelter).

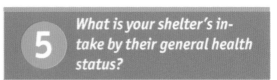

**5** What is your shelter's intake by their general health status?

**WHAT AND WHY?** We suggest that shelters track the general health status of their animals at intake and at final disposition and compare the two. We discuss our recommendation to record the health status at final disposition and make comparisons to that at the time of intake in Chapter 4. General health status of animals at intake also has a critical impact on a shelter's housing capacity, costs, live release rate and other important factors (Haston, 2015).

One strategy for tracking health status at entry is to use Asilomar classifications (See Asilomar Accords sidebar), but shelters can develop their own system with the assistance of a veterinarian. Regardless of the approach, general health categorization at intake can be useful to assess progress towards saving an increasing number of animals in the various healthy status categories (e.g., those with "treatable" conditions). Using an Asilomar matrix, the shelter in Figure 3.9 realized that the health status of animals entering their shelter was changing. It began receiving a higher percentage of unhealthy-untreatable and treatable-manageable cats in the years following an economic downturn in their community, suggesting that an increasing number of community members could no longer afford veterinary care. These data prompted the shelter to redirect their fund-raising efforts, and to reallocate resources to provide medical care for these additional animals.

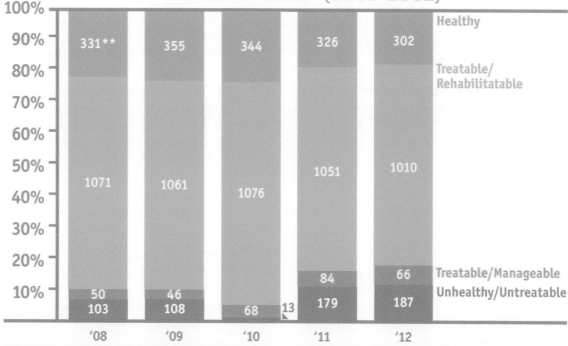

## FIGURE 3.9 ASILOMAR STATUS AT ENTRY OF CATS* (2008-2012)

*Owner-surrendered, stray and transferred-in cats. In this shelter transferred-in cats were very rare.

**The numbers in the bars represent the number of cats.

# ASILOMAR ACCORDS

In August of 2004 representatives from approximately 20 shelters and animal welfare groups met at the Asilomar Conference Center in Pacific Grove, California. The meeting was designed to increase cohesiveness among groups with disparate animal welfare philosophies, develop relationships, and facilitate progress towards ending the euthanasia of healthy and treatable dogs and cats in the United States. One component of the Accords created a structure for gathering and sharing statistical data about animal intake and outcomes that was tied to the general health status of shelter animals and how reasonable, caring owners in communities might manage their care.

The general health status of animals for data gathering purposes was divided into 4 categories: healthy, treatable-rehabilitatable, treatable-manageable, and unhealthy-untreatable (Maddie's Fund, 2016). Each of these categories was defined in broad, general terms, but the specific diseases, conditions or behavioral issues that would be associated with each category were left to individual shelters. Shelters were counseled to describe the medical and behavioral conditions that would be linked to each category in their shelter based on how reasonable, caring owners might care for animals with these conditions in their community. For example, if reasonable caring owners in a community would treat a cat with feline hyperthyroidism, a shelter cat with feline hyperthyroidism from that community could be categorized as a treatable animal in the shelter's Asilomar statistics. If, on the other hand, most caring owners in the community would euthanize a cat with feline hyperthyroidism, then a similar cat in the shelter would be categorized as an unhealthy-untreatable cat. The medical and behavioral issues defined for each category by a shelter was labeled the Asilomar matrix for that organization and each shelter was encouraged to create its own matrix. By examining the percentage of animals released alive (or euthanized) in each Asilomar category over time, shelters could monitor their progress towards achieving their goal of ending the euthanasia of healthy and treatable animals.

**DATA NEEDED** Specify the time frame to which the data pertain, intake numbers by general health status (e.g., Asilomar or other classification) and by species.

**HELPFUL HINTS** Previously we mentioned the importance of maintaining a log of important decisions or events that might influence the interpretation of shelter statistics. Changes in a shelter's Asilomar matrix (or other health definitions) should be recorded in this log, as well as changes to the medical staff that may interpret the matrix differently over time.

The Asilomar Accords and the development of Asilomar matrices are controversial. One source of concern centers on the means by which shelters determine how reasonable, caring pet owners in their community might care for animals with particular issues. Another concern revolves around whether shelters can or should be expected to provide the same level of care as a "reasonable, caring owner" who is present beyond the business hours of shelters and who usually has only one or a few animals for which to provide care. We don't recommend comparing Asilomar statistics between shelters because we share some of these concerns. We do, however, encourage shelters to develop a general health matrix that categorizes animals into broad health categories at intake and exit. This enables the shelter to monitor changes in the health status of animals entering the shelter from the community over time (like the shelter in Figure 3.9) and to evaluate progress towards releasing alive a growing percentage of "treatable" animals. The nature of the categories and manner by which your shelter determines which animals are

placed in those categories (e.g., what is "treatable") is left to your shelter. This approach helps individual shelters monitor their progress if the matrix is used consistently. **It is not intended to guarantee comparability with other shelters.** Health matrices are discussed further in Chapter 6.

> **6** *What is the shelter's annual returned adoption rate (RAR) over time?*

**WHAT AND WHY?** We prefer to report and count returned adoptions with shelter intake data although it could be argued that "being returned" after adoption is a revised outcome. We like to include returned adoption numbers in intake because these animals will

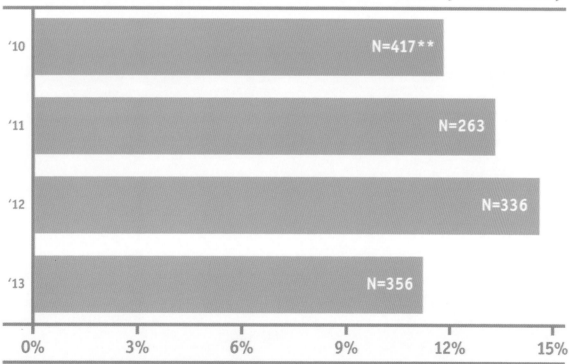

## FIGURE 3.10 ANNUAL RETURNED ADOPTION RATE*
## FOR OWNER-SURRENDERED AND STRAY DOGS (2010-2013)

*Number of dogs returned within 60 days of adoption divided by all adoptions in the year. Note that the percentages in the horizontal axis have been restricted and do not span the range of 0 to 100%.

**Total number of owner-surrendered and stray dogs adopted for each year.

undergo another outcome; these animals occupy cage space (when considering capacity calculations); and they factor into summary length-of-stay calculations.

Returned adoption data are important to monitoring the shelter's "success" in matching animals and people. Numerous programs exist (e.g., Meet Your Match) that enhance the likelihood that animals find a permanent home. If a shelter's returned adoption rate is consistently high, it suggests that finding strategies to reduce that proportion should be a priority.

**DATA NEEDED** Retrieve the number of adoptions per year by species, number of returned adoptions by species for the year.

**HELPFUL HINTS** Every shelter should have a definition of what constitutes a returned adoption. In the shelter in Figure 3.10, a returned adoption is one that occurs within 60 days of adoption from that shelter. If a standard definition is not used, the intake category into which animals are put will vary with the staff member accepting the animal, making it will be difficult to monitor trends over time.

Depending on the number of adoptions occurring monthly and the number of returns, the returned adoption rate could be calculated for different periods of time (e.g., monthly or seasonally). Getting the correct data for these calculations can be difficult depending on the definition of a returned adoption. This is because the number of adoptions that should go in the denominator may be difficult to identify with your software. Even when calculating the RAR for a year, technically the total adoptions should be counted starting at 60 days before (for our example above) the beginning of that year. To simplify the calculation, we ignore this and divide the returned adoptions by those adopted in the same time frame.

Also, remember to record the dates of special adoption events (in your Log of Events) where many animals are adopted in a short period of time. Returned adoptions could cluster in the weeks following such events. Having the date of the event will help you interpret the data months later and compare the "success" of adoptions at these special events with that usually experienced.

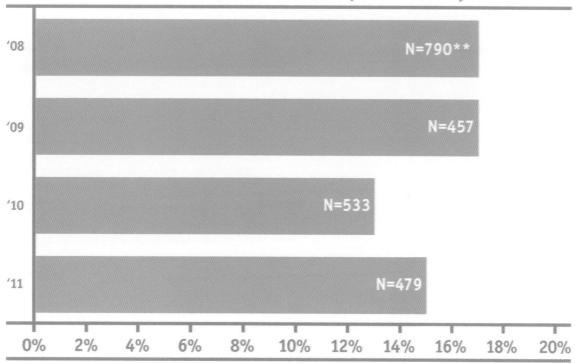

## FIGURE 3.11 ANNUAL INTAKE PERCENTAGE*
## OF PIT BULL-TYPE DOGS (2008-2011)

'08    N=790**

'09    N=457

'10    N=533

'11    N=479

0% 2% 4% 6% 8% 10% 12% 14% 16% 18% 20%

* Note that the percentages in the horizontal axis have been restricted and do not span the range of 0 to 100%.
**Total intake of owner-surrendered and stray dogs for each year.

# RECOMMENDED QUESTIONS

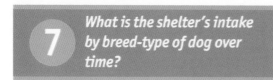

**7**   *What is the shelter's intake by breed-type of dog over time?*

**WHAT AND WHY?** The intake numbers of certain breeds or breed-types of dogs (e.g., Chihuahua-type, pit bull-type) are high in some parts of the country. If dogs of particular breeds or breed-types are more plentiful and less adoptable than other dogs, shelters must often euthanize them; or they contribute disproportionately to average length of stay calculations. In order to diminish the intake numbers of

these dogs, some shelters have developed preventive strategies (such as breed oriented spay/neuter or educational programs). The effectiveness of these initiatives can be evaluated by tracking the numbers and percentages of these breed types entering the shelter over time. The shelter in Figure 3.11 obtained a grant to sterilize pit bull-type dogs in its community in 2008-2009. Both the number and percentage of pit bull-type dogs entering the shelter declined after 2008 among owner-surrendered and stray dogs.

In order to track metrics relating to the success of intake reduction or enhanced adoption programs for targeted breed-types, shelters must define those breeds and breed-types that are of concern. Obviously, identifying dogs' breeds and their breed-types is imperfect, but if the shelter trains its staff members to be consistent in its identification process, trends can be monitored.

**DATA NEEDED** Specify the time frame to which the data pertain, intake numbers of particular breed type dogs, intake of owner-surrendered plus stray dogs from the community to serve as the denominator.

**HELPFUL HINTS** We recognize that some shelters are reluctant to label dogs as a particular breed-type because it might limit their adoptability. If your shelter has a program(s) aimed at specific breed types, then it already has some definition. And it has invested resources into that program. If the shelter is to assess whether the resources are being spent wisely, then the advantages of labeling dogs to facilitate monitoring may outweigh the disadvantages. Also, the labels can be used internally and not made public.

If the intent is to monitor the intake of certain breed-type dogs from the community where preventive programs have been implemented, remember to remove dogs in categories that may not be relevant to monitor (e.g., seized, public assistance, DOA, Department of Health holds or owner-intended euthanasias).

# QUESTIONS FOR YOUR CONSIDERATION

**8** *What are the reasons that animals are surrendered to the shelter?*

**WHAT AND WHY?** For many shelters, owner surrendered animals represent a large percentage of intake. Understanding why animals are surrendered can be used to plan preventive programs and then to track their success. Obtaining accurate information as to why owners surrender pets is notoriously difficult, but

encouraging people to record *all* of the reasons leading to surrender can help. Your software package may have a list of possible surrender reasons that you can tailor to include reasons that you've historically seen in your shelter (e.g., "allergies", "aggression", "litter box issues"). Shelters (with or without software) can capture reasons for surrender in a questionnaire; data can then be entered into a spreadsheet or another format. Discussing the many ways to collect these data is beyond the scope of this guide, but we encourage using questionnaires or checklists. Several studies of relinquishment are referenced at the back of this guide for your perusal (Patronek et al, 1996a, 1996b; Salmon et al, 2000; Scarlett et al, 1999; New et al, 1999; Weiss et al, 2014) to assist you with assembling a list of surrender reasons. Leave space for owners to record "other" reasons not included in your list to ensure the completeness of these data. We have not included an example in this guide because none of the shelters with which we currently work have computerized reasons for surrender.

**DATA NEEDED** Specify the time frame to which the data pertain, intake numbers of owner-surrendered animals by reasons for surrender and by species.

**HELPFUL HINTS** Shelters frequently record a *single* reason for animals being surrendered (e.g., "moving," or "litter box problems"), but in reality, reasons for surrendering animals are often more complex (DiGiacomo et al, 1999; Salman et al, 2000; Scarlett et al, 1999; Weiss et al, 2014). For this reason, we urge you - if you intend to collect information regarding reasons for surrender - to set up your database in such a way as to be able to record *multiple* reasons. **Over-simplifying the data can mask important factors surrounding animal surrender. We believe that without including multiple reasons for surrender, there is little or no reason to collect these data.**

# FIGURE 3.12 ANNUAL DOG* INTAKE & INTAKE RATE PER 1000 HUMAN POPULATION** (1990-2011)

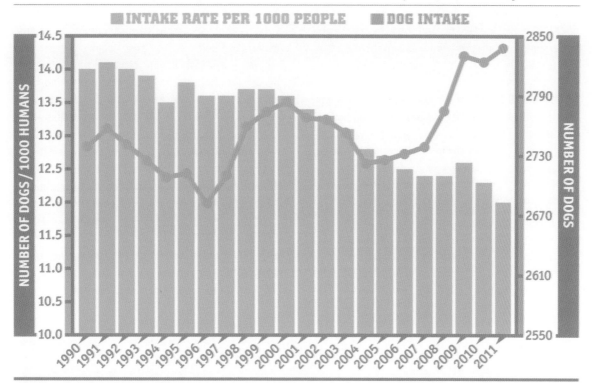

*Owner-surrendered and stray dogs only
**Source of human population estimates: U.S. Census data using yearly estimates

**9** How many animals per 1000 people (based on human population of service area) are entering the shelter?

**WHAT AND WHY?** Changes in the size of the human population in a community usually affect the size of the homeless animal population in that community. Calculations of intake, live release or euthanasia rates per 1000 people can be useful when looking at trends over time for a particular shelter. This is especially true when the human population may have changed significantly in numbers, age distribution, or other ways that could influence pet ownership or relinquishment.

ANNUAL INTAKE PER 1000 HUMANS CAN BE CALCULATED AS FOLLOWS:

**(ANNUAL INTAKE ÷ TOTAL HUMAN POPULATION) X 1000 DURING A SPECIFIC TIME PERIOD**

For example, look at the hypothetical scenario for the only shelter serving a small rural county in Figure 3.12. Note that the intake of dogs increased dramatically after 2007, suggesting that the shelter's preventive programs (e.g., spay / neuter, obedience training) were not effective at diminishing dog intake. When the growth in human population was taken into account, however, the shelter's per-capita intake rate actually fell from 14 dogs entering the shelter per thousand people in 1990 to 12 dogs/1000 people in 2011. Graphing the intake per 1000 human population suggests significant progress for the shelter.

**DATA NEEDED** Specify the time frame to which the data pertain and within that time frame the human census for the defined geographic area (www.census.gov), and the number of animal intakes by species for owner-surrendered and stray animals.

**HELPFUL HINTS** Comparing intakes per 1000 humans over time for one shelter or between shelters should be done *with great caution*. The number of people in an area certainly can affect the size of the homeless animal population, but accounting only for the sizes of human populations oversimplifies differences be-

tween and within communities over time. Other factors such as the availability of pet-friendly housing, age of the human population or the local economy can influence pet ownership and relinquishment and vary by time and between communities. Similarly, many geographic areas (that would correspond to defined areas with human census data) are served by several shelters or rescue groups, making comparing shelter intake across time and communities even more hazardous. **If multiple animal shelters and rescue organizations serve a community, their data should be pooled. The human census data for the area can be used to correct the combined intake data for possible changes in the human population.** Also, if your shelter's service area experiences significant fluctuations in the human population over the course of a year (e.g., in a community with an influx of college students, vacationers), calculating the intake per 1000 residents over shorter periods of time (e.g., academic year, season) may be useful.

# FIGURE 3.13 MAPPED INDIVIDUAL CAT INTAKE AT A MUNICIPAL SHELTER (2014)

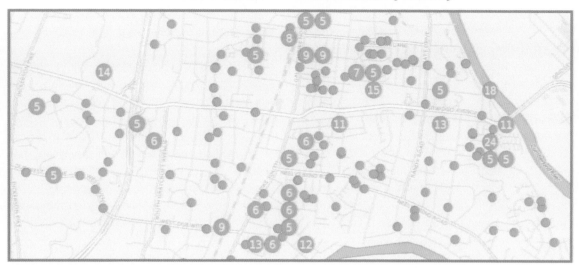

* Numbers in the bubbles are the number of cats from that location. Small bubbles represent < 5 cats.

## 10 From which geographic areas do your animals originate?

### USING GEOGRAPHIC INFORMATION SYSTEM (GIS) DATA TO MAP SHELTER INTAKE

**WHAT AND WHY?** Several studies have demonstrated no or only a modest effect of S/N programs on shelter intake in the areas served by the S/N initiative(s) (Frank & Carlisle-Frank, 2007; Scarlett & Johnston, 2012; White et al, 2010). In order to target their S/N programs more specifically to areas contributing disproportionately large numbers of animals to intake, some shelters have tracked the geographic origin of animals by zip code. In many communities, however, zip codes encompass large, diverse areas and mask sub-areas making substantial contributions to intake. To avoid this limitation, some shelters have turned to Geographic Information Systems (GIS) technology. GIS is computer software that enables data to be analyzed and mapped geographically (http://www.esri.com/what-is-gis). Data that are associated with exact locations (e.g., an address or a GPS coordinate) can be "fed" into a GIS program and mapped not only to the level of a neighborhood or street, but to specific houses and apartment complexes. Having this degree of specificity facilitates finely targeted spay/neuter efforts, TNR programs, or other intake-reduction efforts. Figure 3.13 depicts a map of feline intake in a particular zip code in Nashville, TN. The larger "bubbles" in the map contain numbers representing the number of cats entering the municipal shelter from those specific locations. This map enabled the municipal shelter and their spay-neuter clinic partner to target spay-neuter efforts at a variety of levels: neighborhoods, intersections, housing developments, and specific apartment buildings. This map was generated with freely available web-based software (www.carto.com). These tools are relatively easy to use for anyone who has some experience using spreadsheets. Similar maps can be developed for sources of stray dogs, owner-surrendered animals or other groups of interest, to improve the effectiveness of prevention efforts.

Understanding the power of this technology, the ASPCA has developed a series of PDFs available on the ASPCA Professional website (ASPCAPro, 2013a, 2015b). Their information explains how to prepare your shelter's data for use in GIS, where to find assistance, and provides examples of GIS uses in shelters. There is also an online webinar to get your shelter started.

**DATA NEEDED** The most important piece of information to maximize the use of GIS technology is an *exact* location (or as exact as possible) where each animal originated. For surrendered animals this is most likely the home address of the owner. In the case of strays, this can be difficult, depending on how well the person finding the animal knows the area; the landmarks available; the time of day; and other factors. It is important to pinpoint locations as accurately as *possible*. When using a GIS system, addresses or even two cross streets are the "raw data" that are *geocoded* (i.e. addresses are translated into specific coordinates) and then mapped.

**HELPFUL HINTS** University or community college campuses --particularly those with geography or urban planning departments--are good places to look for GIS technicians. Also, municipal shelters often have access to GIS technicians that assist in city planning. Targeted education and spay/neuter services are likely to reduce animal control costs for the city and may provide a persuasive argument when trying to convince city administrators to authorize a GIS technician to work with shelter data.

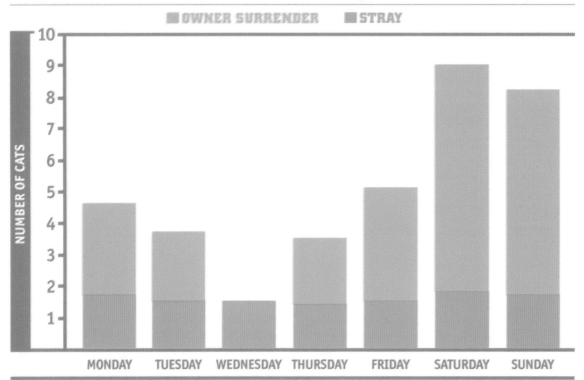

## FIGURE 3.14 AVERAGE DAILY INTAKE OF CATS* BY DAY OF WEEK** AND SOURCE (7/1/11 - 8/31/11)

*Excludes kittens < 8 weeks of age.
**Shelter is closed to the public on Wednesdays.

from the adoption floor. By scheduling the number of animals entering each day, knowing their average length of stay and the average number of animals leaving by day of the week, the shelter can estimate how many animals to have in the holding area ready to move to the adoption area (e.g., vaccinated, sterilized) on the weekends (or whatever days animals are most likely to leave).

# TIMING AND FREQUENCY OF REPORTS

There are no hard-and-fast rules about when and how frequently the data addressing many of the questions presented in this chapter should be run. We make suggestions regarding this topic in Appendix 3 based on our experience and what shelters have told us they are doing. Ultimately the timing and frequency should meet the needs of your shelter.

**SUMMARY** Intake data can be used for many purposes including characterizing your shelter, goal setting, monitoring progress towards achieving goals, planning for staffing needs and for use in prediction models. Reviewing these data should be a routine task for designated management and staff members. Sharing pertinent data with staff, volunteers, board members and other stakeholders is essential. Everyone should clearly understand the current state of the shelter with regards to intake and understand the rationale and nature of a shelter's intake-related goals. This facilitates participation of staff, volunteers and Board members in achieving the goals and promoting them in the community.

Regularly monitoring your data for evidence of progress towards achieving goals can be motivating, facilitate the celebration of achievements and, when necessary, lead to revising strategies that don't work.

| **11** | *How does intake vary by the day of the week?* |

**WHAT AND WHY?** For shelters scheduling (or thinking of scheduling) owner-surrendered intakes, looking at the numbers of animals entering and leaving the shelter by days of the week can help manage use of space in the shelter. The shelter in Figure 3.14 receives the largest number of cats on Saturday and Sunday, and these animals are housed in holding areas. Although the largest number of animals also leaves on Saturday and Sunday, the animals leaving predominantly exit

# OUTCOME

## OBJECTIVES, GOALS, AND QUESTIONS

We believe strongly that the use of most metrics (including outcome-related metrics) should be tied to shelter objectives and goals. While shelters may have different types of outcome-related goals, most share the core objectives of 1) releasing as many animals alive as possible and 2) decreasing the euthanasia rate. As has been true in previous chapters, the outcome metrics a shelter chooses should assist that shelter in setting, and monitoring progress towards, its outcome-related goals.

**DEFINE YOUR OUTCOMES** Similar to what we discussed in the Intake chapter, a shelter's outcome categories and subcategories must be thoughtfully defined and clearly understood by everyone associated with the data. This enables the shelter to analyze and interpret its outcome metrics in the context of its goals. For example, the category "returned-to-owner," can require explanation. Some shelters include not only stray animals returned to their owner, but also those animals that are surrendered and then quickly reclaimed when an owner changes her mind. If a shelter has the goal to monitor its success returning strays to their owners, we recommend that the "return-to-owner" category be defined for stray animals only.

**MAKE YOUR QUESTIONS SPECIFIC** As was true of intake-related questions, outcome-related questions must be clearly and specifically crafted in order to facilitate retrieval of the appropriate data. In other words, certain animals should or should not be included in various counts and rate calculations, depending on the question. For example, suppose your shelter's Board of Directors wants to know whether the return-to-owner rates for cats has increased after the initiation of a 2010 community program encouraging cat owners to place identification on their cats. Asking "Have return-to-owner rates increased since 2010?" or "Is the program working?" is not sufficiently specific to determine the data needed to address the question. A more specific question would be "Has the shelter's return-to-owner rates for stray cats increased over the period 2008 – 2013?" This question specifies the intake category relevant to the question (e.g., stray) and the time period of interest. The years 2008-2010 were included in order to assess whether there were trends in the return-to-owner rates beginning before initiation of the program that should not be attributed to the program.

For most goal-associated questions in this chapter, the outcomes of legally seized animals and those entering shelters through special programs (e.g., TNR or temporary housing programs) are separated from those of owner-surrendered, stray, transferred-in, and returned-adoption animals. We prefer this approach because seized animals and those in special programs are usually associated with different objectives of the shelter. For example, a legal seizure that is returned to an owner may not be a good outcome. Similarly, animals in special programs rarely even belong to the shelter. When asking a question regarding outcome rates, specify the outcomes of interest and also the intake and in-shelter groups to which the question pertains. This insures that the correct numerators and denominators are identified.

As discussed earlier, some outcome types are predetermined (e.g., animals dead on arrival or those euthanized at an owner's request). These animals should be tracked separately and not included in the calculation of general outcome metrics (e.g., adoption rates). In the case that a shelter changes the mind of an owner who wanted an animal euthanized, then that animal should be recorded as an owner-surrendered intake (unless changing owners' minds is an outcome of interest). Note: Henceforth, in this Guidebook we use the terminology "owner-intended euthanasia" in place of "owner-requested euthanasia" as suggested by the former National Federation of Humane Societies (ASPCApro, 2013b).

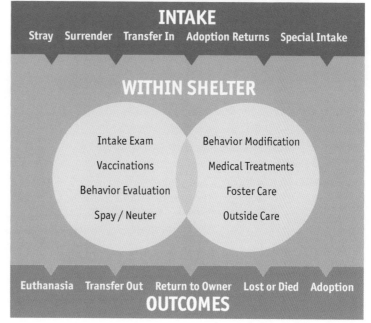

## FIGURE 4.1 SHELTER FLOW

**INTAKE**

Stray    Surrender    Transfer In    Adoption Returns    Special Intake

**WITHIN SHELTER**

Intake Exam

Vaccinations

Behavior Evaluation

Spay / Neuter

Behavior Modification

Medical Treatments

Foster Care

Outside Care

Euthanasia    Transfer Out    Return to Owner    Lost or Died    Adoption

**OUTCOMES**

# POSSIBLE OUTCOMES IN ANY TIME PERIOD: DESCRIBING THE "BIG PICTURE"

Taking a step back and thinking in broad terms, animals can undergo only one of three general outcomes by the end of a given time period. They can (1) be released alive; (2) experience an undesirable outcome; or (3) remain in the shelter system (which includes within foster and other offsite locations). Outcome data can (and should!) be further divided into subcategories (e.g. adopted, euthanized). Let's look first at these three general outcome types.

**LIVE RELEASE** – Animals may leave the shelter alive. The most common forms of live release in shelters are adoptions, returns-to-owners, and transfers to Adoption Guarantee agencies or rescue groups (Figure 4.1). Some shelters have another live release category for free-roaming cats placed back into the community.

**UNDESIRABLE OUTCOMES** The two most common categories of undesirable outcomes are euthanasia and death. Another, often overlooked, undesirable outcome is animal loss. Animals can be lost – either literally (e.g., escaped from shelter) or figuratively (e.g., in the "paperwork"). These animals may technically have "escaped alive," but allowing animals to escape is not an outcome any shelter should tolerate. Similarly, losing animals in the paperwork suggests poor management that should be remedied. These animals are included in the undesirable outcome category because a well-managed shelter should not "lose" animals.

**Note: While we call euthanasia and death from natural causes "undesirable," it is important to note that some euthanasias are necessary (e.g., animals that are very ill or are unsafe), and some**

**deaths may be unavoidable (e.g., fading kittens).** The reasons for euthanasia and causes of shelter deaths should be carefully recorded. This enables shelters to track their progress towards saving as many lives as possible without jeopardizing human health or perpetuating animal suffering.

**STILL-IN-SHELTER** At the end of a specific interval, animals may remain in the shelter's care and are referred to as still-in-shelter (SIS). Their outcome for that interval is SIS.

Animals still in a shelter's care may be in foster care, housed at offsite adoption or satellite locations, or reside in the main shelter facilities. Therefore, a large number of SIS animals should not necessarily be interpreted as bad, but rather these numbers must be viewed in relation to the shelter's total capacity to provide quality care and its length of stay statistics (see Chapter 5). On the other hand, the size of the SIS population is crucial to monitor; when the SIS population increases steadily with time, it is likely that bottlenecks to animal flow exist in the shelter that often lead to overcrowding and increases in average length of stay. More on this in Chapter 5.

Most outcome-related numbers and rates reported by shelters today don't take into account the outcomes of all animals in the shelter during a period of interest. They ignore the animals remaining in the shelter at the end of a period. Instead, they estimate the percentage of animals that have experienced a particular outcome (e.g., euthanasia) among animals that have a final disposition in that period or only among those that entered during that period. We believe that members of the general public and most Board members don't understand what these metrics actually represent. Rates usually convey probabilities. In our experience, *most believe that an outcome rate (e.g., adoption rate) represents the chance that an animal will be adopted during the interval.* Consider the following example for a shelter that only accepts owner-surrendered and stray cats (Figure 4.2). A shelter begins the month of August with 30 cats. Fifty more enter during the month. At the end of the month, 39 cats have been adopted, 4 have been euthanized and 2 were returned to their owners. What is the adoption rate for August in this shelter?

The first adoption metric (86.7%) in Figure 4.2 is the largest, but only reflects what happened to cats that experienced a final outcome. It does not represent the probability (or chance) that a cat will be adopted in August. If this method is used, then it should be described as the percentage of cats that were adopted among those <u>that had a final disposition</u>.

# FIGURE 4.2 POSSIBLE ADOPTION RATE CALCULATIONS

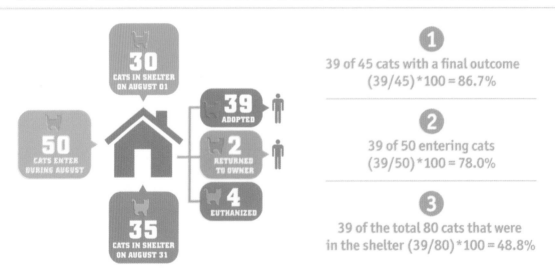

**30** CATS IN SHELTER ON AUGUST 01

**50** CATS ENTER DURING AUGUST

**39** ADOPTED

**2** RETURNED TO OWNER

**4** EUTHANIZED

**35** CATS IN SHELTER ON AUGUST 31

**①** 39 of 45 cats with a final outcome
(39/45)*100 = 86.7%

**②** 39 of 50 entering cats
(39/50)*100 = 78.0%

**③** 39 of the total 80 cats that were
in the shelter (39/80)*100 = 48.8%

The second adoption metric (78.0%) theoretically pertains to cats that entered. However, some of the 39 that were adopted may not have been among those that entered in August. Animals in the numerator must be in the denominator to be considered a rate. For this reason, this metric can be difficult to interpret, particularly for short periods of time.

The third adoption metric (48.8%) represents the proportion of cats that were in the shelter (at risk of adoption) that were adopted. It is mathematically the probability of a cat being adopted from this shelter during August. We prefer the third approach for calculating the adoption rate because it most closely corresponds to what people think an adoption rate represents. That said, if this approach is used, it is important to explain that numerous outcomes (not just adoption and euthanasia) are possible. People should not jump to the conclusion that animals not adopted were euthanized.

**Regardless of the approach shelters use to calculating outcome rates, they must make transparent to consumers how the metrics should be interpreted.**

# STRONGLY RECOMMENDED QUESTIONS

**1** *How would you describe your annual outcome data in a "sound bite"?*

We start this section with a shelter **Outcome Profile** that reports the "outcome" status of all animals in a shelter by the end of a period of time (e.g., year). To obtain rates (e.g., euthanasia rate), the number of animals with each type of outcome <u>is divided by all animals that could have experienced an outcome during the interval</u>. These "outcome-eligible" animals can be thought of as "at risk" of experiencing an outcome.

*Note: Since the rates calculated in this chapter are expressed as percentages we use the two terms, percentage and rate, interchangeably (see Appendix 1 for more discussion).*

**WHAT AND WHY?** A shelter's annual **Outcome Profile** serves to summarize data related to outcomes for a year. When paired with a shelter's annual Intake Profile, a robust picture of the shelter begins to emerge. An example of an annual Outcome Profile is shown in Table 4.1.

**DATA NEEDED** A key challenge to producing this outcome profile is defining the specific group of animals that could undergo an outcome in a given time frame - that is, the denominator for each rate. It includes animals that enter the shelter during the interval, as well as those that were in the shelter at the start of the same time frame. We discuss the advantages of this approach, over more common approaches to calculating the live release rate and other outcome rates, at the end of this chapter.

**HELPFUL HINTS** NOT included in the numerator or denominator for a shelter's general Outcome Profile (Table 4.1) are animals that enter via legal means, those entering through special programs, and those with outcomes not determined by the shelter (e.g., dead-on-arrival, owner-intended euthanasias).

Photo Credit: Adrian Budnick Puptography

# TABLE 4.1 SHELTER OUTCOME PROFILE (2014)

TOTAL OUTCOMES: 2132
SHELTER DESCRIPTION: Open Admission
ANIMAL CONTROL CONTRACT: Yes
CRUELTY INVESTIGATION: Yes

| OUTCOME CATEGORY | 🐕 TOTAL = 545* | | 🐈 TOTAL = 1,587* | |
|---|---|---|---|---|
| SOURCE | # | % | # | % |
| **Released Alive** | **464** | **85.1** | **1348** | **84.9** |
| Adoptions | 265 | 48.6 | 1301 | 82.0 |
| Transfers-out | 9 | 1.7 | 0 | — |
| Returned to owner | 190 | 65.7† | 47 | 8.3† |
| **Not released alive, or lost** | **59** | **10.8** | **165** | **10.4** |
| Euthanized | 58 | 10.6 | 136 | 8.6 |
| Died in shelter | 1 | 0.2 | 28 | 1.8 |
| "Lost" | 0 | — | 1 | 0.0 |
| **\*\*Still in Shelter** | **22** | **4.0** | **74** | **4.7** |

\* Excludes seized animals; includes intakes in 2014 plus animals Still-in-Shelter on 1/1/14

\*\* Includes animals still in shelter system on 12/31/14

† Rates calculated among stray animals only

Categories of animals that are typically considered "outcome-eligible" and those that are not included in the Outcome Profile are summarized in Table 4.2.

A similar tabulation of outcomes for seized animals and those in special programs should be generated separately. Both the numerator and the denominator data of any rate must relate to the same group of animals (e.g., seized, special programs) and the same time frame. Also, the shelter whose data were used in Table 4.1 did not have a category for cats returned to the community because they didn't have such a program.

The outcome definitions adopted by a shelter should reflect categories that are useful to that shelter. Outcome categories must be clearly defined for the staff members who record them.

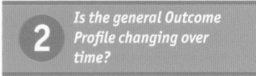

## 2 Is the general Outcome Profile changing over time?

The three broad outcome categories described above can be monitored by graphing their relative contributions to outcomes over time using a stacked bar graph (Figure 4.3).

In January 2010, the shelter in Figure 4.3 set out to reduce its daily census and length-of-stay for

# TABLE 4.2 WHO'S OUTCOME-ELIGIBLE AND WHO ISN'T?

## IN A GIVEN PERIOD OF TIME (E.G., MONTH/YEAR)

| WHO'S OUTCOME-ELIGIBLE? | WHO'S *NOT* OUTCOME-ELIGIBLE? |
|---|---|
| Animals in the shelter at the very beginning of the interval | Privately owned animals coming to the shelter strictly for shelter provided services (e.g., spay/neuter) |
| Animals in the shelter's foster network at the start of the interval | Animals entering for owner-intended euthanasia |
| Stray intakes | Animals seized by a shelter |
| Owner-surrendered intakes | Privately owned animals being held for rabies observation |
| Incoming transfers | Animals being housed temporarily at the shelter as part of a special service or program (e.g., programs that provide housing for the pets of domestic abuse victims) |
| Returned adoptions | |
| Those born in the shelter | Animals entering the shelter DOA (dead on arrival) |

cats. By the end of the year 2010 and continuing through 2011, the rate of animals still in the shelter at year's end had dropped significantly, strongly suggesting that the shelter's efforts were working.

**HELPFUL HINTS** Notice that this graph monitors rate changes among the broad outcome groups over time. This analysis should be accompanied with a review of the actual numbers of animals in each outcome group each year. The percentage contribution of any category (e.g., still-in-shelter) may change, but the absolute numbers of animals in that category could remain the same or change in a direction different from the change in rates. This might happen if the total number of animals in the shelter (i.e., the denominator) changed over time.

The following questions relate to the subgroups within each of the 3 broad outcome types. By answering them, you can construct an Outcome Profile similar to that depicted in Table 4.1.

**3** *What is the rate of animals leaving the shelter alive and is this percentage increasing?*

**WHAT AND WHY?** Arguably, one of the most common goals among shelters is that of releasing a high percentage of animals alive. Historically, there have been several "Live Release Rate" (LRR) or "save rate" calculations used to determine the percentage of animals

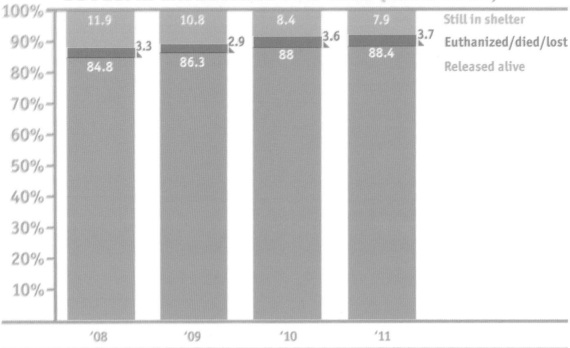

## FIGURE 4.3 ANNUAL DISTRIBUTION OF OUTCOME CATEGORIES FOR CATS (2008-2011)*

*Numbers in bars are percentages.

leaving alive. Since the term "Live Release Rate" does not have a single, standardized definition, we use the term Risk-based LRR (RLRR) to describe the percentage of animals that are released alive during a given time interval from among those that were eligible to leave alive. For more background on other definitions of "Live Release Rate" used by shelters see the section entitled "Comparing Live Release Rate Calculations" at the end of this chapter.

Tracking the RLRR enables your shelter to monitor progress towards your live release goals. Failure to see progress should trigger an examination of why this is so.

**DATA NEEDED** Remember that "live outcomes" typically include adoptions, transfers to other agencies (that guarantee that transferred animals will be not euthanized), and returns-to-owners. The number of animals released alive is used in the numerator of the formula for RLRR. **The denominator includes *all* animals that entered during the interval plus those that were in the shelter at the beginning of the interval that were eligible for a live outcome.** These outcome-eligible animals include the sum of animals surrendered, returned (after adoption), strays and those transferred-in, *plus* the number of animals present at the beginning of the first day of the time period (in these categories).

### THE RLRR IS DEFINED AS:

### (NUMBER OF ANIMALS WITH LIVE OUTCOMES ÷ OUTCOME-ELIGIBLE ANIMALS)

### X

### 100 DURING A SPECIFIC TIME PERIOD

By calculating the RLRR over the course of several months or years, trends can be monitored (Figure 4.4). Graphing the RLRR over time facilitates monitoring trends, but summarizing them in tabular form is also helpful. The key is regular calculation and monitoring.

**HELPFUL HINTS** When evaluating trends, it is always important to ask if there are extenuating circumstances (e.g., a severe canine distemper outbreak introduced by transferred dogs) that may explain the results. The RLRR for dogs dropped in 2013 and then increased again in 2014 (Figure 4.4). When patterns like these arise, they naturally lead to the question of "why", which leads to discussion, engagement of the staff, and often additional analyses of the data.

For shelters accustomed to reporting their Live Release Rate using the Asilomar, final disposi-

tion-based or intake-based approach, you will notice that the Risk-Based Live Release Rate is almost always smaller than these calculations for short time periods (e.g., month). This is because those SIS have been added to the denominator. See the discussion of the four approaches at the end of the chapter and examples of how the different approaches compare to one another.

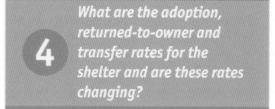

**4** *What are the adoption, returned-to-owner and transfer rates for the shelter and are these rates changing?*

**WHAT AND WHY?** Earlier, we discussed the three ba-

## FIGURE 4.4 ANNUAL RISK-BASED LIVE RELEASE RATES FOR CATS AND DOGS (2011-2014)

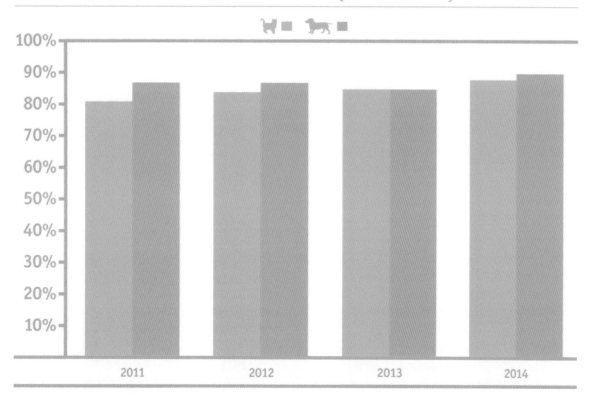

sic outcomes that can occur in any particular time frame once an animal enters the shelter. The most common desirable outcomes – "live releases" – are adoption, being returned to an owner, and being transferred to a facility that guarantees adoption. In some communities, cats returned to the community is a 4th important category. These subcategories of desirable outcomes should be examined separately.

## THE RATES FOR THE DESIRABLE OUTCOMES CAN BE CALCULATED AS FOLLOWS AND CONVERTED TO PERCENTAGES BY MULTIPLYING BY 100:

**ADOPTION RATE** The adoption rate includes adoptions in a time period divided by outcome-eligible animals (Table 4.2) in that time period.

An increase in the adoption rate is indicative of progress toward the goal of increasing the probability of animals being adopted in your shelter. A subtlety here is that some animals may not be eligible for adoption or transfer in a particular period (e.g., animals on their stray hold). In the interest of keeping the calculations straightforward, this distinction is ignored. Your shelter can refine its calculation of adoption rates taking this into account if this is helpful.

**RETURN-TO-OWNER RATE** The return-to-owner rate includes stray animals returned to their owners in a time period <u>divided by stray animals</u> in the shelter during that period.

The animals in an intake category that are eligible to be returned to their owners are strays. An increase in the return-to-owner rate represents progress towards increasing the probability that lost pets are reunited with their families. If animals enter the shelter as owner- surrenders and are then re-adopted immediately by the same owner, this situation does not represent progress toward the goal of returning more lost animals to their owners. If this special group of returned-to-owner group is of interest to your shelter, track it separately.

**HELPFUL HINTS** Many shelters calculate their return-to-owner rates by dividing the animals returned to their owners by the total shelter intake of

animals in the same interval. If only strays are used in the denominator, the returned-to-owner metric represents the probability that a stray animal in the shelter's care will find its way back home. Using the total intake in the denominator is particularly problematic in shelters with a large number of animals transferred-in or surrendered by owners, compared to their stray intake. In these shelters, if the total intake is used in the denominator the shelter will grossly underestimate its success in returning stray animals to their owners.

Notice that in Figure 4.5, the return-to-owner rates for cats are more than 2 times higher if only outcome-eligible stray cats are considered in the denominator rather than total cat intake for the period. This is not an exercise in making the return-to-owner rates look better. Rather it is a more accurate reflection of how a shelter is doing in returning its stray animals to their owners.

**TRANSFER-OUT RATE** Animals that are transferred to an adoption-guarantee agency or rescue group have undergone a "live release." If your shelter partners with such agencies/groups, then outcome-eligible animals have a chance to undergo this particular outcome. The transfer-out rate includes all animals transferred out in a time period divided by all outcome-eligible animals in that time period.

**HELPFUL HINTS** Some animals may not technically qualify for transfer, but to simplify calculations all animals possibly eligible for an outcome are included in the denominator. Shelters can refine this calculation if they desire.

> **5** What are the rates of getting "lost", dying or being euthanized in the shelter?

**LOST RATE** The lost rate includes animals lost in a time period divided by outcome-eligible animals in that time period.

When shelters lose animals – either literally or in the "paperwork" – this suggests management issues that require immediate attention. Eliminating the number of animals lost should be a goal in all shelters.

**MORTALITY RATE** The mortality (or death) rate includes natural deaths in a time period divided by outcome-eligible animals in that time period. In Table 4.1 these are the animals that died in shelter.

**EUTHANASIA RATE** The euthanasia rate includes animals euthanized in the period divided by outcome-eligible animals in that time period.

**HELPFUL HINTS** We believe that animals dying in the shelter should be tracked separately from animals that are euthanized. Both of these categories should

be tracked separately from lost or missing animals. In addition to reducing the number of animals that are euthanized, shelters should have the goal of maximizing the welfare of the animals in their care. One of the most basic "measures" of welfare is whether or not animals are suffering from preventable disease or suffering without hope of recovery. When animals die of preventable disease or are allowed to die when euthanasia could have ended suffering, these animals are not being managed humanely. Management protocols must be re-examined.

As is true for all rates, both the numbers and rates of animals being euthanized should be examined over time. We believe that graphing these values makes monitoring easier and more informative

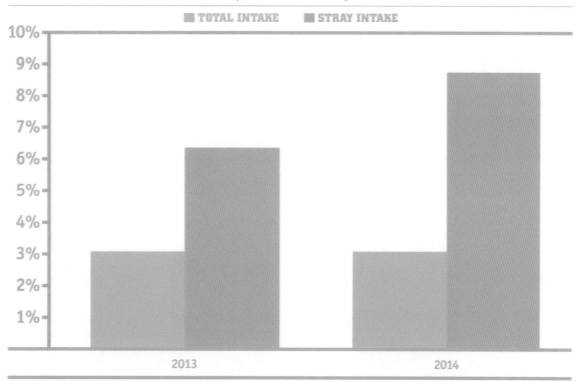

## FIGURE 4.5 RETURN-TO-OWNER RATES CALCULATED USING TOTAL SHELTER INTAKE OF CATS VERSUS OUTCOME-ELIGIBLE STRAYS IN THE DENOMINATORS* (2013-2014)

*The percentages in the vertical axis have been restricted to 0-10%.

# FIGURE 4.6 ANNUAL EUTHANASIA RATES (2012-2014)

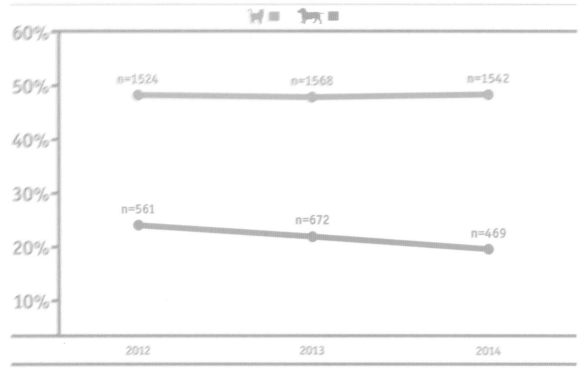

*Numbers represent the denominator of the euthanasia rates.

in comparison to presenting the data in tables or lists. The shelter in Figure 4.6 tracked its euthanasia rates by species for the interval 2012-2014. Some progress was made in reducing the euthanasia rate of dogs, but the euthanasia rate of cats remained stubbornly constant.

The euthanasia rate based on outcome eligible animals will usually be lower than that calculated using the Asilomar, final disposition-based, or intake-based calculations for short periods of time (e.g., month). The four methods produce similar rates for longer periods (e.g., year).

We strongly advocate for shelters to track and monitor the reasons their animals are euthanized as well. By doing so, the shelter can track progress towards eliminating euthanasia for space. It can also identify categories for euthanasia (e.g., behavior, infectious disease) that, with better preventive/control/treatment measures, might be minimized

over time. The Adoption Guarantee shelter in Figure 4.7 separated behavior as a reason for euthanasia into two groups (aggression and other behavioral issues) in 2010 to plan for more behavior modification for their dogs. Using this graph, the shelter knows the probability of dogs being euthanized for specific reasons each year. (Notice that the denominator is not all animals that underwent euthanasia).

> **6** *What is the still-in-shelter rate among outcome-eligible animals at the end of a time interval?*

**WHAT AND WHY?** Remember, *still-in-shelter* refers not only to those animals within the "walls" of the shelter but to any animals in the shelter's care (i.e., in foster care or at satellite locations). Knowing your shelter's

# FIGURE 4.7 PROBABILITY OF DOGS BEING EUTHANIZED FOR VARIOUS REASONS* (2008-2012)

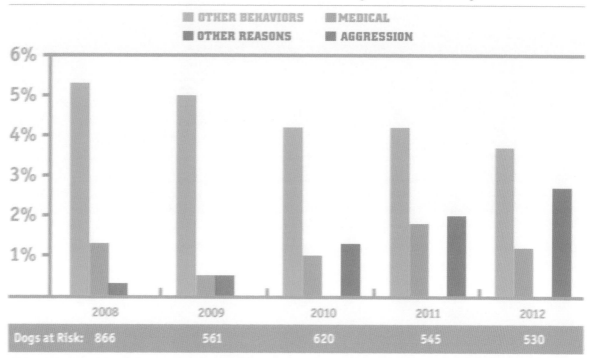

Legend: OTHER BEHAVIORS, MEDICAL, OTHER REASONS, AGGRESSION

| Dogs at Risk: | 866 | 561 | 620 | 545 | 530 |

*The percentages on the vertical axis have been restricted to 0 to 6%.

*still-in-shelter* rate is often an indicator of how efficiently animals are moving through the shelter system.

**DATA NEEDED** Most shelter management programs have the ability to count the number of animals in your shelter on a given day, including those still in the shelter at the end of the final day of any time period.

**HELPFUL HINTS** Don't be confused by when to use the still-in-shelter count at the end versus the beginning of a period. See Table 4.3 *"Which Still-In-Shelter Number?"* for further explanation and an example. Also recognize that the category still-in-shelter may need to be further subdivided. This would be true if your shelter's goal was to reduce overcrowding in all of its associated facilities. In this instance, those remaining within the shelter's walls would be monitored separately from those offsite

(e.g., in foster care, at PetSmart). Also, remember that some animals (e.g., seized, special programs) are best monitored separately. If present in large numbers they may need to be included/excluded in the SIS calculation depending on how the shelter is using this information.

# TABLE 4.3 WHICH STILL-IN-SHELTER (SIS) NUMBER?

The number of animals still in the care of a shelter (SIS) is used in calculations of three general types. Look at the data for dogs from a hypothetical shelter below.

| INTAKE AND OUTCOME OF DOGS IN JULY | NUMBER OF DOGS |
|---|---|
| Intake in July | 75 |
| Euthanasias | 8 |
| Released alive | 69 |
| Still in shelter at the start of July 1 | 20 |
| Still in shelter at the end of July 31 | 18 |
| Still in shelter during July 12 | 25 |

**1** Use the "Still-in-Shelter" number at the start of the interval when you want to assemble all animals that are outcome-eligible for an event in that interval and add them to those entering during the period.

FOR EXAMPLE, THE EUTHANASIA RATE FOR DOGS
DURING THE MONTH OF JULY CAN BE CALCULATED AS FOLLOWS:
(NO. OF EUTHANASIAS) ÷ (INTAKE IN JULY + STILL IN SHELTER JULY 1)
APPLYING THE DATA FROM THE TABLE ABOVE:
EUTHANASIA RATE =
$8 ÷ (75 + 20) = 8 ÷ 95 = 0.084 \times 100 = 8.4\%$

**2** Use the "Still-in-Shelter" number at the end of the interval when you want to estimate the rate of animals that did not leave the shelter during that period (i.e., had the outcome of remaining in the shelter).

FOR EXAMPLE, CALCULATE THE "STILL-IN-SHELTER" RATE AT THE END OF JULY:
(NO. OF DOGS STILL-IN-SHELTER AT THE END OF THE DAY ON JULY 31)
÷ (DOG INTAKE + DOGS STILL IN THE SHELTER
AT THE BEGINNING OF THE DAY ON JULY 1)
APPLYING THE DATA FROM THE TABLE:
STILL-IN-SHELTER RATE =
$18 ÷ (75 + 20) = 18 ÷ 95 = .189 \times 100 = 18.9\%$

**3** Use the "Still-in-Shelter" number on a particular date to evaluate the shelter population in relation to its capacity for providing care. We will discuss this further in Chapter 5.

FOR EXAMPLE, THE NUMBER OF DOGS ON JULY 12 IN THE SHELTER
CAN BE COUNTED (BY SOFTWARE OR BY PEOPLE)
FROM THE TABLE:
SIS DOGS ON JULY 12: 25 DOGS

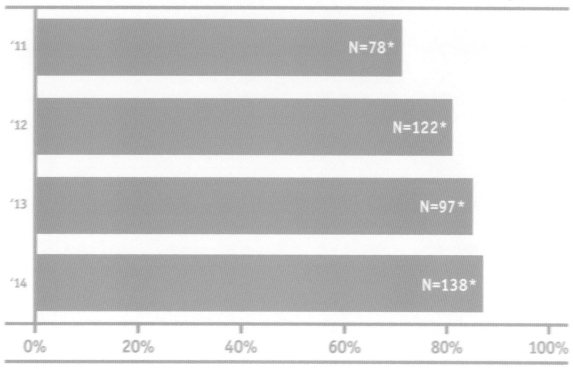

## FIGURE 4.8 RISK-BASED LIVE RELEASE RATE AMONG FOSTER CARE KITTENS 0-4 WEEKS (2011-2014)

'11    N=78*

'12    N=122*

'13    N=97*

'14    N=138*

0%   20%   40%   60%   80%   100%

\* Total number of kittens that were outcome eligible.

# RECOMMENDED QUESTIONS

Answering the *Recommended* questions adds refinements to the understanding of outcomes.

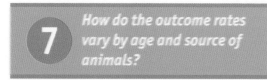

**7**   *How do the outcome rates vary by age and source of animals?*

**WHAT AND WHY?** The age and source of animals (e.g., owner-surrendered, stray) often have a powerful influence on their outcome. For example, in many shelters, kittens and puppies have a higher likelihood of adoption, while adult animals may linger in the shelter and be euthanized for lack of space. Similarly, the issues of dogs from owners (e.g., behavioral & physical health)

compared to those entering as strays may vary, resulting in different outcome rates for those groups.

**DATA NEEDED** In order to look at outcome rates by different parameters (e.g., age group, source) your data must be broken into subsets; most software programs enable users to subset outcome data by age group and source.

*RLRR By Age Group:* After looking at the 71% RLRR from foster care for kittens less than 5 weeks of age in 2011, the shelter in Figure 4.8 revised its foster care book and training sessions to help providers improve the care of their un-weaned kittens. By 2014 the RLRR for this age group had improved to 87% and efforts continue to push this rate even higher.

*Outcome rates by Intake Type:* By keeping track of outcome rates by source (i.e., intake type), the shelter that generated the data shown in Figure 4.9 realized

# FIGURE 4.9 FINAL ANNUAL OUTCOME RATES
# FOR SURRENDERED AND STRAY DOGS (2011-2014)

## OUTCOME TYPES FOR SURRENDERED DOGS

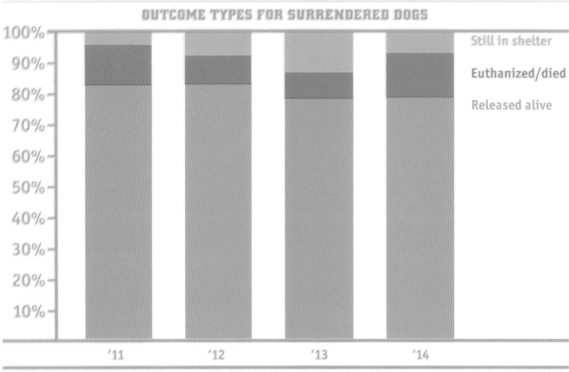

## OUTCOME TYPES FOR STRAY DOGS

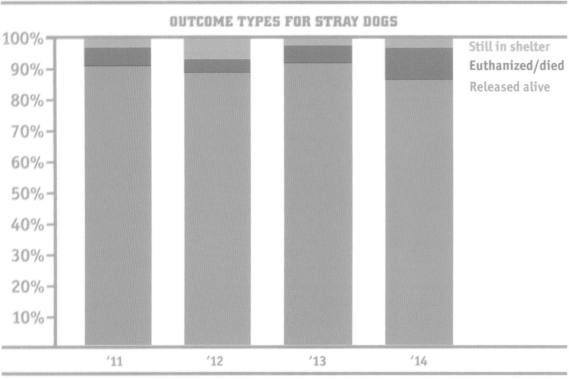

that owner-surrendered dogs were more likely to be euthanized than stray dogs. Then, looking at the reasons for euthanasia, the shelter determined that owner-surrendered dogs had a higher probability of being euthanized for behavioral reasons. This prompted writing a grant to pay a part-time animal behaviorist to create behavior modification plans for dogs displaying undesirable behaviors in the shelter and to provide support for adopters of these dogs.

**HELPFUL HINTS** Besides monitoring outcome rates by age and source, looking at these metrics by time periods other than annually can also be helpful. For example, outcome rates can vary by month and season. Identifying those time frames where the live release or the adoption rates are the lowest can target efforts to improve them.

> **8** *What is the general health status (e.g., Asilomar status) of animals <u>at the time of their final disposition</u> (i.e., when they leave the shelter's care)?*

**WHAT AND WHY?** As mentioned in Chapter 3 (Intake), we recommend recording each animal's general health status at intake and at final disposition. We define final disposition of an animal as its outcome status as it leaves the shelter system's care. We will discuss comparing data regarding the general health status at intake and at final disposition in Chapter 6.

A commonly used means to categorize the general health status of animals in a shelter is that described by the Asilomar Accords (Maddie's Fund, 2016), but any method defined by your shelter may be used. Using the Accords, an animal's general health status is categorized as 1) healthy, 2) treatable-rehabilitatable, 3) treatable-manageable, or 4) unhealthy/untreatable. The shelter in Figure 4.10 suspected that the general health status of their dogs at the time of their final disposition was changing.

**DATA NEEDED** Health status at final disposition.

**INTERPRETATION** The general health status of dogs at their final disposition worsened between 2011 and 2013 in this shelter. That is, the proportion of animals that were unhealthy/untreatable doubled over time. This observation begs the question "why"? Does this reflect worsening care in the shelter, outbreaks of disease that resulted in more undesirable outcomes, a change in the health status of animals entering the shelter or some other explanation?

*RLRR by general health status (e.g., Asilomar Status):* For shelters using general health designations for their animals at exit from their shelter, the risk live release rate should also be monitored by those designations. This enables a shelter to track progress towards increasing the RLRR among healthy and treatable animals. Figure 4.11 shows a graph tracking the RLRR for dogs by their Asilomar status at outcome over a two-year period.

> **9** *What is the Outcome Profile for seized animals?*

**WHAT AND WHY?** Throughout this chapter, we focused primarily on metrics relating to the outcomes of owner-surrendered, transferred-in and stray animals. We treat data regarding seized animals separately (Table 4.4) because these animals do not belong to the shelter (at least until their "case" is resolved) and the shelter's goals relating to them are somewhat different. For example, returning seized animals to their owners is not usually regarded as a positive outcome (as it would be for strays). Also, since seized animals may be severely injured or ill (and require euthanasia to alleviate suffering), inclusion of their outcomes may negatively impact the shelter's outcome statistics for homeless animals from the community.

**HELPFUL HINTS** Differences in the rates of outcomes calculated when seized and other shelter animals are combined versus not combined (Figure 4.12) will depend on the ratio at intake of seized to other shelter animals. We presented a separate outcome profile for seized animals because they are often the largest

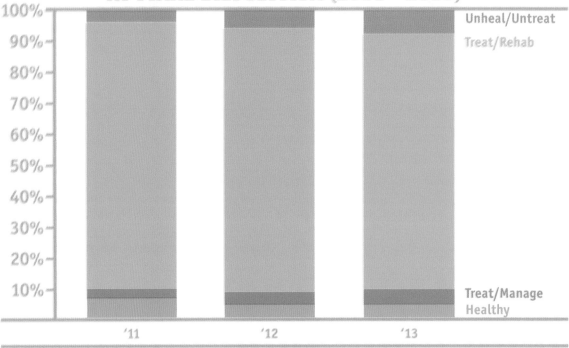

## FIGURE 4.10 ASILOMAR STATUS OF DOGS AT FINAL DISPOSITION (2011 - 2013)

Unheal/Untreat

Treat/Rehab

Treat/Manage
Healthy

'11    '12    '13

group of special shelter intakes. Other intake categories that are "special" might include animals temporarily housed due to natural or man-made disasters or those belonging to special-needs people in the community (e.g., victims of domestic violence). When these animals are returned to their owners, it would not make sense to include them in the shelter's live release rate relating to homeless animals.

The easiest way to separate outcomes for special intake animals is to ensure that they are appro-

priately labeled at intake. You will then be able to include or exclude these animals when looking at various metrics.

# QUESTIONS FOR YOUR CONSIDERATION

**10** *What is the outflow of animals by day of the week?*

**WHAT AND WHY?** As described in the Intake chapter, monitoring intake and outflow by days of the week can facilitate planning for the number of animals

# FIGURE 4.11 ANNUAL RISK-BASED LIVE RELEASE RATE (RLRR) FOR DOGS (2013-2014)

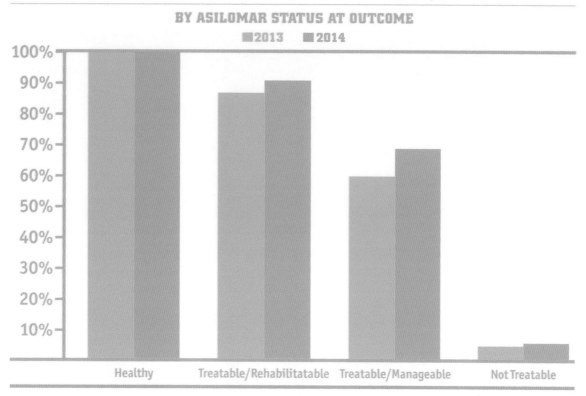

BY ASILOMAR STATUS AT OUTCOME

■ 2013 ■ 2014

to admit daily, and also for how many to have ready to leave the shelter during any given time period. Planning can be especially important for animals to be transferred (to other locations or rescue groups) or to be placed on the adoption floor as your shelter wants to have sufficient animals available (without overcrowding) to maximize the number of animals leaving alive. Planning for transfers will depend on the arrangement each shelter has with its transfer partners and what has been historically true with these partners. Estimating how many animals to have available on the adoption floor is discussed in more detail in Chapter 5. Anticipating the number of adoptions and transfers-out to be expected during a given period can be used to plan for: 1) adequate numbers of adoption counselors, 2) staff working with rescue groups, and 3) using housing space maximally without overcrowding in holding and adoption areas.

The shelter in Figure 4.13 planned to have at least 80-90 cats "available for adoption" every weekend during July and August in 2014.

**HELPFUL HINTS** Notice that having animals "available for adoption" does not necessarily mean that they must all be on the adoption floor simultaneously. As animals are adopted throughout the day (or weekend), other animals can be moved from holding areas to the adoption floor. Since adoption rates may vary by age group, monitoring intake and outflow, and planning by age group, is recommended. Also, when using historical data to estimate what may happen in the present or future, pay attention to events/protocol changes that may be linked to previous adoption rates (i.e., Check your Log of Events or Changes in Protocols, Chapter 3) and adjust your plans accordingly.

# TABLE 4.4 OUTCOME PROFILE FOR SEIZED ANIMALS (2014)

**OVERALL SEIZED OUTCOMES = 234**
**SHELTER DESCRIPTION: Open Admission**
**ANIMAL CONTROL CONTRACT: YES**
**CRUELTY INVESTIGATION: Yes**

| OUTCOME CATEGORY<br>SOURCE | 🐕 TOTAL = 545* | | 🐈 TOTAL = 1,587* | |
|---|---|---|---|---|
| | # | % Outcome Eligible | # | % Outcome Eligible |
| **Released Alive** | 21 | 87.5 | 61 | 29.0 |
| Adoptions | 21 | 87.5 | 0 | 29.0 |
| Transfers-out | 0 | — | | — |
| **Returned To Owner** | 0 | — | 40 | 19.0 |
| **Not released alive or lost** | 3 | 12.5 | 105 | 50.0 |
| Euthanized | 3 | 12.5 | 102 | 48.6 |
| Died in shelter | 0 | — | 3 | 1.4 |
| "Lost" | 0 | — | | |
| **\*\*Still in Shelter** | 0 | — | 4 | 1.9 |

\* Animals seized in 2014 and those seized animals still in the shelter on 1/1/14

\*\* Includes animals still in shelter system on 12/31/14

# SUMMARY

All shelters should be collecting and analyzing the outcomes of their animals on a regular basis. We strongly recommend that shelters use a category that includes animals still in the shelter's care at the end of any time period when examining outcomes. We have encountered too many shelters where the population in the shelter begins to creep upwards over time until it exceeds the shelter's capacity to provide good care. By regularly monitoring animals remaining in the shelter, administrators and staff can act early (if necessary) to curb a rising census before the facility becomes overcrowded.

We also strongly recommend that the numbers of animals with various outcomes be divided by animals that are outcome-eligible. The outcome-eligibles are those animals that are "at risk" of experiencing an outcome. When calculations are made using this approach, the shelter can report the chance or probability that animals in the shelter's care will experience an outcome within specific time frames. We believe that most people looking at shelter outcome rates (regardless of how they are calculated) interpret the information as the chance of the animals experiencing particular outcomes. Also, we believe that Boards of Directors, donors, and the general public are in-

# FIGURE 4.12 ANNUAL OUTCOME RATES
## WHEN DATA FROM SEIZED ANIMALS
## ARE INCLUDED AND EXCLUDED FROM ANALYSES

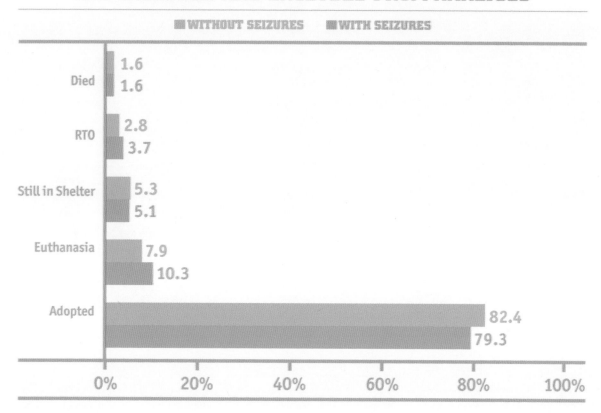

WITHOUT SEIZURES    WITH SEIZURES

| | |
|---|---|
| Died | 1.6 / 1.6 |
| RTO | 2.8 / 3.7 |
| Still in Shelter | 5.3 / 5.1 |
| Euthanasia | 7.9 / 10.3 |
| Adopted | 82.4 / 79.3 |

terested in what happens to all of the animals in a shelter's care, not just a subset (e.g., those released alive). Other approaches to the calculation of outcome rates (e.g., Asilomar, final disposition-based or intake-based) are not wrong. Rather, they answer different questions. Minimally, shelters should report clearly the basis for their calculations and interpret their outcome metrics accordingly.

Many shelters put heavy emphasis on their Live Release Rate (regardless of the method used to calculate it), almost to the exclusion of other metrics when evaluating their performance. Managing animals for optimal welfare is complicated and cannot be measured with one or even a handful of metrics. Shelters can have high live release rates and yet be accumulating animals

beyond their capacity for care. Similarly, shelters can have both high Asilomar LRRs and high mortality rates due to mismanagement. Not only are other metrics important to gauging a shelter's progress towards reaching its many goals, they are necessary for data-driven management and welfare decisions.

As shelters move to making greater usage of their data, they must also begin to evaluate the impact their data has on the welfare of animals in other welfare organizations in their communities. As emphasized in recent presentations (Haston, 2015), when shelters focus only on their own performance and ignore their impact on other shelters in the same community, community animal welfare can suffer. Adoption Guarantee shelters can have high LRRs if they admit only a small

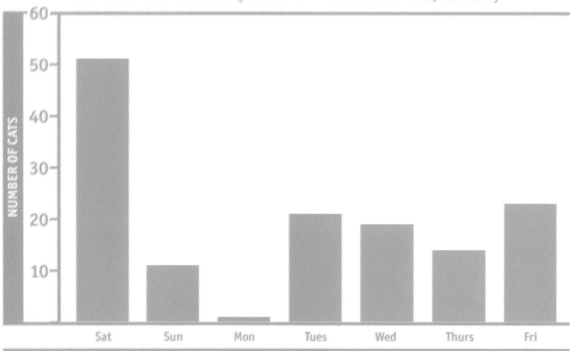

## FIGURE 4.13 AVERAGE NUMBER OF CAT ADOPTIONS BY DAY OF WEEK (JULY 6 - AUGUST 31, 2013)

number of highly adoptable animals, but drive up the intake (and euthanasia rate) of open admission shelters in the same community. Making greater usage of data to improve animal welfare should include efforts to pool information from other welfare organizations in the community. Participation in Shelter Animal Count (shelteranimalcount.org) is beginning to facilitate this process. The common goal should be to save and improve the lives of as many animals as possible in the entire community, not just in a particular organization. Monitoring progress towards shelter- and communi-

ty-level goals requires accurate and complete data regarding all outcomes and an assessment of multiple welfare-related metrics. This approach helps address the question of what is happening to ALL of the animals in a shelter's care and facilitates evaluating the overall welfare of animals in communities.

# COMPARISON OF METHODS TO CALCULATING LIVE RELEASE

In this section we present several different live release rate calculations, but shelters use similar methods to calculate other outcome rates (e.g., adoption, euthanasia) as well. Therefore, comments

## TABLE 4.5 DESCRIPTIONS OF THE NUMBERS INCLUDED IN THE DENOMINATOR OF 4 DIFFERENT LIVE RELEASE RATE CALCULATIONS

| NAME OF THE CALCULATION | COUNTS OF ANIMALS INCLUDED IN THE DENOMINATOR OF THE CALCULATION |
|---|---|
| Asilomar Accords LRR | Adoptions + transfers-out + returns-to-owners + euthanasias of shelter animals + owner-intended euthanasias in Asilomar healthy and treatable categories |
| Final disposition-based LRR | All animals that have left the shelter's care (that is, have experienced a final disposition) |
| Intake-based LRR | All animals that have entered the shelter's care (that is, all intakes into the shelter) |
| Risk-based LRR | All animals that have entered the shelter's care + those that were present at the beginning of the interval |

made regarding the LRR calculations also pertain to other outcome rate calculations (e.g., adoption) using these approaches.

Most shelters calculate a "Live Release Rate" (LRR) as a means to quantify the proportion/percentage of animals that experience "live outcomes" in their shelter. Yet, no single, standardized definition of this metric is used by all shelters. Some shelters use the Asilomar Accords' definition of Live Release Rate (Maddie's Fund, 2016); others use LRR based on final dispositions or, on intake (ASPCApro, 2014a), and still others use some variation of these calculations. The Asilomar LRR, the intake-based LRR, final disposition-based LRR, and the RLRR define animals "released alive" identically, and sum the number of animals adopted, transferred-out, and returned-to-their-owners for their numerators. (The numbers of stray cats released back into the community or barns may also be included in the numerator of some shelters). The methods, however, differ by the denomina-

tors used. Another term, the "save rate," is used less frequently and is discussed last.

All of the rates pertain to a specified time period and all are converted to percentages by multiplying the fractions by 100.

Each of the methods mentioned above has advantages and disadvantages. Selecting among these definitions depends on the question(s) your shelter wants answered, the information it wishes to convey, and (we believe) what your constituencies want to know. Descriptions of the denominators used in each of the LRR calculations are presented in Table 4.5.

### The Asilomar Accords' Live Release Rate (LRR$_{AA}$)

The LRR$_{AA}$ answers the question: "Of the animals that experience an Asilomar-defined outcome in a given time period, what percentage leave the shelter alive?"

Drawbacks to the LRR$_{AA}$ include: 1) It does not account for those remaining in the shelter; 2) it does not account for animals that die or are lost in the interval; and 3) it confuses what happens to shelter-owned animals with those that belong to community members. Drawbacks 1 and 2 can mask serious issues within the shelter that (if present) should be addressed for the welfare of the animals. For example, since still-in-shelter animals are excluded, the LRR$_{AA}$ may remain high while animals accumulate beyond the shelter's capacity to provide good care. Also, since animals that die are not included in the LRR$_{AA}$, animals could be left to die naturally, rather than be euthanized, resulting in unnecessary suffering. Likewise, hypothetically, opening the door and allowing animals to escape (i.e. become "lost") could also preserve a high LRR$_{AA}$. In well-managed shelters where animals are neither lost nor die in high numbers, these latter concerns are less relevant.

By including some owner-intended euthanasias in the denominator of LRR$_{AA}$, the probability of being euthanized after entering a shelter is confused with the shelter's policy to euthanize healthy or treatable animals from the community. Also, shelter staff rarely evaluates the health or behavior of owned animals presented for euthanasia to nearly the same extent as those belonging to the shelter. We, therefore, regard the inclusion of these animals in the shelter's outcome data as a drawback. We prefer that shelters report and track their owner-intended euthanasias separately because this information tells the public exactly what the shelter is doing for the community. It enables the shelter to straightforwardly report the outcomes of the homeless, shelter-owned animals as well.

What is potentially deceptive about LRR$_{AA}$ is that it is not a true measure of the probability or "chance" of being released alive (or inversely, of being euthanized) from a shelter in a defined period. It is simply the percentage of animals having a particular outcome among those experiencing an Asilomar-defined outcome of interest during the period.

In summary, the LRR$_{AA}$ provides information about the percentage of animals undergoing an Asilomar-defined outcome that are released alive during a specified time period. Unfortunately, many in the shelter community don't understand the nuances of the LRR$_{AA}$, let alone members of the public.

It does not account for all animals entering the shelter during the time period, remaining in the shelter, or those animals that die or are lost by the shelter. Its interpretation is further obfuscated by the inclusion of owned, healthy and treatable animals euthanized at the owner's request in shelters performing owner-intended euthanasias.

**Final Disposition-based Live Release Rate (LRR$_{FD}$)**
The LRR$_{FD}$ uses the total number of animals that have had a final disposition as its denominator. It is similar to the LRR$_{AA}$, except that it does not include owner-intended euthanasias, and it does include animals that were lost or died within the time interval of interest. It answers the question during a particular time period, "What percentage of all animals leaving the shelter's care, left the shelter alive?" It does not represent the risk of leaving the shelter alive and could mask animals accumulating in the shelter. For shelters that use this approach it is important to explain what the metric means.

**Intake-based Live Release Rate (LRR$_{intake}$)** The denominator of the intake-based LRR is all animals entering the shelter during the time period of interest. It is used by the ASPCA in their partner shelters (ASPCApro, 2014a). This calculation does not account for animals in residence at the beginning of the interval that could experience an outcome during the interval. Therefore, the probability of an

animal experiencing a particular outcome during the interval cannot be directly calculated.

Notice that the intake-based calculations can include outcomes for animals in the numerator that are not in the denominator. As a consequence, the intake-based LRR is not a true percentage and is, therefore, difficult to interpret. It is possible that the numerator could exceed the denominator if the shelter conducted a highly successful adopt-a-thon and moved most of the animals in the shelter out by the end of a short time period. This could happen because animals in the shelter are the sum of both those entering during the time interval plus those that were still present at the beginning of the interval.

**Risk-based Live Release Rate (RLRR)** The denominator of the RLRR includes all animals in the shelter's care during the interval of interest. This metric represents the probability that animals in the shelter's care (at the beginning of the period plus those entering) were released alive. If the RLRR is 80% for July 2014, animals in the shelter during that month had an 80% chance of leaving alive. We believe that this information is what most people think calculations of LRR represent.

*Examples: All four approaches to the calculation of Live Release will produce very similar (if not identical) results for any long period of time (e.g., year).* This is because the number of animals in the shelter at the beginning and end of a long time period will be only a small fraction of total intake. Also most animals in the shelter will have experienced an outcome by the end of a long period. An exception to this would be for a shelter that euthanizes a large number of healthy and treatable animals at their owner's request and uses the Asilomar definition of LRR. As time frames of interest become shorter (e.g., month, season), the percentage of animals remaining in the shelter is larger in relation to the total intake and those undergoing final outcomes. Therefore, the four calculations can diverge. It is easier to understand the differences among these methods by looking at a comparison. The raw data for Shelter A for one year (2014) are provided in Table 4.6. The live release metrics for this shelter are provided in Table 4.7. All four annual live release calculations for this shelter (79.6%, 79.2%, 79.2% and 78.7%) are very similar, as are their euthanasia rate estimates (20.4%, 20.0%, 20.0, 19.9%). This is because the numbers of cats in the shelter on January 1, 2014 and those remaining on December 31, 2104 are each a small fraction (< 1%) of the total annual intake. [**NOTE:** many shelters using intake-based, final disposition-based, and LRR$_{AA}$ calculations include seized animals as well. We have removed them for the reasons discussed earlier.]

If we look at another shelter, Shelter B, using data for one month (e.g., June )(Table 4.8), the four calculations produce more discrepant estimates shown in Table 4.9. This happens because the proportion of animals remaining in this shelter at the end of a month is much larger in relation to the total intake and total number of outcomes for the month. As predicted, the RLRR is considerably smaller (42.4%) than the Live Release Rates calculated using the other three methods (66.7%, 72.0% and 65.4%). This is because the total number of animals in the denominator of the RLRR is larger (including all animals eligible to experience an outcome). Notice, however, that for the same reason, the euthanasia rate (calculated using all animals eligible to experience an outcome) is considerably smaller (14.1%) than those calculated using the other approaches (33.3%, 24.0%, 21.8%). To reiterate, we prefer the Risk LRR and accompanying outcome rates because they represent probabilities (or the chance) of being released alive or experiencing other outcomes during an interval (e.g., June).

**SAVE RATE** Another metric, the Save Rate, has been used to characterize the percentage of animals leaving a shelter's care alive. One definition subtracts animals that were euthanized from those that entered the shelter and divides this difference by the number of entering animals during an interval (ASPCApro, 2013b). It does not include animals that were still in the shelter at the beginning of the time interval and it assumes that all outcomes other than euthanasia in the interval were desirable (e.g. dying). Other save rate definitions exist. Always describe how save rate and LRR calculations were done.

## TABLE 4.6 OUTCOME AND INTAKE DATA FOR CATS FOR SHELTER A (2014)

| DESCRIPTION | SHELTER A |
|---|---|
| STILL IN SHELTER ON 1/1/14 | 56 |
| **INTAKE (TOTAL)** | |
| Owner-Surrender | 4923 |
| Stray | 4028 |
| Return Adoption | 779 |
| Transfers-In | 0 |
| Born in Shelter | 10 |
| **Intake Total** | **9740** |
| **OWNER-REQUESTED EUTHANASIA (ORE)** | |
| Healthy + Treatables | 20 |
| Unhealthy/Untreatable | [80] |
| ADJUSTED TOTAL INTAKE (ASILOMAR) | 9760 |
| **OUTCOMES** | |
| Adoptions | 7172 |
| Returns-to-Owner | 538 |
| Transfers-Out | 0 |
| **Total Live Outcomes** | **7710** |
| **EUTHANASIAS (IN SHELTER)** | |
| Healthy | 0 |
| Treatable - Rehabilitatable | 99 |
| Treatable - Manageable | 598 |
| Unhealthy/Untreatable | 1253 |
| **Total Euthanasias** | **1950** |
| **OWNER-REQUEST EUTH (ORE)** | |
| Healthy + Treatables | 20 |
| Unhealthy/Untreatable | [80] |
| **Adjusted Total Euthanasias (Asi-lomar)** | **1970** |
| **Died/Lost In Shelter** | **76** |
| STILL IN SHELTER ON 12/31/14 | 60 |

## TABLE 4.7 COMPARISON OF LRR CALCULATIONS IN SHELTER A (2014)

| DESCRIPTION | SHELTER A |
|---|---|
| LRR (ASILOMAR) | 79.6% (7710/9680 |
| Euthanasia (Asilomar) | 20.4% (1970/9680) |
| LRR (final disposition-based) | 79.2% (7710/9736) |
| Euthanasia (final disposition-based) | 20% (1950/9736) |
| Died/Lost (final disposition-based) | 0.8% (76/9736) |
| LRR (intake-based) | 79.2% (7710/9740) |
| Euthanasia (intake-based) | 20% (1950/9740) |
| Died/Lost (intake –based) | 0.8% (76/9740) |
| LRR (risk-based) | 78.7% (7710/9796) |
| Euthanasia rate | 19.9% (1950/9796) |
| Died/lost in shelter | 0.8% 76/9796 |
| STILL IN SHELTER ON 6/30 | 0.6% (60/9796) |

## TABLE 4.8 INTAKE AND OUTCOME DATA FOR THE MONTH OF JUNE 2004 FOR SHELTER B

| DESCRIPTION | SHELTER B |
|---|---|
| STILL IN SHELTER ON 6/1 | 30 |
| **INTAKE (TOTAL)** | |
| Owner-Surrender | 26 |
| Stray | 27 |
| Return Adoption | 2 |
| Transfers-In | 0 |
| Born in Shelter | 0 |
| **Intake Total** | **55** |
| **OWNER-REQUESTED EUTHANASIA** | |
| Healthy + Treatables | 6 |
| Unhealthy/Untreatable | [14] |
| ADJUSTED TOTAL INTAKE (ASILOMAR) | 61 |
| **OUTCOMES** | |
| Adoptions | 30 |
| Returns-to-Owner | 6 |
| Transfers-Out | 0 |
| **Total Live Outcomes** | **36** |
| **EUTHANASIAS (IN SHELTER)** | |
| Healthy | 0 |
| Treatable - Rehabilitatable | 0 |
| Treatable - Manageable | 3 |
| Unhealthy/Untreatable | 9 |
| **Total Euthanasias** | **12** |
| **OWNER-REQUESTED EUTHANASIA** | |
| Healthy + Treatables | 6 |
| Unhealthy/Untreatable | [14] |
| ADJUSTED TOTAL EUTHANASIAS (ASILOMAR) | 18 |
| **Died/Lost In Shelter** | 2 |
| STILL IN SHELTER ON 6/30 | 35 |

## TABLE 4.9 COMPARISON OF LRR CALCULATIONS FOR THE MONTH OF JUNE

| DESCRIPTION | SHELTER B |
|---|---|
| LRR (ASILOMAR) | 66.7% (36/54) |
| Euthanasia (Asilomar) | 33.3% (18/54) |
| LRR (final disposition-based) | 72.0% (36/50) |
| Euthanasia (intake-based) | 24.0% (12/50) |
| Died/Lost (intake-based) | 4.0% (2/50) |
| LRR (intake-based) | 65.4% (36/55) |
| Euthanasia (intake-based) | 21.8% (12/55) |
| Died/Lost (intake –based) | 3.6% (2/55) |
| LRR (risk-based) | 42.4% (36/85) |
| Euthanasia rate | 14.1% (12/85) |
| Died/lost in shelter | 2.3% (2/85) |
| STILL IN SHELTER ON 6/30 | 41.2% (35/85) |

# FLOW & CAPACITY

## INTRODUCTION

In Chapter 3 we discussed intake metrics primarily as they related to the common objective of reducing shelter intake of homeless animals from the community. In Chapter 4 we discussed metrics relating to releasing as many animals alive as possible. In this and the next chapter, we look at metrics that are associated with the welfare of the animals within a shelter system's care. Specifically, we discuss metrics that relate to length of stay, shelter housing and staff capacity, and medical data. We think of the shelter system as encompassing all areas where animals can reside and events through which animals can pass when in the shelter's care (Figure 5.1). This can include time or residence in foster care, at offsite adoption sites, in veterinary clinics for surgery, in the main or satellite shelter facilities, or

in other places where animals are taken before being permanently released.

### FIGURE 5.1 SHELTER FLOW

**INTAKE**

Stray   Surrender   Transfer In   Adoption Returns   Special Intake

**WITHIN SHELTER**

Intake Exam

Vaccinations

Behavior Evaluation

Spay / Neuter

Behavior Modification

Medical Treatments

Foster Care

Outside Care

Euthanasia   Transfer Out   Return to Owner   Lost or Died   Adoption
**OUTCOMES**

# TABLE 5.1 FIVE FREEDOMS: INDICATORS OF GOOD ANIMAL WELFARE

| TYPE OF FREEDOM | DESCRIPTION |
| --- | --- |
| Freedom from hunger and thirst | by ready access to fresh water and a diet to maintain full health and vigor. |
| Freedom from discomfort | by providing an appropriate environment including shelter and a comfortable resting area. |
| Freedom from pain, injury or disease | by disease prevention or rapid diagnosis and treatment. |
| Freedom to express normal behavior | by providing sufficient space, proper facilities and company of the animal's own kind. |
| Freedom from fear and distress | by ensuring conditions and treatment which avoid mental suffering. |

Source: Farm Animal Welfare Council. Accessed March 25, 2013. http://www.fawc.org.uk/freedoms.htm

While we cannot easily quantify good "welfare", we know from experience and studies that the nature of a shelter's facilities and management protocols influence welfare as defined by the "five freedoms" originally espoused for livestock species (Newbury & Hurley, 2013, McMillan, 2013; Farm Animal Welfare Council, n.d.). These five freedoms, also presented in the ASV's Shelter Guidelines, are outlined in Table 5.1 (ASV, 2010).

The welfare of shelter animals, assessed using these freedoms, is directly affected by time spent in the shelter, by the type, size and quantity of animal housing, and the availability of staff (ASV, 2010). Certainly, these are not the only aspects of shelters that affect welfare, but we concentrate on these because they are among the most influential. Despite our focus on these factors, we encourage you to identify all aspects of your shelter system that affect animal welfare and track your progress towards making improvements to them.

This chapter is divided into 2 parts: Animal Flow and Capacity. The Animal Flow section discusses metrics related to the time it takes for animals to move through the shelter system. The Capacity section discusses metrics related to the number of animals that can be humanely housed and that can receive basic care within the shelter.

The objective of this chapter is to explain metrics that can assist in setting goals regarding length of stay and shelter capacity and to monitor progress towards their achievement. Strategies to manage time spent by animals in shelters and to increase capacity are discussed elsewhere (www.millioncatchallenge.org).

# TERMINOLOGY

Since the terminology used by shelters varies, we have defined certain areas (Table 5.2) and events (Table 5.3) to clarify what we mean when we use various terms throughout this and the next chapter. We are not advocating that your shelter adopts this terminology; rather we want to communicate clearly with you. We realize that not every shelter has all of the areas or performs all of the tasks listed in the tables; however, this chapter should be useful even if your shelter does not "fit" this model exactly.

# TABLE 5.2 DEFINITIONS OF
# COMMON SHELTER AREAS WITH HOUSING SPACE

| AREA | DEFINITION |
|---|---|
| Holding | Area that houses animals after they enter the shelter, but before they are placed on the adoption floor. Holding is sometimes called "pre-adoption" as it houses animals before they are ready to be placed on the adoption floor. Shelters often have multiple holding areas (e.g., stray hold, legal hold). |
| Quarantine | Area(s) housing animals that appear healthy, but may be incubating disease. It is usually used in shelters transporting animals in from other parts of the country. |
| Isolation | Area(s) housing sick animals with communicable disease. These areas commonly house animals with upper respiratory tract disease, dermatophytosis/ringworm or parvovirus. Other medical areas may house animals with non-communicable conditions. |
| Surgery | Area associated with a surgery suite for animals either awaiting or recovering from surgery. Typically, these housing units are intended for short-term stays (<24 hours). This may also be a holding area for animals awaiting transport to community veterinarians for surgery. |
| Adoption floor | Area where potential adopters view and interact with animals. In some shelters, animals might be made available for adoption prior to physically arriving on the adoption floor. |
| Foster | Foster care is provided for animals outside of the shelter facility by a qualified individual/household. It provides care for animals that are recovering from a medical procedure, undergoing medical treatment or behavior modification, or are simply too young to be in the shelter. It is included here because animals in foster care are still within the shelter system. |

# TABLE 5.3 DEFINITIONS OF COMMON SHELTER 'EVENTS'

| EVENT | DEFINITION |
|---|---|
| Intake | The date/time of intake marks the start of each animal's path through the shelter system. It is important to accurately record intake data (date, time, intake type) to facilitate monitoring an animal's progress through the system. We discuss intake types extensively in Chapter 3. |
| Intake exam | The intake exam is the initial exam performed by medical personnel or trained non-medical staff. It usually includes a physical exam and vaccination. It also commonly includes the administration of deworming medication, topical anti-parasitics, and infectious disease testing (e.g. FeLV/FIV, heartworm, etc.) depending on the area of the country and shelter resources. |
| Spay / neuter | Many shelters routinely spay and neuter animals before adoption which affects the time that animals spend in a shelter's care. Surgery is performed within the shelter or by offsite veterinarians. The time and resources associated with these procedures must be considered when evaluating costs, time in the shelter, and capacity of the shelter. |
| Behavior evaluation | Some shelters routinely evaluate the behavior of their animals to identify aggressive animals and enhance matches to appropriate adopters. This procedure also affects costs, time in the shelter and shelter capacity. |
| Outcome | All animals entering the shelter eventually have a final outcome. It is important that outcome data (e.g., date, reason) be accurately and completely recorded in order to evaluate time spent in the shelter system and assess the efficiency of animal transit. We discuss outcome types extensively in Chapter 4. |

We have not partitioned the questions in this chapter by levels of recommendation (as is true in other chapters) since most of the discussion centers on basic measures of ALOS and capacity.

# PART I. ANIMAL FLOW

## TABLE 5.4 SHELTER FLOW PROFILE FOR DOGS AND CATS (ALL AGES) (2014)

**TIME FRAME: 2014**
**SHELTER DESCRIPTION: Open Admission**
**ANIMAL CONTROL CONTRACT: Yes, 5 day hold for strays**
**CRUELTY INVESTIGATION: Yes**

| INDICATORS OF FLOW | 🐕 AVERAGE LOS** | | 🐈 AVERAGE LOS | |
|---|---|---|---|---|
| | 0-S* | STRAY | 0-S* | STRAY |
| Time from entry to exit | 22 | 25 | 29 | 30 |
| Time to adoption | 24 | 21.5 | 32 | 35 |
| Time to euthanasia | 11 | 14.5 | 9 | 7 |
| Time to transfer*** | 17.5 | 8 | -- | -- |
| Time to return-to-owner | -- | 2 | -- | 4 |
| Time to first exam | 1.5 | 1.5 | 2 | 2 |
| Time to S/N | 6 | 6.5 | 5.5 | 8.5 |
| Time ON adoption floor | 16 | 13.5 | 24.5 | 25 |

* 0-S : owner/guardian surrender. Excludes unweaned animals in foster care, legally held and special program animals (e.g., pets of domestic violence victims, seized animals).

**LOS : length of stay calculated using the intake-based method.

*** Shelter does not transfer cats.

As in previous chapters, we suggest creating a **Shelter Flow Profile** that provides a quick summary of the average time animals take to common events.

# THE ANNUAL SHELTER FLOW PROFILE

**WHAT AND WHY?** The annual **Shelter Flow Profile** (Table 5.4) serves to summarize time-to-event data each year. It provides a summary of the average (or median – see Appendix 1) time animals spend in a shelter, and it also breaks down the length of time (or speed) it takes for animals to experience com-

mon events (such as behavior evaluation or spay/neuter surgery). Monitoring these metrics can highlight possible impediments (or bottlenecks) to animal flow that, in turn, may suggest strategies to decrease transit time. The shelter in Table 5.4 has animal control contracts and a mandatory hold period of five days for stray animals. For this reason, owner-surrendered and stray animals were separated. In shelters that don't accept strays, the stray information would be eliminated; for shelters with large transport programs a column could be added to reflect transit times of transferred animals that may require more time in your shelter (e.g., quarantine, medical treatment for heartworm infection). We also recommend that the average length of stay of seized animals, unweaned kittens and puppies, and those in special programs be evaluated separately from other intake groups to monitor their flow. **Monitoring the ALOS and average time to events is likely to be most helpful if done frequently (e.g., monthly, seasonally).** Frequent assessments help identify and problem-solve bottlenecks quickly. As always, data in the profile should reflect information that is most helpful to your shelter, so modify these profiles to meet your shelter's needs.

Ideal transit times through a shelter vary because shelters differ by factors (often beyond their control) that influence animal transit time. For ex-

ample, shelters with a mandatory eight-day hold for stray animals are likely to have a higher average length of stay (ALOS) for their strays than shelters in areas with a five-day hold. For us, the most important question for all shelters viewing a particular metric is "Can we improve this metric in our shelter? If so, are we making progress? By how much? Over what time period?"

# LENGTH OF STAY IN THE SHELTER

**WHAT AND WHY?** The **length of stay (LOS)** of an animal is the amount of time (typically measured in days) that she or he spends in the shelter system. It is the time spent from intake until final disposition (i.e., adoption, transfer out, euthanasia) and includes time in foster care or at other offsite locations. It can also be thought of as the speed at which an animal moves through the system. The faster an animal moves, or "flows through", the shorter his LOS; the more slowly he moves through, the longer his LOS.

Note that if you subtract the intake date from the outcome date, then one day in the shelter may be lost. For example, imagine that a cat is found as a stray on January 2nd and is adopted on January 10th. January 10th minus January 2nd yields eight days. If that cat was housed and fed on the 10th and on the 2nd, it actually received 9 days of care. When calculating length of stay for each animal we add one day to our calculations to account for this (Formula 1). Using this approach, animals with zero days in the shelter are counted (e.g., those returned to their owner the same day as they entered, or those euthanized on the day they entered the shelter).

FORMULA 1:

**LENGTH OF STAY = (DATE OF FINAL OUTCOME – DATE OF INTAKE) + 1 DAY**

## TABLE 5.5 REASONS TO MINIMIZE THE TIME ANIMALS SPEND IN A SHELTER

| REASON | EXPLANATION |
|---|---|
| Risk and duration of stress | Shelters are inherently stressful for animals and chronic stress leads to suffering. |
| Risk of disease development | Stress can lower the body's immune defenses and time in a shelter increases the likelihood of exposure to disease organisms, both leading to more disease. Disease causes suffering. |
| Risk of behavioral deterioration | Stress and failure to meet an animal's basic needs can lead to mental deterioration, negatively affecting behavior and likelihood of adoption. |
| Cost of care | More days in the shelter increases the cost of care per animal. |
| Decreased efficiency of cage space | The longer one animal occupies a housing space, the fewer animals can be housed in that housing unit over a period of time. |
| Decreased need for co-housing | Moving animals through the shelter more quickly decreases the need for co-housing that may increase stress. |

Minimizing the time spent in a shelter is important for reasons listed in Table 5.5. Residing in any shelter is stressful to animals because they are confronted with unfamiliar and often frightening stimuli (e.g., other animals, noises, smells, procedures).

Stress can lower an animal's ability to resist disease and lead to mental distress that can lead to poor quality of life (McMillan, 2000, 2013). Increased LOS has been associated with an increased risk of upper respiratory tract infections and overcrowding (Dinnage & Scarlett, 2009; Edinboro et al, 2004). Overcrowding can lead to behavioral deterioration, and both disease and behavioral distress lead to suffering, poor welfare, and lowered adoptability (Kessler and Turner, 1999, Rochlitz, 2005, Griffin & Hume, 2006). Avoidable suffering and poor welfare are not consistent with any shelter's humane mission. Time in the shelter is also related to the average cost of care per animal. If animals spend less time in the shelter and animal costs decline, then more money can be diverted to other shelter priorities (e.g., targeted spay/neuter). Also, more animals can be helped with the same resources. Another, perhaps less appreciated, consequence of shortening animals' LOS is a gain in your shelter's efficiency of housing unit use.

# FIGURE 5.2 FREQUENCY DISTRIBUTION OF THE LENGTHS OF STAY FOR CATS IN A SHELTER (2014)

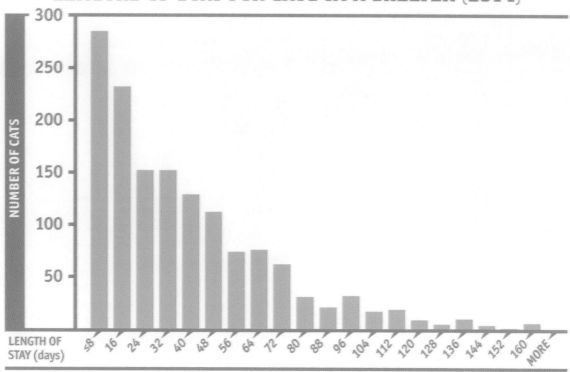

**AVERAGE LENGTH OF STAY (ALOS)** At the time of writing of this Guidebook, shelter software packages summarize the length of stay of all (or subsets of) animals in a shelter using the average length of stay (ALOS). For a given group of animals, it is calculated as follows:

FORMULA 2:

## ALOS = SUM OF THE LOS FOR ALL ANIMALS IN THE GROUP ÷ TOTAL NUMBER OF ANIMALS IN THE GROUP DURING A GIVEN TIME PERIOD

The ALOS may not be the best summary measure of the length of stay, *depending on the purpose for which it is being used*. We say this because in all of the shelters we have looked, the frequency distributions of lengths of stay have not assumed a bell-shaped or Gaussian distribution. They are skewed to the right similar to Figure 5.2. That is, a high percentage of animals stay relatively short periods of time and a smaller percentage stay longer periods. If this is true for your shelter, the average does not represent the middle of the data where half of the animals have lengths of stay below the average and half above. The more appropriate metric is often the **median** which by definition divides a distribution of values into two equal parts (see Appendix 1 entitled "The Math of It" for more details). It is important to graph the distribution of the lengths of stay in your shelter to better understand the flow of your animals.

# FIGURE 5.3 MONITORING CHANGES IN THE AVERAGE LENGTH OF STAY* FOR CATS** (BASED ON INTAKE DATE) (2008 – 2012)

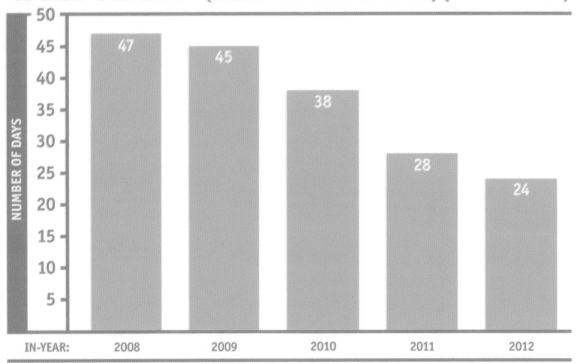

*ALOS was calculated according to the intake-based method.

**Excludes unweaned kittens, those held for legal reasons (e.g., seized/rabies hold) and in special programs (e.g., temporarily housed owned animals).

Since the average length of stay is calculated by shelter software today, the following discussion uses this metric (but median LOS could be substituted for ALOS). Where we think that using the ALOS is potentially misleading, we will alert you.

Since LOS essentially measures the speed at which an individual animal moves through the shelter, ALOS measures the *average* speed at which animals move. It is a measure of the efficiency of animal movement. When describing the passage of animals through the shelter, Newbury & Hurley (2013) coined the terminology of animal "flow-through." We shortened the terminology to "flow" for brevity, but the concept is identical. Shelters want to release as many behaviorally and physically appropriate pets in as short a time frame as possible without sacrificing good welfare. This is not an easily or quick-

ly achieved goal, but it should be a goal of every animal shelter. To do this, shelters should monitor the average length of residence of animals in their care and use these data to identify impediments to flow. The data in Figure 5.3 are taken from a limited admission shelter that had the goal of reducing its average length of stay for cats. The shelter made progress towards its goal over a period of four years.

Interestingly, ALOS is also related to how many animals a shelter can house in a given time period. By minimizing the ALOS of animals in your shelter, you can maximize the use of your housing space. For example, if you had only two cat cages in your shelter, you could house 2 cats in a given month if each cat stayed an average of 30 days. If each cat had an average length of stay of 15 days however, you could theoretically house 4 cats in the same month. If your

ALOS was 7.5 days, then you could house 8 cats during the month. By shortening your animals' ALOS your shelter can reduce stress, risk of disease, and risk of behavioral deterioration. It can also increase the number of animals the shelter can manage in a given time period. If this translated into less suffering and more lives saved, that would be highly desirable!

The word "theoretically" is used here because there is obviously a limit to how much the ALOS can be decreased and animals still receive good care, undergo sterilization, behavioral evaluation and other important events in the shelter. When we (and others) advocate for reducing ALOS, shelter personnel often worry that we are advocating for decisions that will ultimately change an animal's outcome – say, from a live release to euthanasia – simply for the sake of reducing the average length of stay. This is not the intent of this recommendation. Generally speaking, the goal when monitoring ALOS is to determine if there are particular areas or events in the shelter where animals are lingering longer than necessary. Addressing these "bottlenecks" can lead to *more rapid* outcomes, not less desirable outcomes. For example,

animals destined for the adoption floor might have their ALOS reduced by decreasing the amount of time to their first examination or by shortening the time they wait for spay/neuter surgery. Similarly, animals slated for transfer to other agencies could have their average lengths of stay reduced by streamlining the paperwork and other logistical matters. In our experience, reducing the ALOS (and freeing up housing units) tends to increase the live release rate rather than decrease it. Strategies that shelters can adopt to reduce their average length of stay are described in detail elsewhere (www.millioncatchallenge.org, Newbury, Hurley, 2013). We have not included metrics related to costs in this guide, but longer average lengths of stay are associated with higher costs per animal, another important reason to minimize ALOS in shelters.

Average length of stay data should minimally be evaluated by age group and source of animals as these characteristics usually affect ALOS. Juvenile animals (excluding the unweaned) usually have a lower ALOS compared to adult animals. Stray animals often have a higher ALOS compared to owner-surrendered animals because of their stray hold. Examining ALOS information by these characteristics, specific areas in the shelter (e.g., adoptions), and by average times to specific procedures (e.g., S/N) can help target interventions and facilitate capacity calculations. Also realize that ALOS often varies over time (e.g., by season, year), so we recommend monitoring it frequently.

When answering the question, "How is the shelter doing, overall?" average length of stay is a metric that must be considered along with other measures discussed in this guide.

**NOTE** When ALOS is used to monitor progress over time, remember that it can be potentially misleading if a few animals stay very long periods of time. This is because the average is sensitive to extreme values. For example, the ALOS might not change (or even increase) because of a few animals that lingered in the shelter, while the median LOS actually declined. That is, most animals left faster, but the ALOS was unduly affected (i.e., increased) by the long stay of a few animals.

Photo Credit: MACC Nashville, TN

# METHODS OF CALCULATING ALOS

Calculating ALOS is trickier than it may first appear, depending on how you plan to use the metric. There are three approaches to calculating ALOS: 1) based on the intake or entry date; 2) based on the outcome or final disposition date; 3) based on days spent in the shelter (care-days) during the period. The calculation and uses for each of these approaches are explained in more detail at the end of Part 1. Each approach answers a different question. Using the intake-date approach addresses the question: "Among cats entering the shelter in a specific period (e.g., January 2013), what was their average length of stay?" Using the outcome-date ALOS calculation answers the question: "Among cats that had a final disposition in a specific period (e.g., January 2013), what was their average length of stay?" The care-day ALOS answers the question: "Among cats in the shelter system during a specific period (e.g., January 2013), what was their average length of stay *in that time frame*? All 3 methods produce similar ALOS estimates for long periods of time (e.g., year). For shorter periods (e.g., month), the 3 methods often produce discrepant estimates. When a shelter is working towards shortening its ALOS, any of these calculations can usually be used.

The key is to monitor the same definition consistently and understand the limitations of each metric.

**DATA NEEDED** Time frame to which the data pertain; each animal's date of entry during the time frame and date of exit from the shelter system; total number of animals relevant to your calculation.

**HELPFUL HINTS** In recent years, shelters have paid closer attention to LOS and ALOS, largely due to recommendations from shelter medicine experts (ASV, 2010, Koret Shelter Medicine Program, 2015a). Also the availability of shelter software programs has enabled users to generate reports with these metrics. **It is imperative, however, that you understand which method or methods your software uses to calculate ALOS.** A software provider at the time of writing this chapter, for example, enabled users to specify either "intake" or "outcome" depending on whether they wanted to know the ALOS of animals entering (intake-date ALOS) or exiting (outcome-date ALOS) their shelter during a specified interval.

Shelters without dedicated software programs can use a spreadsheet to track intake and outcome dates and calculate the ALOS of all animals entering or leaving the shelter. When presenting the ALOS, always specify the method used to make the calculation. Of course, having accurate data regarding the date of intake and date of final outcome for each animal is *essential* to generating accurate length of stay information.

Also, note that if the intake-date ALOS is used, sufficient time must have passed to allow animals to have experienced a final disposition in order to obtain an unbiased estimate of the ALOS for animals entering during a particular period.

## TABLE 5.6 COMMON REASONS* FOR BOTTLENECKS IMPEDING FLOW OF ANIMALS THROUGH A SHELTER

| COMMON BOTTLENECKS | POTENTIAL REASONS FOR DELAY |
|---|---|
| Delays to intake exam | Insufficient staff |
| | An unusually large number of animals (e.g., seizure) enter in a given time frame |
| Delays to behavioral assessment | Insufficient staff, particularly behavioral |
| | An unusually large number of animals (e.g., seizure) enter in a given time frame |
| Delays to spay/neuter surgery | Insufficient staff, particularly medical staff |
| | An unusually large number of animals (e.g., seizure) enter in a given time frame |
| Illness | Insufficient staff |
| | Ineffective biosecurity or non-existent protocols. |
| | Overcrowding |
| Overcrowding in adoption | Ineffective marketing. The community is unaware of the nature and characteristics of animals available in the shelter. |
| | Potential adopters are overwhelmed by the number of choices (paradox of choice) (Schwartz, 2004). |
| | The shelter is not managing intake. |
| Animal has no plan of movement | There is no systematic monitoring of animal movement. |
| | No one has responsibility for ensuring that each animal is moving. |

*Lack of or poor protocols for moving animals will impede flow for all of the reasons listed.

# BOTTLENECKS AFFECTING FLOW

**WHAT AND WHY?** If flow refers to the speed of an animal's path through the shelter system, then bottlenecks are areas or procedures along the way where animals fail to flow efficiently and may cause back ups in the system. If animals are moving through the shelter such that they are spending minimal time and receiving appropriate care, then the shelter's flow is fast or efficient. Conversely, if animals are lingering in areas where the transit time could be improved, then flow is slow or inefficient. Bottlenecks common to many shelters are listed in Table 5.6.

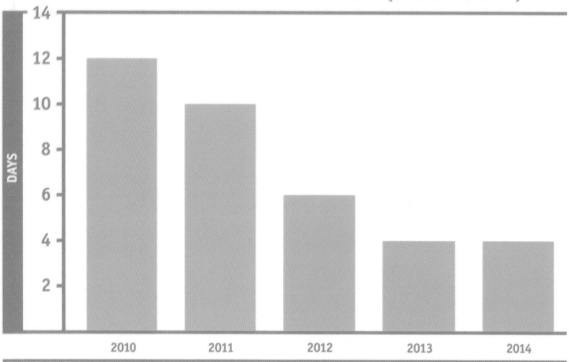

## FIGURE 5.4 AVERAGE TIME FROM ENTRY TO SPAY/NEUTER SURGERY FOR CATS (2010 – 2014)

**IDENTIFYING BOTTLENECKS** Identifying potential bottlenecks and monitoring your progress towards increasing flow through them can be done using several approaches. One approach is to look at the average time from entry to each common event (e.g., first exam) or procedure (e.g., behavioral evaluation) (Table 5.4). With these data, you can brainstorm the question "How can this time be reduced?" We suggest initially answering this question without considering current resources. If there is any possibility that resources can be increased in the future, goals can be set to mitigate the bottleneck when resources are identified. If one potential bottleneck can't be addressed immediately, then problem-solve reducing the time to another until all have been examined. Where progress might be made immediately, draft your strategy for reducing time to completion of that event or procedure. Progress can be monitored over

time by calculating the average time to completion of each problematic event or procedure. The shelter in Figure 5.4 hired an additional part-time veterinarian in 2011 to assist with surgeries, alleviating the chronic backlog of cats awaiting surgery.

Another approach to identifying bottlenecks is to partition the total length of stay into its component parts for animals taking various paths through the shelter. The overall LOS of an animal is the sum of time from entry to physical exam, time from physical exam to behavioral evaluation, time from behavioral evaluation to spay/neuter surgery and so forth, depending on the particular path an individual animal is taking. Calculating the time spent in these intervals by animals taking the most common pathways can increase insight into potential areas where efficiency can be increased. It can also identify pathways that are particularly problematic. The

# FIGURE 5.5 AVERAGE TIME TO EVENTS AND PROCEDURES IN CATS THAT WERE ADOPTED (2010 - 2014)

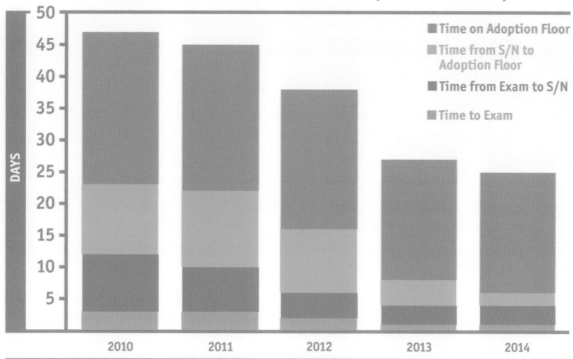

average times between common events (e.g., first exam to S/N surgery) are graphed in Figure 5.5 to illustrate what progress over a four-year period might look like for a fictitious shelter. The disadvantage of this approach is that for many shelters the dates of all events are not recorded in the software, and the data can be difficult to retrieve. Also, similar graphs would be needed for animals taking other pathways (e.g., those not requiring S/N surgery). If shelters are attentive to entering the appropriate data and software improves (making it easier to obtain time estimates between common events), it will become realistic to produce routinely a graph similar to that in Figure 5.5.

The next goal for the shelter in Figure 5.5 might be to shorten its cats' time on the adoption floor. If only one or two areas or events are problematic, then data regarding time spent in only these areas (or get-

ting to these events) can be monitored. Your analyses should reflect what makes sense for your shelter.

**DATA NEEDED** Time frame to which the data pertain; date of entry, date of first exam, date of behavioral evaluation (if applicable), date of spay / neuter surgery, date entering the adoption floor, date of adoption (or other final disposition) or dates of other events important to your shelter. The dates are then subtracted from one another (e.g., date of adoption – date entering the adoption floor + 1 day) for each animal, averaged, and plotted by time period (e.g., year).

**HELPFUL HINT** Some software packages enable shelters to get estimates of time to events (e.g., "Stage reports"). If these are not available or incomplete, monitoring time to events may require a spreadsheet in which staff record dates of events

# FIGURE 5.6 CHANGES IN THE AVERAGE NUMBER OF DAYS TO EUTHANASIA IN A SHELTER FOR DOGS AND CATS (2011 – 2014)

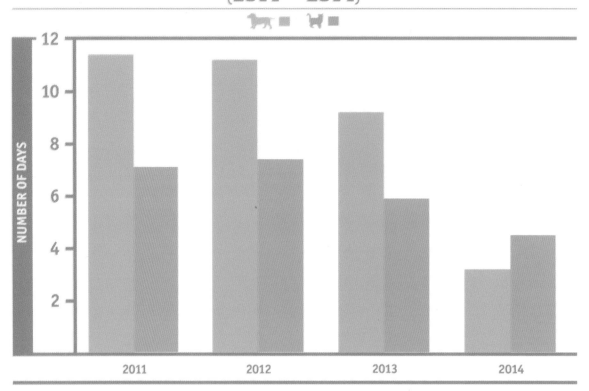

(e.g., entry, surgery) such that they can monitor progress. Similarly, time in particular areas (e.g., adoptions) in a shelter can be calculated if staff faithfully and accurately record location whenever an animal is moved.

If shelters never try to identify and resolve impediments to flow or are not persistent in their efforts, the delays will almost certainly persist and continue to retard animal movement. The potential benefits to improving flow can be so great, that addressing impediments, however difficult, is warranted.

**Detailed analyses are often unnecessary. Shelters frequently know where their primary bottlenecks are and they only need to problem-solve them.** The effectiveness of their efforts can often be monitored by evaluating only the overall ALOS.

# MEASURING THE TIME TO EUTHANASIA

**WHAT AND WHY?** For animals that must be euthanized the time should be as short as possible. Decisions to euthanize should be made in a timely manner such that animals are minimally stressed and do not get sick (and suffer) before they are euthanized. For the shelter in Figure 5.6, turnover of the staff providing behavioral assessments resulted in delays in euthanasia decisions that led to an increased ALOS in 2011 – 2012. Following the employment of a new behaviorist in mid-2012, the average length of time to euthanasia for behavior rea-

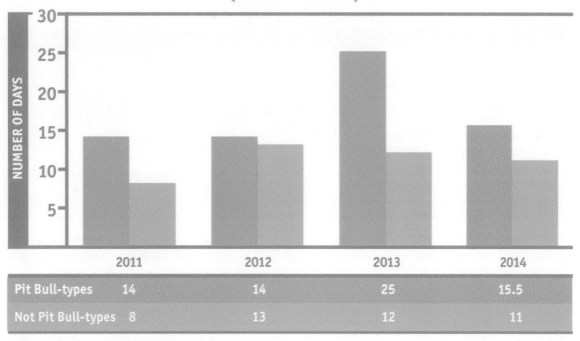

## FIGURE 5.7 AVERAGE LENGTH OF STAY* BY BREED: PIT BULL-TYPE COMPARED TO NON-PIT BULL-TYPE DOGS (2011 – 2014)

| | 2011 | 2012 | 2013 | 2014 |
|---|---|---|---|---|
| Pit Bull-types | 14 | 14 | 25 | 15.5 |
| Not Pit Bull-types | 8 | 13 | 12 | 11 |

*ALOS was calculated using the intake-based approach.

sons (and for all reasons combined) decreased dramatically for dogs and somewhat for cats.

**DATA NEEDED** Time frame to which the data pertain, date of euthanasia, date of intake, (date of euthanasia – date of intake +1) for all animals euthanized (excluding owner-intended).

If the dates of entry and of euthanasia are recorded for each animal euthanized, these calculations can be done in a spreadsheet. Alternatively, your management software may do this for you.

# CHARACTERISTICS THAT IMPACT ALOS

**WHAT AND WHY?** Other characteristics of shelter animals often have an important effect on length of stay,

including intake type (e.g., stray, owner-surrendered), breed (e.g., pit bull type or not), size, age group, season of intake, and Asilomar status. **Like most of the metrics we discuss, evaluating ALOS by subgroups and by area in the shelter are likely to be more helpful than looking at overall ALOS alone.** For example, "fast-tracking" certain types of animals like kittens and previously altered, owner-surrendered animals is one approach to decreasing ALOS (Newbury & Hurley, 2013). Examining the ALOS of subgroups can identify groups that are moving quickly; conversely, it can identify groups whose transit time is slow and could benefit from creative solutions to lower their ALOS. In Figure 5.7, the shelter was interested in monitoring the ALOS of pit bull-type dogs, as they recognized that these dogs often remained on the adoption floor longer than other breed types. Despite efforts to market these dogs more progressively, however, the ALOS failed to change. Failed plans, if identified, are opportunities to problem-solve current strategies and seek new solutions based on input from all relevant personnel.

**DATA NEEDED** Time frame to which the data pertain, the definition of pit bull-type dogs in your shelter (or other breed mixes of interest); intake and exit dates of pit bull-type and non pit bull-type dogs; average length of stay for pit bull-type dogs and non pit bull-type dogs by year.

**HELPFUL HINTS** We particularly like to review the ALOS of animals by age group (always looking at unweaned animals separately), source (e.g., stray, seized), and breed-type (if a shelter has a problematic breed type). Monitoring the average time spent in particular areas (e.g., adoptions) can signal areas where new strategies to accelerate flow would be helpful. Estimates of ALOS in specific areas can also be used to estimate the housing capacity in those areas.

Also, it is not uncommon to see increases (or decreases) in average length of stay during particular years (as is true in Figure 5.7 for 2013) that are not sustained over time. This can be due to legal seizures in cruelty cases or other factors that result in periodic variability in the data. Always keep this in mind when interpreting data. After examining data over a period of years, the usual variability in your data will become apparent.

# CHOOSING THE APPROPRIATE AVERAGE LENGTH OF STAY ESTIMATE

As mentioned earlier in this chapter there are three approaches to calculating the average length of stay of shelter animals and each method answers a

# FIGURE 5.8 TWELVE CATS AND THEIR LENGTH OF STAY IN A HYPOTHETICAL SHELTER DURING MAY – JULY

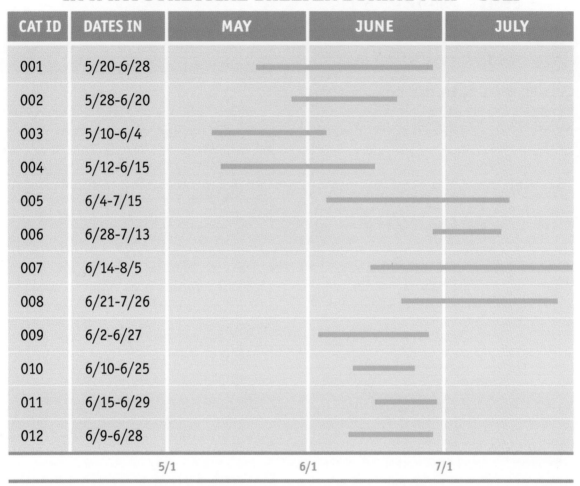

| CAT ID | DATES IN | MAY | JUNE | JULY |
|--------|----------|-----|------|------|
| 001 | 5/20-6/28 | | | |
| 002 | 5/28-6/20 | | | |
| 003 | 5/10-6/4 | | | |
| 004 | 5/12-6/15 | | | |
| 005 | 6/4-7/15 | | | |
| 006 | 6/28-7/13 | | | |
| 007 | 6/14-8/5 | | | |
| 008 | 6/21-7/26 | | | |
| 009 | 6/2-6/27 | | | |
| 010 | 6/10-6/25 | | | |
| 011 | 6/15-6/29 | | | |
| 012 | 6/9-6/28 | | | |

5/1     6/1     7/1

different question. To understand the differences among the three approaches, study Figure 5.8.

The vertical lines (in white) in the figure separate May from June from July and represent the first day of each of these months. The horizontal lines (in green) represent individual cats with the beginning of the line (reading from left to right) being the day a cat entered the shelter and the end of the line representing the day the cat left the shelter. Cat #001 entered the shelter on May 20 and was adopted on June 28; cat #002 entered the shelter on May 28 and was adopted on June 20; cat #003 entered the shelter on

May 10 and was returned to her owner on June 4, and so forth. In this shelter let's assume that a total of 12 cats were in the shelter at some time during June.

**Intake-date ALOS** is calculated by averaging the lengths of stay of all cats that entered during a particular period of time. It omits cats that entered before the beginning of the period.

**Outcome-date ALOS** is calculated by averaging the lengths of stay of all cats that left the shelter (i.e., had a final disposition) during a particular period of time. It omits cats that have not yet left the shelter system's care.

**Care-day ALOS** is calculated by averaging the lengths of stay of all cats during a particular period of time that they were in the shelter.

To clarify the differences among these three methods, look at calculating the average length of stay for the month of June using Figure 5.8.

**USING THE INTAKE-DATE METHOD** The lengths of stay for cats entering the shelter in June (cats #5 – 12) are summed and divided by the number of cats entering the shelter in June.

## INTAKE-DATE ALOS

## 224/8 = 28.0 DAYS

**USING THE OUTCOME-DATE METHOD** The lengths of stay for cats leaving the shelter in June (cats #1 – 4; 9 - 12) are summed and divided by the number of cats leaving the shelter in June.

## OUTCOME-DATE ALOS

## 202/8 = 25.3 DAYS

**USING THE CARE-DAY METHOD** In order to estimate the average number of days spent in the shelter in June by all 12 cats in the shelter, the total number of care-days must be divided by the total number of cats in the shelter. (A **care-day** is a day or fraction of a day that an animal spends in the shelter and requires care and cage space. Two cats spending 2 days in a shelter contribute 4 care-days to the total number of care-days for cats **in that period**).

So, cat #001 spent 28 days in the shelter (i.e., June 28-June 1+1) in June; cat #002 spent 20 days in the shelter (June 20-June 1+1) in June; cat #007 spent 17 days in the shelter (June 30-June 14+1) in June; etc. Summing over all 12 cats, 201 care-days (or cage-days) were occupied in this shelter during June. Divide this number by the number of cats that were in the shelter (i.e., 12 cats in this example) to obtain the ALOS of cats in the shelter in June. The

care-day based calculation of average length of stay (ALOS) in the shelter for these cats was 16.8 days.

## CARE-DAY ALOS

## (201/12) = 16.8 DAYS

To summarize, the methods of calculating ALOS based on intake-date (or outcome-date) omit animals that did not enter (or exit) during the period of interest, yet occupied cage space during the time frame. In the example above, notice that of the 12 cats in the shelter in June, only 8 entered during June and the intake-date ALOS uses only these 8 cats. Similarly, the ALOS of cats leaving the shelter in June uses only the 8 cats that exited in June. Therefore, each of these calculations fails to include 4 cats that spent time in the shelter and occupied cage space in June. Also, both of these ALOS calculations include time the cats spent in the shelter outside of the month of June.

The results of the three methods of ALOS calculation for this hypothetical shelter are summarized below.

## INTAKE-DATE ALOS
## =
## 28.0 (224/8) DAYS

---

## OUTCOME-DATE ALOS
## =
## 25.3 (202/8) DAYS

---

## CARE-DAY ALOS
## =
## 16.8 (201/12) DAYS

*Of the three possible calculations of ALOS, the care-day based ALOS is the most appropriate when calculating housing capacity.* It represents the

## TABLE 5.7 ANOTHER APPROACH TO ESTIMATING THE CARE-DAY ALOS FOR ANIMALS IN A SHELTER DURING A PERIOD OF TIME

| | |
|---|---|
| 1 | Using shelter software, obtain animal count data for animals in the shelter for each day in the period of interest. |
| 2 | Sum the daily counts to obtain the total number of care-days provided. |
| 3 | Obtain the number of animals entering the shelter during the period and add that to the number present on day 1. These are the animals housed during the period. |
| 4 | Divide the number of total care-days by the number of animals in the shelter during the period. This is an estimate of the care-day ALOS during the period. |

ALOS of animals in the shelter (or particular area) during a period of time. When predicting needed housing capacity for short periods of time (e.g., month), it is critical to use the care-day method or capacity estimates may be biased.

# OBTAINING THE CARE-DAY ALOS

Most shelters will need a shelter software package to get the numbers needed to estimate the care-day ALOS of animals during a particular period (e.g., June). The method described above is one approach to obtaining the total number of care-days that animals spent in a shelter. Another approach is suggested in Table 5.7.

**HELPFUL HINTS** When using the approach in Table 5.7, the count in step # 1 must include (or closely approximate) ALL animals that were in the shelter each day. Remove counts of animals in foster or from other offsite locations. (Check your software to identify the report that provides this information). By summing the counts across all days in the period, you get the total care-days for animals in the shelter. Dividing this number by the total number

of animals in the shelter during the period provides an estimate of the care-day ALOS. **Notice that this approach could be used to get the care-day based ALOS for specific areas in the shelter as well.** The information used in each step would pertain to the area of interest. This will be discussed further in the Capacity section of this chapter.

## TABLE 5.8 DAILY COUNT FOR DOGS (JULY 1 – JULY 7, 2014)

| DATE | CARE-DAYS |
|------|-----------|
| 7/1/2014 | 171 |
| 7/2/2014 | 163 |
| 7/3/2014 | 165 |
| 7/4/2014 | 161 |
| 7/5/2014 | 162 |
| 7/6/2014 | 161 |
| 7/7/2014 | 162 |
| **TOTAL** | **1145** |

An example showing a care-day based ALOS calculation is provided below:

The daily dog count for a 7-day period in a shelter is shown in Table 5.8. A total of 180 dogs (171 present on July 1 plus 9 that entered) resided in the shelter for some amount of time during the period (Table 5.9). Therefore, these 180 dogs stayed an average of 6.4 days (1145/180 = 6.4 days) during the period.

**HELPFUL HINT** In the example presented, the calculations of ALOS were restricted to animals in the shelter; this is particularly important when ALOS is incorporated into calculations of housing capacity (see next section). If the goal is to monitor ALOS for all animals or other subsets, this restriction would not be necessary.

## TABLE 5.9 EXAMPLE OF AVERAGE LENGTH OF STAY CALCULATION BASED ON CARE-DAYS FOR THE MONTH OF JULY

| DESCRIPTION OF DATA | VALUES |
|---------------------|--------|
| Time frame | 7/1 - 7/7 |
| Sum of the daily counts of dogs (care-days) in the shelter during the period | 1145 care-days |
| Total intake for the period | 9 |
| Total dogs in shelter on July 1 at 12 a.m. | 171 |

$$\frac{\text{Total care-days}}{\text{\# of animals that were housed}} = \text{ALOS}$$

Rearranging the formula and plugging numbers in:

?? ALOS X (9 + 171) = 1145 care-days

Solving for ALOS

1145 care-days / 180 dogs = **6.4 days**

**SUMMARY** Any of the ALOS methods can be used to monitor trends in the average length of stay in a shelter. Remember, however, that both the intake and outcome date-based calculations may encompass time in the shelter outside of a particular period of interest. The outcome-date method has the advantage of being produced routinely and is available almost immediately after a period has ended in software packages. The intake-date method requires that sufficient time has passed for a large percentage of animals entering during a specified period to have experienced a final disposition (or the ALOS will be biased downwards). Calculating the care-day based method may currently require more work, but should be used when estimating housing capacity, particularly for short periods of time (e.g., month). For long periods of time (e.g., year) ALOS values (regardless of method of calculation) will be very similar.

Photo Credit: iStock

# PART 2. SHELTER HOUSING AND STAFFING CAPACITY

**WHAT AND WHY?** Shelter capacity can be defined in numerous ways. For example, one could consider the capacity of the parking lot for accommodating the vehicles of potential adopters or the shelter's capacity to hold on-site fundraising events. Even a shelter's capacity to provide animal care can be defined by many factors. For example, the availability of certain resources (e.g., food, towels, medical services) can affect a shelter's capacity to provide care. Measuring every factor that relates to your shelter's capacity for care is not necessary. Pick measurable and influential indicators. In this guidebook, we limit our discussion to animal housing and staffing capacity calculations.

Exceeding the housing (or staffing) capacity of a shelter leads to overcrowding, increased lev-els of stress, behavioral degeneration, disease, and increased average lengths of stay (Pedersen, 1991, Lawler, 1998, McMillan, 2013, Dinnage & Scarlett, 2009). Unfortunately, the number of animals in many shelters exceeds the number for which they can provide adequate care. Even in shelters providing adequate care, there is always the danger for the count to creep up or for ongoing budgetary issues to force staff cutbacks. Consistent monitoring can identify the impact these changes have on capacity. Interestingly, underutilization of space for dogs has also become an issue in some shelters that have experienced sharp declines in dog intake. Underutilization of space or staff can be indicative of lost opportunities to save lives or of wasted resources.

## HOUSING CAPACITY

Capacity is defined as 1) the largest amount or number that can be held or contained; 2) the ability to hold or contain people or things; 3) the ability to do something: a mental, emotional or physical ability (Miriam-Webster, 2014). With regards to housing, we are using the first definition. Housing capacity can be measured at numerous levels – for the whole shelter, areas within the shelter or even at offsite locations (e.g., foster homes). For simplicity, we will talk about whole shelter capacity, but present examples for particular areas because the principles are the same.

Most often people think of the housing capacity in a shelter as the maximum number of animals that can be housed in the shelter <u>at any point in time</u>. Theoretically, this is a static, or unchanging, measure of housing capacity until new housing is constructed so we refer to it as the **static housing capacity**. Since some characteristics of animals influence housing needs (e.g., age, size), and animals entering a shelter with those characteristics can change over time, housing capacity is not really static. For example, during the winter, a shelter with a fixed number of housing units might humanely house 10 cats (all adults), but that same shelter might also humanely house 22 cats in the summer (3 adults and 19 kittens). This makes determining what we call "static capacity" challenging.

**Dynamic housing capacity (DHC)**, in contrast, incorporates a time dimension and relates to the estimated maximum number of animals that a shelter can humanely house in a given period of time (e.g., the month of July). Over time, it can vary for the same reasons as static capacity, but is also influenced by how long animals stay in the shelter and the length of the time period of interest. The dynamic housing capacity of a shelter can be estimated by understanding the relationship between the number of humane housing spaces, the average length of stay (ALOS) of animals, and the length of the period of interest. Formula 3 defines the relationship.

(e.g., too small to enable animals to express normal behaviors) should not be counted when determining capacity. Since not every housing unit is humane for every animal, the shelter needs to have guidelines as to the number of animals with particular characteristics (e.g.; age, group, sizes) that can be humanely housed in each of their housing spaces. (Shelters probably have these already, but they may not be explicitly defined and widely understood).

Notice that when the number of humane housing units is multiplied by days in a time frame, the result is the total cage-days available for housing. In a sense, it is a shelter's "housing currency" and a shelter can choose how it wishes to utilize that currency. The shelter can house a few animals for a long time (have a long ALOS) or more animals for a short time (have a short ALOS) during any time period. Managing the ALOS is critical to efficiently using housing space and saving lives.

## FORMULA 3
## DYNAMIC HOUSING CAPACITY (DHC)
=
## (NUMBER OF HUMANE HOUSING UNITS
X
## THE NUMBER OF DAYS IN THE PERIOD OF INTEREST)
÷
## AVERAGE LENGTH OF STAY

When using Formula 3, the number of housing spaces in the shelter must be estimated for the period of interest. These housing spaces must be humane. We refer to these basic housing units as Humane Housing Units (HHUs). One HHU is a cage, run, room, space in a room or other form of housing (including foster homes) that meets or exceeds current guidelines for housing an animal in shelters referenced by ASV (2010). We use the terminology, Humane Housing Unit, to emphasize that inappropriate housing

# TABLE 5.10 ASSUMPTIONS ASSOCIATED WITH
# THE USEFULNESS OF CALCULATIONS USING FORMULA 3

| 1 | The intake and outflow of animals housed in a shelter (or area) are roughly equal within the time frame of interest. Therefore, the number of animals housed in the shelter (or area of interest) is constant. |
|---|---|
| 2 | Animals entering and leaving the area occur relatively evenly across the time period. For example, if most of the animals entering during a month enter during the first 2 weeks, then the shelter could be overcrowded during the first 2 weeks and relatively empty at the end of the month. |
| 3 | The care-day method of estimating ALOS is used. |
| 4 | The calculation is made taking into account the characteristics of the animals to be housed (e.g., age group, size) and their housing needs. |
| 5 | The average length of stay is fairly constant throughout the period of interest. |

Also, note that if the ALOS can be thought of as the average speed with which animals are moving through a shelter (or area), a shelter's DHC can be thought of as the animal "throughput" during a particular period of time. If throughput is maximized, more animals can be housed and more lives can be saved. This is done, not by crowding in as many animals as possible at one time, but by minimizing their ALOS. This may at first seem counter-intuitive. Remember, however, that overcrowding leads to higher stress for animals and staff, which in turn leads to more disease and behavioral issues, which then leads to longer average lengths of stay, and ultimately to fewer animals passing through the shelter. Formula 3 clarifies how the ALOS, the number of HHUs, and a shelter's dynamic housing capacity inter-relate during a specific period of time. Using the formula, shelters can anticipate how changes in one of these components (e.g., ALOS) will affect others (e.g., DHC). Strategies to lower ALOS and increase throughput are discussed elsewhere (Newbury & Hurley, 2013).

It is important to realize that the valid use of the formula is associated with certain assumptions (Table 5.10). These assumptions should be carefully considered before applying Formula 3. The validity and precision of the capacity estimates obtained will depend on the quality of the data and the degree to which the assumptions apply.

The two examples that follow illustrate 2 useful applications of Formula 3. To digest the examples and ensuing discussion requires some math, time and effort.

### EXAMPLE 1

*The shelter manager and executive director of a limited admission shelter want to reduce the ALOS that their cats spend in the adult holding area from the current 14 days. Their motivation is to increase the number of cats they can house in that area (DHC) and reduce stress during April-September (their highest intake months). They are developing a plan to accomplish their S.M.A.R.T. goal. (See Chapter 2 for discussion of goals.)*

*As part of their plan they want to estimate the number of animals that the shelter could humanely house if they achieve various reductions in their ALOS*

# TABLE 5.11 ESTIMATING DHC IN HOLDING WHEN THE ALOS IS ALTERED

| | STEPS TO ESTIMATING DHC |
|---|---|
| 1 | Count the number of Humane Housing Units for cats in holding. They estimated 50 spaces for cats in holding. |
| 2 | Count the number of days in the period. They counted 183 days in April-September. |
| 3 | Put the numbers in steps #1 and #2 into Formula 3 along with the target ALOS. |
| 4 | Solve for the DHC associated with each target ALOS. |

### SAMPLE CALCULATION

**Formula 3:**
**(HHUs X number of days in the period) ÷ ALOS = DHC**

If the ALOS was reduced to 13 days in holding,
704 cats could be housed there.

**(50 HHUs X 183 days) ÷ 13 days = 704 cats**

\* This calculation assumes that only one cat occupies one housing unit at a time.

---

during the period April – September. (Remember that the dynamic housing capacity is the estimated number of animals that could be housed in a given time period.)

The steps they used are outlined in Table 5.11. First they counted the number of HHUs for cats in the adult cat holding area assuming one cat per housing unit. Then they counted the number of days in the period April-September. Lastly, they put these 2 numbers into Formula 3 along with their target ALOS numbers one-at-a-time. Table 5.11 shows their calculation for a target ALOS of 13 days. They repeated their calculations for target ALOS numbers of 9-12 to generate the numbers in Table 5.12.

Notice that this shelter (with 50 HHUs in holding) could house an average of approximately 78 more cats for each day of reduction in their ALOS during the period April-September. For practice,

replicate the DHC estimates for the other target ALOS values in Table 5.12.

**HELPFUL HINTS** Estimating the number of HHUs in a shelter (or in an area in a shelter as in Example 1) is complicated because the distribution of entering animals of different sizes and age groups (requiring different size housing units) is usually not definitively known when calculations are made. This distribution can be estimated using data from previous time periods, but these characteristics may change with time, resulting in errors in the DHC calculations. Group or colony housing represents another challenge, as definitive guidelines for counting the number of individuals that can be housed in group housing do not exist. Deciding how to count the number of HHUs in relation to the characteristics of your entering animals can be dif-

# TABLE 5.12 ESTIMATES OF THE DYNAMIC HOUSING CAPACITY WITH VARIOUS REDUCTIONS IN THE AVERAGE LENGTH OF STAY OF CATS

### PERIOD OF TIME: APRIL–SEPTEMBER (183 DAYS)

| TARGET ALOS (DAYS) | DYNAMIC HOUSING CAPACITY |
|:---:|:---:|
| 13 | 704 |
| 12 | 762 |
| 11 | 831 |
| 10 | 915 |
| 9 | 1017 |

ficult, may vary over time, and will require judgment.

Also, the ALOS often changes over time (e.g., by season). Before estimating capacity for a relatively long time period, it is wise to examine whether the ALOS values from similar periods remained constant. If ALOS seems likely to vary significantly, capacity assessments should be made for shorter intervals.

The ALOS values evaluated must allow animals to receive good care, undergo sterilization, behavioral evaluation (if done) and other important events in the shelter. Therefore, when using Formula 3 to evaluate the effect of lowering ALOS, choose realistic target ALOS values.

## EXAMPLE 2

*In another shelter, the shelter manager wants to estimate the average number of cats to have on the adoption floor each day in July-August if the shelter achieves various reductions in the average time they spend on the adoption floor. Cats are currently available for adoption an average of 13 days.*

*In Example 1, Formula 3 was used to estimate the DHC of a particular area in the shelter when the ALOS was altered. In this example, DHC during July-August was estimated using the number of animals that were*

Photo Credit: Penny Adams

# TABLE 5.13 ESTIMATING THE NUMBER OF CATS TO HAVE IN ADOPTION HHUs WHEN THE ALOS IS ALTERED

## STEPS TO ESTIMATING THE NUMBERS

| | |
|---|---|
| 1 | Look up the number of cat adoptions from last July-August. The shelter adopted out 190 cats. These are the cats that occupied HHUs on the adoption floor. |
| 2 | Count the number of days in the period. There were 62 days for July-August. |
| 3 | Put the numbers in steps #1 and #2 into Formula 3 along with a target ALOS. |
| 4 | Solve for the HHUs associated with each target ALOS. |

### SAMPLE CALCULATION

**Formula 3:**
**(HHUs X number of days in the period) ÷ ALOS = DHC**

If the ALOS on the adoption floor was reduced to 9 days,
and assuming last year's number of adoptions,

**(HHUs X 62 days) ÷ 9 days = 190 cats**

**(9 X 190) ÷ 62 = 28**

**Number of cats (on average) to have on the adoption floor daily is ~28.**

* This calculation assumes that only one animal occupies one housing unit at a time.

housed in the adoption area last year during the same period (190 cats). The shelter manager in this example wants to estimate the number of cats to have on the adoption floor (occupying HHUs) if approximately the same number of adoptions occur this year, but the ALOS on the adoption floor is reduced. Using Formula 3 she will solve for the HHUs to be occupied. The steps are outlined in Table 5.13. A sample calculation is provided for a target ALOS of 9 days.

Notice that this shelter manager can house fewer animals on the adoption floor if she reduces the average time that her animals are housed there and the adoption numbers remain similar to those of last

# TABLE 5.14 ESTIMATES OF THE NUMBER OF CATS TO HAVE ON THE ADOPTION FLOOR ASSOCIATED WITH VARIOUS TARGET ALOS

### PERIOD OF TIME: JULY-AUGUST WITH 62 DAYS
### ESTIMATED NUMBER OF ADOPTIONS: 190

| TARGET ALOS FOR CATS ON THE ADOPTION FLOOR (DAYS) | NUMBER OF HHUs THAT COULD BE OCCUPIED ON THE ADOPTION FLOOR DAILY |
|---|---|
| 12 | 37 |
| 11 | 34 |
| 10 | 31 |
| 9 | 28 |
| 8 | 24 |

year. Since fewer choices often lead to more adoptions (ASPCA Pro, 2013c), the shelter's adoption rate may increase this year.

Her calculations yield the estimates in Table in 5.14.

**HELPFUL HINTS** Hurley and Newbury have called this calculation "Adoption Driven Capacity (ADC)," and have a spread sheet-based calculator automating the calculation. Their calculator also allows for more refinement of the calculations; it includes options for housing multiple animals per cage and for "fast- and slow-tracked" animals that have different ALOS targets and adoption numbers (Koret Shelter Medicine Program, 2015b, 2015c).

The adoption numbers used in calculations must reasonably represent what will happen in a period of interest. In example 2, if the number of animals housed in adoptions last year was atypical of most years (e.g., an exceptional push for adoptions was made last year), calculations based on its inclusion may produce misleading estimates of the number of animals to have on the adoption floor this year. Consulting your shelter's Log of Events and Changes in Protocols (Chapter 3) is advised to identify any unusual "events" that could affect use of last year's numbers.

Similarly, if the estimate obtained from the calculation in example 2 exceeds the number of HHUs actually available, the adoption floor will be overcrowded, at least part of period. This could happen if the target ALOS selected (despite being reduced from last year) still exceeded the ALOS that was required to avoid overcrowding with last year's adoption numbers. The selection of target ALOS values should be made taking into account the number of HHUs on the adoption floor that could be occupied.

Also, the number of animals to have on the adoption floor is an estimate. The ideal or perfect number of animals to have available for adoption depends on what your adopters are seeking, the number and characteristics (e.g., size, age) of the animals available, the manner in which animals are displayed, the number and character of potential adopters that visit the shelter, as well as on numerous other factors. The ASPCA has an adoption center visitor survey and log that can help shelters better understand what their adopters are seeking (ASPCA Pro, 2014b).

Too many choices can paralyze consumers to the

extent that they do not make a purchase (Schwartz, 2004). It is possible that last year's adoption rate could be improved if fewer animals were available for viewing at any point in time. In one study the transition rate for potential cat adopters increased 40% when the number of cats available for viewing was decreased (ASPCA Pro, 2013c).

**DISCUSSION** These examples serve to illustrate some of the advantages and disadvantages of using Formula 3. The usefulness of calculations based on Formula 3 depends on the validity of the numbers used in the equation and on the degree to which the assumptions for its use are met. Our examples involved two specific areas in shelters, but Equation 3 can be used for other areas/situations, and to solve for any of the variables in the equation when other values in the formula are known or can be estimated.

Calculations using Formula 3 are often influenced by many factors and considerations. These influences can impact the validity and precision of answers obtained, limiting the formula's practical usefulness. We simplified our examples by specifying that all animals required the same humane housing units and assumed that ALOS estimates were constant throughout the periods of interest. Calculations using the equation will be most helpful when applied to specific types of animals (e.g., age groups, source of animals) for short periods of time. By restricting calculations to homogeneous groups of animals, particular areas in a shelter, or short time frames, fewer additional considerations will affect your estimates, making them more accurate.

As discussed earlier in the chapter, the care-day ALOS should be used when making capacity calculations, particularly for short periods of time. If intake- or outcome-ALOS methods are used, the resulting capacity calculations may not accurately estimate the number of animals that can be housed. Also, it is important to check whether the distribution of lengths of stay is Gaussian. If it is not, then using the <u>average</u> length of stay may result in misleading estimates of DHC or HHUs.

Using Formula 3 is not the only approach to assessing shelter capacity. A shelter could, for example, have staff members count the number of animals in

# TABLE 5.15 QUARTERLY STAFF CAPACITY* FOR DELIVERING BASIC CARE FOR ANIMALS IN A SHELTER**

| TIME FRAME | MAX DOG COUNT | AVERAGE WEEKLY STAFF HOURS | HOURS/DAY /ANIMAL |
|---|---|---|---|
| WINTER Jan-March | 25 | 61.2 | 0.35 |
| SPRING April-June | 38 | 66.5 | 0.25 |
| SUMMER July-Sept | 45 | 66.5 | 0.21 |
| FALL Oct-Dec | 37 | 66.5 | 0.26 |

* Includes cleaning and feeding only

** Excludes off-site animals

specific areas each day and record them in a spread-sheet. These "census counts" could be divided by the number of HHUs in those areas and multiplied by 100 to calculate the daily % capacity for them. These capacity numbers could be shared during rounds or at weekly staff meetings and discussed; when appropriate, plans could be made to problem-solve large or chronic deviations from 100% capacity in affected areas. The advantage of this approach is that problems can be identified quickly and shared with the staff most knowledgeable to resolve them. Regardless of the approach, assessments of housing capacity should be done regularly to prevent severe or chronic overcrowding.

## STAFF CAPACITY

We suggest creating a Staff Capacity Profile for your shelter that provides a quick summary of the adequacy of shelter staffing to provide basic animal care (Table 5.15). This profile can be updated quarterly or as often as your shelter requires.

Photo Credit: MACC Nashville, TN

## THE STAFF CAPACITY PROFILE

**WHAT AND WHY?** Housing space is not the only potential limiting factor affecting shelters' ability to provide humane care. Obviously, having sufficient staff is also crucial. The Staff Capacity Profile relates to the staff's ability to provide basic animal care, defined as cleaning and feeding. Staff capacity to provide animal care can be difficult to estimate because an array of people is usually directly or indirectly involved. Some animal care staff members may perform non-animal-related tasks, and some non-animal-care staff members may provide animal care. Quantifying each of these people's contribution to animal care can be challenging and is the subject of ongoing research.

Shelters can begin an assessment of their staff capacity for animal care with a focus on providing basic care: cleaning and feeding. The National Animal Control Association (2009) and the Humane Society of the United States (2010) recommend that a minimum of 15 minutes per day per animal be allocated for basic care. In most shelters, this care is provided by staff. Even when volunteers assist with basic care, their help is often sporadic and in their absence, staffing must be sufficient to care for the animals.

## CALCULATION OF STAFF CAPACITY

Since staffing needs can vary widely (e.g., by season, after a seizure), shelters should evaluate the adequacy of staffing as animal care needs change. To assess your shelter's capacity to provide basic care for any period of time, we suggest first calculating the total daily staff hours recommended for basic animal care

in your shelter. Then compare that number to the total time actually devoted to basic care.

To calculate the time recommended for basic care in your shelter, identify the maximum number of animals that require care on a daily basis in the time period of interest (e.g., month, season); and multiply this number by 0.25 hours (15 minutes) per animal using Formula 4. To calculate the time your shelter actually devotes to basic care, generate a chart with the names of staff members and approximately how many hours each person spends performing basic

---

FORMULA 4

## RECOMMENDED TOTAL DAILY STAFF HOURS
## FOR BASIC ANIMAL CARE

=

## MAXIMUM ANIMALS PER DAY
## EXPECTED IN THE PERIOD
## X 0.25 HOURS OF CARE PER ANIMAL DAILY

---

# TABLE 5.16 CALCULATION OF THE AVERAGE NUMBER OF HOURS DEVOTED DAILY TO BASIC CARE FOR ANIMALS IN A SHELTER

| STAFF MEMBER | SUN | MON | TUES | WED | THURS | FRI | SAT | TOTAL HOURS |
|---|---|---|---|---|---|---|---|---|
| Chris | 8:30-6:00 | 8:00-5:00 | OFF | OFF | 8:30-6:00 | 8:30-6:00 | 8:30-6:00 | 40 |
| Marilyn | OFF | OFF | OFF | 8:30-6:00 | 8:30-6:00 | 8:30-6:00 | 8:30-6:00 | 32 |
| Mike | 8:30-6:00 | 8:00-12:30 | 8:00-5:00 | 8:30-6:00 | OFF | OFF | OFF | 28 |
| Sharon | 8:30-6:00 | 8:00-12:30 | 8:00-12:30 | OFF | OFF | 12:30-6:00 | 12:30-6:00 | 28 |
| Brenda | Front desk | Front desk | 8:00-5:00 | 8:30-6:00 | 8:30-6:00 | OFF | OFF | 25.5 |
| Dave | OFF | OFF | 8:30-11:30 | 8:30-11:30 | 8:30-11:30 | 8:30-11:30 | 8:30-11:30 | 15 |
| Shawna | 8:30-12:30 | 8:00-12:30 | OFF | OFF | OFF | 8:30-12:30 | 8:30-12:30 | 16 |
| Total | | | | | | | | 184.5 |

Total weekly hours =  184.5 hours for basic care

Average hours for daily basic care for animals = 184.5 ÷ 7  =  26.4 hours

The maximum number of animals per day is 79 in the spring;

Therefore: 26.4 hours ÷ 79 = 0.33 hours per animal per day
(within recommended guidelines)

animal care each week as shown in Table 5.16. Sum those hours to obtain the total time weekly provided for basic animal care and divide the total time weekly by 7 to estimate the average time for care per day. Lastly divide this number by the maximum number of animals that will require care per day during the period. This last number will approximate how many staff hours each animal can receive each day when the shelter is most full (0.33 hours in Table 5.16). Compare the recommended number of hours for basic care to those actually provided by your staff.

If you find that staff time for basic care is less than that suggested in the guidelines, the shelter should consider an investment in additional staff positions, cross-training of non-animal-care staff, or a reduction in the numbers of animals in the shelter. If your shelter meets the guidelines, remember that the recommended daily time per animal is a minimum estimate. Many shelters should consider increasing this time to maximize the welfare of the animals in their care.

Of course, many animals also require medical and behavioral care. Given that these needs often vary widely among shelters (or even within the same shelter over time), similar guidelines for basic medical and behavioral care don't exist. Clues to the inadequacy of meeting these needs, however, include high disease or death rates, high return rates for behavioral reasons, or long lengths of stay (e.g., waiting for S/N surgery, behavioral evaluation). Similarly, exercise and socialization with humans are also essential, often largely provided by volunteers. Shelters should strive to have sufficient staff and volunteers to meet the many physical and behavioral needs of their animals (ASV, 2010). If your shelter has insufficient staff to meet even the minimal guidelines for basic care, goals to address this deficiency must be drafted and plans implemented to address them.

**HELPFUL HINTS** If staff members providing basic care have responsibilities other than providing that care, omit those hours from your basic care calculations. Also, it is important to plan to meet basic care standards when people are ill or on vacation. Calculations are most helpful when made by species and by age group because puppies and kittens often require more time for basic care than adult animals (especially for cleaning). Of course, we encourage you to refine these calculations as is appropriate for your shelter.

Numbers can be powerful. If you plan to approach your shelter's Board of Directors or municipal governing body regarding increased funding for needed staff, a chart that summarizes your current staff capacity as compared to nationally recommended guidelines is a useful tool.

# SUMMARY

Minimizing your shelter's average length of stay can improve the welfare of your animals. When reducing the overall average LOS becomes a shelter goal, identifying delays in the flow of animals can be facilitated by calculating the time to various events (e.g., spay/neuter, behavior evaluation) that may retard that flow.

Minimizing animals' average residence in the shelter (without straying from your shelter's mission) can also increase the shelter's capacity to house and manage animals. Overcrowding is a major threat to animal welfare and monitoring a shelter's housing capacity can help eliminate the adverse effects that overcrowding produces. Consciously monitoring ALOS and the capacity of the adoption floor can increase adoptions if ALOS is minimized; and more animals can be offered for adoption. This helps ensure that housing space (overall and in particular areas) is used efficiently. The maximum achievable adoption rate is most often unknown. However, shelters can experiment with factors that may increase their adoption rates (including the number of animals available daily) and evaluate their effects on those rates. Shelters that routinely calculate and monitor their length of stay (including time to important events) and shelter capacity can maximize the numbers of animals saved and enhance the welfare of animals in their care.

Staff capacity to provide basic care is essential to the quality of life (physical and behavioral health) of shelter animals. Both NACA and HSUS recommend a daily minimum of 15 minutes per animal of staff time for feeding and cleaning. This recommendation does not include time for enrichment, medical care, exercise and other basic needs of animals. Some shelters overcrowd their facility beyond their staff members' capacity to provide even minimal care, leading to poor quality of life for their animals. This result is not compatible with the mission of humane animal shelters. Therefore, shelters must be cognizant of their staffing needs and monitor them such that their animals receive at least minimal care, with the goal of exceeding that minimum.

# MEDICAL DATA
## FROM THE INDIVIDUAL TO THE POPULATION

## INTRODUCTION

Optimizing both individual animal and population health is essential to the humane mission of animal shelters, and these two aspects of animal health are inextricably intertwined.The health of an individual can profoundly affect the health of a population, and the health of the population can profoundly affect the health of individual animals. A medical record for each animal is an essential component of both individual and population care.

Shelters record medical data on paper or in electronic medical records or both, similar to the approach used by private veterinary clinics. Data collected with either format can be used to support individual animal and population care. Population care, however, requires calculating summary metrics using data from many individuals, and computers make this process considerably easier. Shelters using only paper records can certainly do the same calculations, but the process will be more laborious and time-consuming.

The focus of this chapter is on recording and using summary metrics to enhance shelter population care. Veterinarians and veterinary technicians may wish to skip to the section entitled "Population care: managing the health of a population of animals," page 5.

## THE MEDICAL RECORD

### WHY DO MEDICAL RECORDS MATTER?

Individual animal and population care begins with the medical record. The following list -- in no particular order -- outlines some of the reasons that maintaining up-to-date, accurate medical data is vital to managing your shelter animals' health.

**OPTIMAL CARE** Medical records provide a recorded history of the health of each animal while in the shelter. If the records are complete and regularly updated, staff can review them at any time to assess what each animal has received and determine what additional care he or she requires. We strongly recommend that shelters have a protocol describing the nature, extent and timing for entry of medical data that is expected for every record.

**CONTINUITY OF CARE** If all preventive measures (e.g., vaccinations), treatments, and surgical procedures are recorded, all staff members can be equally informed. This is especially important because mul-

help strengthen relationships with local veterinarians. Often the medical records accompanying new adopters and their pets are the only direct contact local veterinarians have with the shelter. The goal is not to "impress" the local veterinary community but to recognize that animal welfare is a team effort. Good medical records are important pieces of communication between the shelter and the community.

# COMPARISON OF INDIVIDUAL ANIMAL AND POPULATION CARE

The process of providing care for a population has a lot in common with treating individual animals (Table 6.1). When an animal is presented to a veterinarian she takes a thorough history, examines the animal, and records what is normal and abnormal. When abnormalities are found she develops hypotheses (i.e., proposes explanations) as to the cause, plans additional diagnostic tests if necessary, interprets the test results, develops a plan of treatment, and monitors the effectiveness of that treatment. Often she also counsels the owner as to how he can prevent this or similar diseases in the future.

Tending to the health of a population is similar. A veterinarian (or other responsible person) must first become familiar with the history of that population (e.g., the recent entry of dogs from another part of the country). She then assesses the health of the population by examining the frequency (most often incidence) of diseases common to that population, their severity, and mortality rates (e.g., overall, cause-specific). If disease rates are unacceptably high, the veterinarian develops hypotheses to explain the high frequency and attempts to verify her suspicions by further characterizing the incidence rates by age group, breed type, time frame or other pertinent factors. Often diagnostic tests are run on several animals. These data are reviewed and once she is satisfied that she has a good

tiple people provide care. Missed or duplicate "care" should be avoided, as it can jeopardize the health of an animal or waste money and staff time.

**LEGAL ISSUES** A medical record is a legal document. While an animal is in your care, the shelter is responsible for not only administering care, but accurately recording it as well. The old adage, "If it's not in the record, it never happened" is a good one to keep in mind when thinking about the need for a complete medical record.

**RELATIONSHIPS WITH THE PUBLIC** Shelters with complete and accurate medical records can easily summarize an animal's health and medical care in the shelter for potential and new adopters. This information enables potential adopters to make informed decisions about animals that require ongoing medical care, reducing the risk of return for such animals. A complete record also helps the new owner avoid paying for duplicate veterinary care (e.g., vaccinations administered at intake). Finally, good medical records speak to the shelter's commitment to quality animal care.

**RELATIONSHIPS WITH LOCAL VETERINARIANS** Local veterinarians working with new adopters can use medical information from the shelter to avoid duplication of care. Also, complete medical records

## TABLE 6.1 COMPARISON OF APPROACH TO EXAMINATION AND DIAGNOSIS OF DISEASE IN AN INDIVIDUAL ANIMAL AND A POPULATION OF ANIMALS

| INDIVIDUAL ANIMALS | POPULATION OF ANIMALS |
|---|---|
| Collection of a pertinent history | Collection of history of events (e.g., transfer of new animals from another shelter) that may impact the population's health |
| Physical examination (*Look for disease signs*) | Identify the diseases present<br>Assess their frequency<br>Calculate disease incidence and mortality rates |
| Formulate list of differential diagnoses | Formulate hypotheses to explain disease frequency |
| Run diagnostic tests | Characterize disease rates by age, length of stay, neuter status, etc.<br>Run diagnostic tests |
| Interpret test results | Interpret test results |
| Plan for treatment | Plan for implementing, changing or enhancing adherence to disease prevention/control protocols |
| Treatment | Implement or make protocol changes or enhance adherence to current protocols |
| Monitor effectiveness | Monitor effectiveness (e.g., using disease incidence) |
| Recommendations to prevent this disease in the future or for provision of ongoing care | Recommendations to sustain the changes or make new recommendations |

understanding of the disease problem, she develops a plan for control and prevention. After the plan is implemented, the rates of disease are monitored at an appropriate interval(s) to evaluate the effectiveness of the plan. If the plan proves effective, the veterinarian makes recommendations either to maintain current disease control measures or to seek to reduce disease development even further in the future. If the plan fails to control the disease, it is reassessed and another is developed.

Notice that caring for a population depends on good individual care and recording of medical information (e.g., the cause of disease, diagnostic testing). Managing disease in individual animals and in populations both require a systematic approach to disease recognition, identification, treatment, monitoring, final assessment and recommendations to prevent reoccurrences in the future.

# POPULATION CARE

## MANAGING THE HEALTH
## OF A POPULATION OF ANIMALS

An essential component of a population health care plan is disease surveillance (see sidebar). This component is akin to doing a physical examination on an individual animal. The surveillance program identifies the diseases present, assesses their frequency and their distribution among subgroups in the population.

# DISEASE SURVEILLANCE

Disease surveillance is defined as 1) the ongoing systematic collection, orderly consolidation, analysis and interpretation of health-related data in populations; and 2) the prompt dissemination of this information to the people who are in a position to act on that data (Dwyer et al, 2014). Surveillance data are used to plan, implement and evaluate preventive and control measures for disease in populations (Salmon, 2003; Scarlett, 2012).

Disease surveillance programs include good individual animal identification, clear definitions of diseases to be included, a medical records system, a clear understanding of why monitoring is important, incentives to report, and a clear management plan for affected animals. Regular timely analyses, interpretation, and the dissemination of data to pertinent parties are essential.

Surveillance requires calculations of metrics that summarize the frequency of medical "events" in individuals. These events most often include diseases, conditions, euthanasias and deaths, but may also include clinical signs, treatments, outcomes (e.g., recovered), medical and surgical procedures, complications (surgical and medical) or the results of diagnostic tests (Figure 6.1). Computerization of the medical data greatly facilitates this process, but is not essential.

# FIGURE 6.1 COMMON MEDICAL EVENTS THAT COMPRISE MEDICAL CARE IN ANIMAL SHELTERS

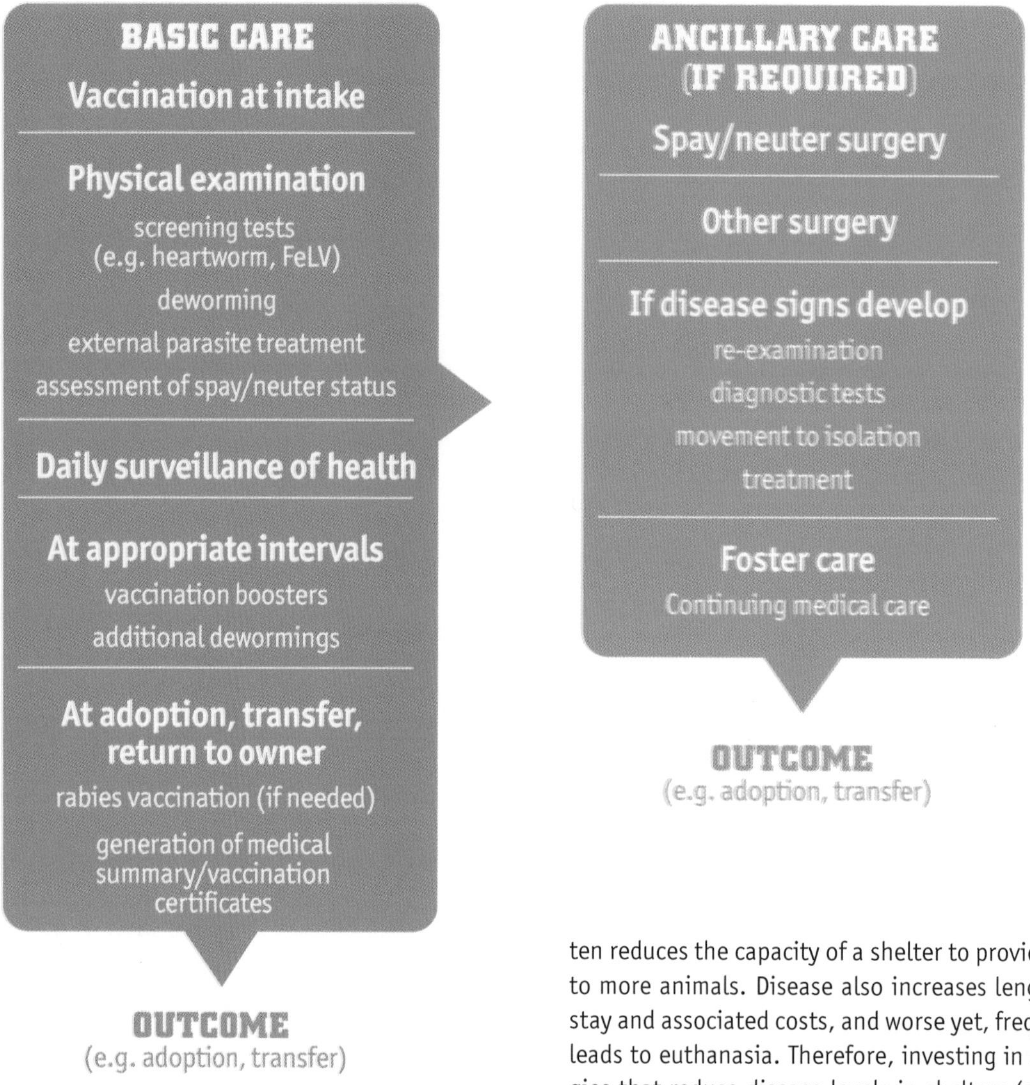

**BASIC CARE**

**Vaccination at intake**

**Physical examination**

screening tests
(e.g. heartworm, FeLV)

deworming

external parasite treatment

assessment of spay/neuter status

**Daily surveillance of health**

**At appropriate intervals**

vaccination boosters

additional dewormings

**At adoption, transfer, return to owner**

rabies vaccination (if needed)

generation of medical summary/vaccination certificates

**OUTCOME**
(e.g. adoption, transfer)

**ANCILLARY CARE (IF REQUIRED)**

**Spay/neuter surgery**

**Other surgery**

**If disease signs develop**

re-examination

diagnostic tests

movement to isolation

treatment

**Foster care**

Continuing medical care

**OUTCOME**
(e.g. adoption, transfer)

Shelters should strive for quality population care and efficiency of the delivery of that care, not only to reduce costs but also to reduce suffering and increase the proportion of animals released alive. A high frequency of disease in shelters induces suffering in affected animals, increases costs, and of-

ten reduces the capacity of a shelter to provide care to more animals. Disease also increases lengths of stay and associated costs, and worse yet, frequently leads to euthanasia. Therefore, investing in strategies that reduce disease levels in shelters (such as computerizing disease data and monitoring disease frequency) can have huge benefits. We discuss metrics that shelters can calculate and monitor to enhance their disease-reducing efforts below.

**NOTE ABOUT TERMINOLOGY** Software programs and even veterinarians vary in how they use the terms "diagnosis, condition, clinical signs and symptoms." When recording data it is important that this terminology is standardized within your shelter to ensure consistency. *Rather than use these four words – disease, condition, sign or symptom - we use the word "disease" in the following pages to encompass all of these terms.* (As an aside, many in the shelter community use the word "symptom" because people report symptoms (e.g., "my stomach hurts; I have a headache"). Since animals only have "signs" that humans can recognize, the word "symptom" is not used in veterinary medicine).

# STRONGLY RECOMMENDED QUESTIONS

> ## 1 How would you characterize the health of your population of animals in a sound bite?

## THE ANNUAL MEDICAL PROFILE

**WHAT AND WHY?** The annual **Medical Profile** (Table 6.2) enables the medical director or committee (whoever is ultimately in charge of the health of the population) to assess the annual status of disease in the shelter, set goals, and track progress towards improving the population's health on an annual basis. The contents of the annual **Medical Profile** should reflect the medical information that your shelter wishes to monitor/report annually. The shelter whose data appear in Table 6.2 chose to include: a condensed summary of the major infectious diseases in its facility, the frequency of natural mortality, and the number and percentage of euthanasias for medical reasons. **Without a clear understanding of the frequency of common diseases and causes of death, the shelter is making medical policy decisions and drafting medical protocols for the population based on impressions and opinions. This is akin to prescribing treatments for an animal without doing a physical exam. This is not acceptable for individual animal care, and it should not**

**be an acceptable practice in modern shelter population care.** A summary of the frequency of common diseases in your shelter is also a basic component of a disease surveillance program that is essential to population health management.

Also, as was true for intakes and outcomes, having a document that summarizes the health of your shelter animals to present to board members and other constituencies enhances communication. It highlights progress and continuing medical challenges for the shelter. Data can also enhance your shelter's success in securing funds to improve care and reduce the frequency of disease.

**INTERPRETATION** The annual **Medical Profile** for the shelter in Table 6.2 summarizes the annual incidence of the most common infectious diseases in this shelter. It includes: the prevalence of FeLV, FIV and heartworm infections among incoming animals; the overall annual mortality; and the number and proportion of animals euthanized for medical reasons. **The decision as to which diseases and other medical information that your shelter includes in its Annual Medical Profile should be made on the basis of the frequency, severity and importance to your shelter.** We discuss possible components of the Medical Profile and their rationale further below.

The percentages of dogs and cats diagnosed with coccidiosis, giardiasis, and sarcoptic mange in Table 6.2 were among those animals with clinical signs of these diseases that had a fecal examination (coccidiosis, giardiasis) or a skin scraping (sarcoptic mange). These tests (i.e., fecal examination or skin scraping) were ordered by the shelter's veterinarian because she suspected that their signs could be due to one of these agents. To get these percentages the numbers of animals with these parasites were divided by those *that were tested*. When interpreting these numbers, it is important to remember that the percentages were among animals with clinical signs (that might have been associated with these infections) and that were "tested" for these organisms. We interpret each percentage as **cumulative incidence** (see discussion below), but recognize that the organisms may not have been the cause of the

# TABLE 6.2 ANNUAL MEDICAL PROFILE IN AN ADOPTION GUARANTEE SHELTER: 2014

| DISEASE | # | % AFFECTED | # | % AFFECTED |
|---|---|---|---|---|
| Coccidiosis* | 43 | 22.8 (43/189) | 22 | 18.3 (22/120) |
| Giardiasis* | 22 | 11.6 (22/189) | 10 | 8.3 (10/120) |
| Sarcoptic mange* | – | – | 8 | 8.2 (8/98) |
| URI/kennel cough** | 249 | 15.8 (249/1575) | 11 | 2.2 (11/501) |
| Heartworms*** | – | – | 3 | 0.8 (3/393) |
| FeLV*** | 15 | 1.0 (15/1532) | – | – |
| FIV*** | 6 | 0.04 (6/1532) | – | – |
| Mortality (all causes) | 25 | 1.7 (25/1443) | 3 | 0.7 (3/447) |
| Euthanasias for medical reasons | 97 | 6.2 (97/1575) | 5 | 1.0 (5/501) |
| Treatable**** | 0 | – | 0 | – |
| Non-Treatable | 97 | 6.2 (97/1575) | 5 | 1.0 (5/501) |

*Animals positive for this organism among those tested with signs possibly associated with this disease.

** Disease that developed among the shelter animals while they were in residence in the shelter.

*** Animals positive for this organism among those tested during the intake examination.

**** Could be treated in the future with additional resources.

clinical signs in some animals. Since only clinical animals were evaluated, the number of animals that were infected is probably underestimated. Similarly, the cumulative incidence is probably overestimated because only animals with signs were tested. Despite these limitations, trends in the occurrence of these parasites can be examined if the rationale for testing does not change over time.

The percentages **(or prevalence)** of animals testing positive for heartworm disease, FeLV or FIV are among animals tested during their intake examination. The majority of dogs entering this shelter are tested for heartworm (excluding those too young to harbor adult parasites). Similarly, most cats are tested for FeLV and FIV (excluding most feral cats and some that are euthanized because of severe illness at entry). Knowledge of these exceptions should be factored into interpretation of the data. If shelters keep a log of test results, these percentages are easy to calculate. For shelters using software programs, the denominators should be among animals tested.

The percentages (cumulative incidence) of cats and dogs that developed feline upper respiratory disease and kennel cough, respectively, are shown in in Table 6.2. Cumulative incidence calculations are discussed later in this chapter and in Appendix 1.

The most frequent infectious diseases in the shelter in Table 6.2 are common in many shelters. Feline upper respiratory tract infections were by far the most frequent cause of illness in this shelter. In some shelters kennel cough would be more common. The intestinal parasites giardia and coccidia were common causes of diarrhea, especially in young animals (breakdown by age not shown). The **prevalence** estimates of FeLV, FIV and heartworm infections were low in this community as evidenced by their low prevalence among incoming animals. This shelter monitors the frequency of these infections in order to inform its policies (e.g., planning for heartworm treatment, finding adopters) with regards to infected animals. The overall mortality is low in this shelter in both cats and dogs, mostly occurring in un-weaned kittens (data not shown). The risk (or probability) of being euthanized because of

a medical issue is about 6% for cats and only 1% for dogs. This shelter treats all animals with "treatable" conditions according to their Asilomar matrix and therefore, has no animals that were euthanized for other than non-remediable diseases.

**HELPFUL HINTS** For many of these metrics, the most difficult challenge is determining which animals should go in the denominators, and then how to get those numbers. Determining these denominators is discussed in pertinent sections below.

---

**2** *How many new cases of infectious disease arise in a given time period?*

---

**WHAT AND WHY?** The most useful medical metrics for evaluating population health are measures of the incidence of various diseases. Incidence either measures the risk of developing a particular disease in a population (**cumulative incidence**) or the speed with which a disease is moving through a population (**incidence density**) in a specified time period. (Incidence density is used in research. See Appendix 1 for more discussion). The calculation of both incidence measures begins by identifying all cases of a disease that were diagnosed in a defined time frame. These newly diagnosed cases are called "incident cases" of that disease. Notice that an animal that develops a disease is counted only on the day of first diagnosis, regardless of the length of his illness. For example, if your shelter sees 28 newly diagnosed cases of feline upper respiratory infection (URI) in the month of April, then you could say, "In April, the number of incident cases of URI is 28." By itself, the number of incident cases is potentially misleading as it is unclear among how many cats these cases developed (e.g., 30, 300, 519?).

**DATA NEEDED** As a first step, the diagnosis (and its date) of each disease of interest must be recorded in each affected animal's medical record; then the numbers of newly diagnosed cases must be counted during the particular time period of interest (e.g., month, season). The total number of new cases during a period of time can be summed by your shelter software, in a spreadsheet that you maintain, or by some other method of your choosing. Regardless of the method, the diagnosis, its date, and a unique identifier for each affected animal must be collected for each disease in your surveillance plan. Obviously, this can become a laborious process if every possible diagnosis that could occur in a shelter was monitored. To make the process manageable, we recommend tracking only the most frequent or severe diseases occurring in your shelter. Software packages are increasingly facilitating counting disease cases for defined periods of time. The intent (regardless of method) is to enable counting the number of new diagnoses of particular diseases occurring within a specified period of time.

**FREQUENCY OF DISEASE MONITORING** How often particular diseases are monitored (defined as counted, graphed and reviewed) depends on many factors. Usually, frequently occurring diseases are monitored more often than rarely occurring health issues. For example, feline upper respiratory tract infections are usually monitored on a monthly basis, whereas the number of canine parvovirus cases might be reported only annually if they rarely develop in your shelter. In the midst of outbreaks, however, the incidence of the cause of the outbreak might be monitored much more frequently (e.g., daily) to track the effectiveness of control measures in bringing the epidemic under control.

**HELPFUL HINTS** *Multiple Disease Occurrences* For diseases that can occur more than once in an individual animal (e.g., upper respiratory tract infections) during a particular time frame, only the first episode is usually counted as an incident case. If your shelter has an interest in reoccurring illnesses in a particular time frame, second occurrences can be counted and reported separately. If second occurrences are monitored during time period of interest, the denominator should include only animals with a first occurrence in that time frame. Fortunately, since animals do not reside in a shelter long enough to

experience a second infection of most diseases, the numbers of second infections are usually ignored.

***"Diagnoses" vs. "Clinical Signs"*** Another issue complicating the collection of medical data is the failure to reach a diagnosis in many animals. For this reason, some software programs enable shelters to collect both "diagnoses" and "clinical signs" (check the nomenclature used by your software). From a disease surveillance standpoint, an actual diagnosis is preferable when it can be made. However, this is often not possible in shelters and recording and monitoring important clinical signs is the next best approach. Clinical signs such as diarrhea, vomiting, coughing or weight loss are not diagnoses, but rather common indicators of underlying abnormalities. When a diagnosis cannot be made, recording and counting animals on the day of first recognition of common clinical signs (e.g., diarrhea) that impact the health of your populations is advisable. The risk of developing important clinical signs can then be assessed by calculating the cumulative incidence of each of the signs. These signs should not be captured in a "diagnosis" list, but rather in a separate "signs" list. The discussion below can also pertain to "signs" when we use the terminology "diseases or diagnoses."

***Keep a Manageable List of Diagnoses*** Shelters can track the number of animals diagnosed with diseases of interest using their software, a spreadsheet, or by hand. Regardless of the method, diagnoses of interest must be agreed upon, defined and recorded in a standard fashion by members of the medical staff. We suggest that shelters consider monitoring only those diagnoses that are of greatest concern to them in their surveillance programs. Attempting to monitor too many diseases can overwhelm staff and lead to failure to record findings consistently, and ultimately to inaccurate, incomplete or inconsistent data. *We believe that it is better to collect and monitor data for a few important diseases well, than to attempt to monitor many diseases and do it poorly.*

Diseases and signs whose frequency we believe should be considered for tracking in most (if not all) shelters are listed in Table 6.3. How often the fre-

## TABLE 6.3 DIAGNOSES AND CLINICAL SIGNS TO CONSIDER FOR INCLUSION IN A DISEASE SURVEILLANCE PLAN FOR YOUR SHELTER

| DISEASES | 🐕 | 🐈 |
|---|:---:|:---:|
| Upper respiratory tract disease | ✔ | ✔ |
| Canine distemper | ✔ | |
| Canine parvovirus | ✔ | |
| Panleukopenia | | ✔ |
| Ringworm | | ✔ |
| Feline leukemia virus (FeLV) | | ✔ |
| Feline immunodeficiency virus (FIV) | | ✔ |
| Feline infectious peritonitis (FIP) | | ✔ |
| Heartworm disease | ✔ | |
| **CLINICAL SIGNS (DIAGNOSIS UNCLEAR)** | 🐕 | 🐈 |
| Weight loss | ✔ | ✔ |
| Diarrhea | ✔ | ✔ |
| Vomiting | ✔ | ✔ |
| Coughing | ✔ | ✔ |

quency of each disease (or sign) is updated will vary by the factors discussed earlier. Once the diseases your shelter wishes to monitor are identified, protocols should be developed (e.g., documenting what should be entered, when and by whom) to enhance the likelihood that they are identified and entered consistently when they occur.

For shelters with lists of diagnoses that they are already using, target collection of data regarding those that are most important to your shelter; standardize the definitions of those diseases; and remove redundant terms for the same condition. Once this is done, train your staff to use the standardized terminology. If and when the shelter makes changes to disease definitions or diagnosis lists, record when and why the changes were made in your Log of Events and Changes in Protocols (Chapter 3). This will enhance your ability to interpret the medical data in the future.

*Recording Less Common Diseases* From a data management standpoint, diseases not monitored on a regular basis can be handled in a variety of ways. If your shelter uses shelter software, these diagnoses can be entered into text fields and/or they can be recorded in broad categories (e.g., cancer, congenital defect) or in an "other" category that includes many conditions (whose exact nature can be retrieved if needed from text fields). Researchers often partition disease into "definite" and "presumptive" categories depending on the quality and completeness of the data surrounding the diagnosis. We are not aware of shelter software at this time that enables shelters to make this distinction and, except for research purposes, seems of little practical importance to shelters.

## MORE ABOUT MONITORING DISEASE IN SHELTERS WITHOUT COMPUTERIZATION OF MEDICAL INFORMATION

As mentioned earlier, if your shelter does not use computer software or software that enables collection of medical diagnoses, the frequency of diseases of interest to the shelter can be monitored by hand or in a spreadsheet. First, decide which diseases in each species are most important to the shelter (e.g., most frequent, most severe, most costly). Then record each affected animal's unique identifier, the diagnosis (e.g., upper respiratory tract infection), and the first date of diagnosis in a notebook, spreadsheet or by some other means. Newly diagnosed diseases can then be totaled for various time periods (e.g., month of August).

**3** | *What is the risk of animals developing disease while in your shelter?*

**WHAT AND WHY?** The risk (or probability) of an animal in your shelter developing a particular disease while in residence is measured by calculating the **cumulative incidence** (also called **incidence proportion**) of that disease (Rothman, 2012, Gordis, 2014, Fletcher et al, 2014). Cumulative incidence (CI) and incidence proportion are the terms used by epidemiologists, but most of the veterinary literature refers to these summary metrics as "incidence" or "incidence rates." We prefer to use the epidemiologic terminology as it distinguishes clearly between this calculation and that of the other measure of incidence, often called **incidence density** or **incidence rate** (Rothman, 2012, Gordis, 2014, Fletcher et al, 2014). To calculate cumulative incidence, you need to know the number of incident cases of the disease of interest and the number of animals at risk of developing (or eligible to develop) that disease in a specified time frame. Without understanding the population at risk of developing disease, it is difficult to interpret the number of incident cases.

More specifically, cumulative incidence is calculated by dividing the number of newly diagnosed cases of a disease by the number of animals at risk of that disease in a specified time period. For example, if 28 new cases of feline URI are diagnosed in the month of April and there are 140 cats at risk (i.e., that could develop URI) in the shelter during that time, then the cumulative incidence of feline URI for the month of April would be 28/140 or 20%. In April, 20% of susceptible cats developed URI or the probability of cats developing URI in April while in the shelter is 20%.

> ## CUMULATIVE INCIDENCE (CI) OR INCIDENCE PROPORTION IS DEFINED AS
>
> ### THE NUMBER OF NEWLY DIAGNOSED CASES OF A DISEASE ÷ TOTAL NUMBER OF ANIMALS AT RISK TO DEVELOP THAT DISEASE IN A SPECIFIED TIME PERIOD
>
> CUMULATIVE INCIDENCE IS OFTEN EXPRESSED AS A PERCENTAGE BY MULTIPLYING THE PROPORTION DEFINED ABOVE BY 100.

## TABLE 6.4 CATEGORIES OF ANIMALS IDEALLY REMOVED FROM THE POPULATION ELIGIBLE (OR AT RISK) OF DEVELOPING A DISEASE OF INTEREST

Those that already have the disease at the beginning of the interval

Those that enter the shelter in the interval with the disease

Those that have already had the disease in the shelter and recovered

Those that were euthanized or otherwise removed from the shelter almost immediately after entering (i.e., had no opportunity for exposure)

**IMPORTANT NOTE** Technically, cumulative incidence is NOT the most appropriate incidence measure when using shelter data. This is because shelter animals have varying lengths of stay (i.e., periods at risk) in a shelter; the calculation of CI assumes that all animals have equal periods of risk. In our experience, however, CI calculations give similar answers to incidence density calculations (that account for varying periods of risk) when monitoring trends in disease frequency in shelters. They are also far easier to understand and more informative than using words such as "a lot or a moderate amount or very little" disease (e.g., upper respiratory tract infections) to define disease frequency. CI calculations are not appropriate for use in most shelter research. See Appendix I for more discussion and references to further reading.

**DATA NEEDED** New cases are identified and recorded as described above in Question 2. The challenge is to count all of the animals that could have developed (or were "at risk of") the disease of interest and that were in the shelter during the same period in which the cases developed. The animals in the shelter that already have the disease or have recovered from the disease while in the shelter should ideally not be counted in the "at risk" population. Note that animals "at risk" can be thought of as "outcome eligible" as described in previous chapters. The outcome in this case is the disease of interest.

*Which animals can develop (are at risk of) the disease and should be included in the denominator?* For most diseases the answer to this question is impossible to know definitively. That said, the "at risk" population can be estimated using the best information at hand. Start first by getting intake counts for the period of interest *and* identify the number of animals that were in the shelter at the beginning of the period. Some of these animals will not be at risk of developing URI during the period of interest. Categories of animals that should ideally be removed from calculations are described in Table 6.4. We have not included animals

## TABLE 6.5A EXAMPLE OF THE CALCULATION OF THE CUMULATIVE INCIDENCE OF URI AMONG CATS IN A SHELTER IN JULY

| DESCRIPTION OF DATA | VALUES |
|---|---|
| Time frame | July |
| Number of newly diagnosed URI cases that developed in the shelter during July | 26 |
| Cats that entered in July with URI | 7 |
| Cats in the shelter at the start of July 1 with URI | 9 |
| Cats in the shelter on July 1 that had recovered from URI while in the shelter prior to July 1 | 2 |
| Total intake of cats in July | 98 |
| Total cats in shelter at the start of July 1 | 42 |

**CI = # of newly diagnosed cases / population at risk**

**Number of newly diagnosed cases = 26**

**Population at risk: [(cat intake – those entering with URI) + (cats in the shelter on July 1 – cats with URI on July 1 – cats recovered from URI while in the shelter prior to July 1)]**

Plugging into the formula:

CI = 26 / (98 – 7) + (42 – 2 – 9)
= 26 / 122
= 0.213 or 21.3 %

---

that have been vaccinated since vaccination histories are often questionable; many vaccinations (e.g., respiratory) provide limited protection; and vaccinations in the shelter may not yet have induced a protective immunity. Also, since we have rarely observed a second URI in cats while in a shelter, we consider cats that have recovered from URI in the shelter immune for purposes of incidence calculations. If second infections occur frequently in your shelter, cumulative incidence of second infections can be calculated separately using cats that have recovered from a first infection in the denominator.

## TABLE 6.5B THE STEPS TO THE CALCULATION

**1** Identify the total intake for the period (e.g., July). (= 98)

**2** Subtract cats that entered the shelter with URI from those entering in July (Q 1). (98 – 7 = 91) These are cats at risk of URI that entered in July.

**3** Get the cats present at the start of July 1. (= 42)

**4** Count the number of cats with URI on July 1 (do not include cats entering the shelter with URI on July 1). (= 9)

**5** Count the cats in the shelter on July 1 that have recovered from URI. (= 2 ) This is often a small number and if so, can be ignored.

**6** Add the cats with URI on July 1 (Q 4) to those that have recovered from URI (Q5) (9 +2  = 11)  These cats are not at risk of URI in July.

**7** Subtract the sum of those with URI on July 1 and recovered from URI on July 1  - those in Q 6 – from the cat census on July 1 (42 – 11 = 31). These are the cats in the shelter on July 1 that remain at risk of URI.

**8** Now add the cats entering the shelter at risk to those in the shelter at risk on July 1.  (91 + 31 = 122).  These are all of the cats at risk in July of developing URI.

**9** Of these 122 cats at risk, 26 or 21.3% developed URI (26/122 X 100%).

---

Data for a theoretical shelter are provided in Table 6.5A and steps to calculate CI are in Table 6.5B.

**INTERPRETATION:** Among cats that had not yet developed URI in this shelter by July 1, the risk of developing URI in July was approximately 21% or ~ every 2 of 10 cats in the shelter developed URI in July. As discussed in Appendix 1, this is obviously not a perfect measure of the risk of acquiring disease, but it provides a reasonable estimate of the probability of developing disease in this example.

**HELPFUL HINTS** Looking at Table 6.5A, note that a number of factors contribute to the degree of accuracy associated with the calculation of cumulative incidence. However, depending on the size of some of the components, they may not be strictly necessary to produce a reasonable estimate. Often the numbers of cats entering a shelter with URI, recovered from URI, or those currently suffering from URI are quite small. If any of these numbers are small (in relation to the total number of animals that are "at risk"), the CI calculations will not change much if they are ignored. For example, if the 2 cats in Table 6.5A that had recovered from a URI before July 1 were not removed from the denominator, the CI estimate 26/128 (20.3%) would change very little from the more accurate 21.3%. *If all of these numbers are relatively small in relation to the total "at risk" population, the denominator can be simplified*

# FIGURE 6.2 ANNUAL CUMULATIVE INCIDENCE OF URI IN CATS BY AGE GROUP** (2014)

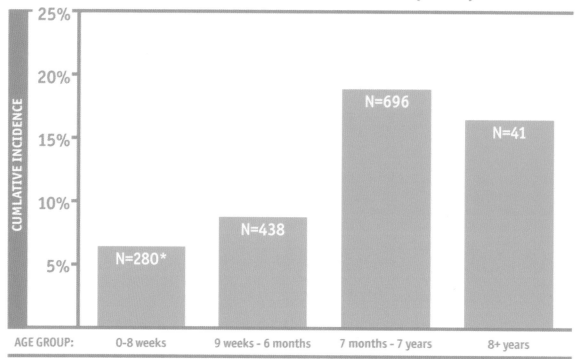

CUMLATIVE INCIDENCE

25%
20%
15%
10%
5%

N=280*
N=438
N=696
N=41

AGE GROUP:  0-8 weeks  9 weeks - 6 months  7 months - 7 years  8+ years

*Numbers in the bars represent the denominators of the incidence calculations.
**The percentages on the vertical axis have been restricted to 0-25%.

by adding the census on day 1 of the time frame to the number of animals entering the shelter during the time frame. For most shelters with which we currently work, just starting to quantify the risk of developing URI (albeit crudely) is helpful to the shelter if they use the same approach consistently. As shelters gain familiarity with obtaining and using medical data from their database, the incidence estimates can be refined.

The cumulative incidence data from a previous year(s) can be used to anticipate what might occur in the future if the characteristics of entering animals (e.g., age), and conditions within the shelter do not change much from year to year. For example, a shelter could ask "What is the probability that a cat entering the shelter will develop URI this July?" If little has changed from the previous year, the shelter could calculate the cumulative incidence of

URI among cats entering the shelter last July and predict what *may* happen this year. To do this the denominator of cats at risk would be restricted to only those entering the shelter without URI last July. The actual probability of developing URI among entering cats this year can be calculated (in August or later this year), by dividing the number of cats that developed URI in July this year by the number entering the shelter without URI in July this year.

For readers interested in enhancing their understanding of the calculation of incidence measures in epidemiology, particularly if they are conducting research, read Appendix 1 and consult with the references cited there.

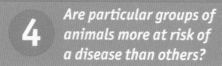

**4** *Are particular groups of animals more at risk of a disease than others?*

# FIGURE 6.3 COMPARISON OF THE ANNUAL CUMULATIVE INCIDENCE OF UPPER RESPIRATORY TRACT INFECTIONS AMONG OWNER-SURRENDERED AND STRAY CATS** (2013-2014)

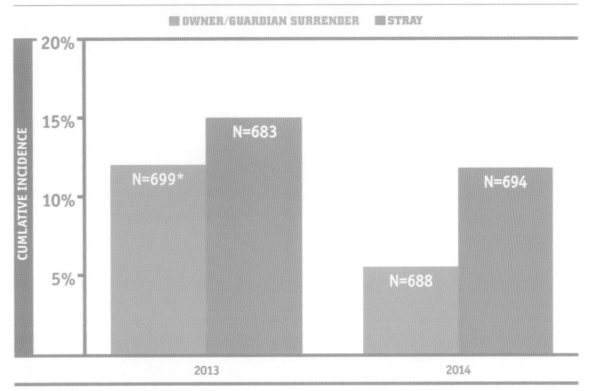

■ OWNER/GUARDIAN SURRENDER    ■ STRAY

*Numbers in the bars represent the denominators of the incidence calculations.

**Percentages on the vertical axis are restricted to 0-20%.

In order to refine preventive and control protocols, shelter staff should understand how disease risk varies across subgroups of animals. We present examples of evaluating risk differences across age and source categories of animals below, but this can be done for other subgroups as well. We chose to illustrate sub-

groups of age and source because (in our experience) disease risk is likely to vary within these subgroups.

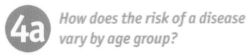

### 4a  How does the risk of a disease vary by age group?

**WHAT AND WHY?** One of the most important **host factors** often affecting disease risk is age. Host factors are characteristics of animals or humans such as age, gender, neuter status, and breed that may affect their risk of disease. In the shelter in Figure 6.2, un-weaned and older kittens had a lower risk of developing URI than adult animals.

Photo Credit: iStock

# FIGURE 6.4 NUMBER OF CATS DIAGNOSED WITH UPPER RESPIRATORY INFECTIONS (URI) BY SEASON (2014)

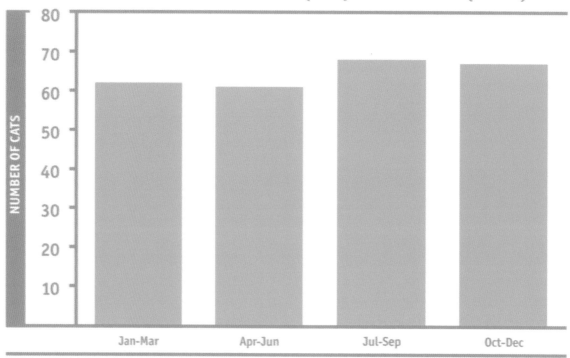

**INTERPRETATION** Graphs such as this one raise questions such as "*Why* is the risk lower in kittens when we generally think of them as being more susceptible to many infectious diseases, including URI?" In this shelter, the discrepancy is probably due to differences in stress and exposure between kittens and adults, as many of the kittens spent time in foster care away from the stresses and exposures of the shelter. They were also adopted more quickly once in the shelter.

Looking at cumulative incidence data among subgroups of animals refines the ability of the medical staff to direct their preventive and control efforts.

**4b** *Does the risk of developing a disease vary by the source (owner-surrendered or stray) of the animal?*

**WHAT AND WHY?** Since owner-surrendered and stray cats often have very different medical histories (e.g., vaccinations, natural infections) the shelter in Figure 6.3 examined the risk of developing URI between owner-surrendered and stray cats.

**INTERPRETATION** Stray cats were more likely to develop URI than owner-surrendered cats during 2013-2014 in this shelter. While it is beyond the

Photo Credit: iStock

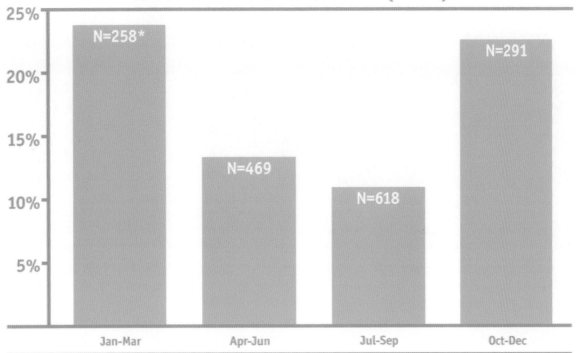

# FIGURE 6.5 CUMULATIVE INCIDENCE OF URI AMONG CATS BY SEASON** (2014)

| | | | |
|---|---|---|---|
| N=258* | N=469 | N=618 | N=291 |
| Jan-Mar | Apr-Jun | Jul-Sep | Oct-Dec |

*Numbers in the bars represent the denominators of the incidence calculations.
**Percentages on the vertical axis are restricted to 0-25%.

scope of this Guide, the comparison could be evaluated using a statistical test to separate the element of chance from what is likely to be a real difference in risk between groups. Practically speaking, shelters can make comparisons and monitor their progress towards reducing disease without using statistical tests. Recognize, however, that large differences between incidence rates are more convincing than small ones, and differences that are sustained and grow over time are of most importance. Also, as discussed previously, natural variations in the data will be observed.

**DATA NEEDED** The calculations necessary in Figures 6.2 and 6.3 require that the disease and intake data be partitioned by age group and source. Ideally animals not at risk of URI should be removed from the denominators of these calculations. This may not be accomplished easily with current versions of shelter

software, but even crude estimates (consistently measured) can be very helpful to shelters.

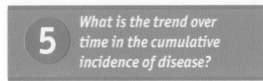

**5** **What is the trend over time in the cumulative incidence of disease?**

**WHAT AND WHY?** The risk of developing many diseases changes over time —— during an outbreak, seasonally, in response to changes in protocols, etc. It is important to understand the trends in disease frequency for a variety of reasons. These include targeting preventive measures, identifying the onset of outbreaks, assessing the effectiveness of changes in protocols, anticipating space requirements in isolation wards, and assessing staffing needs. The trend in the number of upper respiratory tract infections (URI) in cats over a year is graphed by season for a shelter in Figure 6.4.

# FIGURE 6.6 MONTHLY CUMULATIVE INCIDENCE RATES OF URI IN CATS (2013-2014)

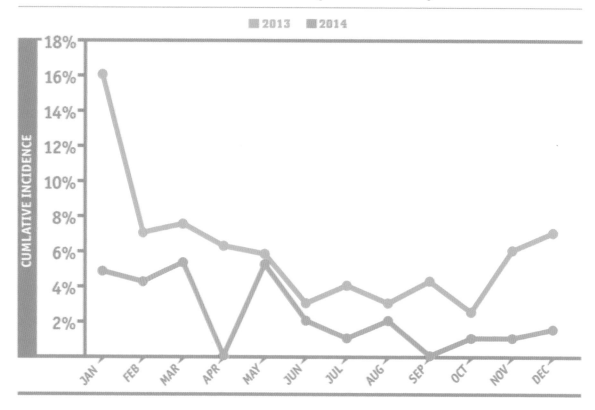

2013 ▦ 2014

**INTERPRETATION** Not surprisingly to the staff of the shelter in Figure 6.4, the highest number of cases of URI in cats occurred during the summer months. As discussed previously, however, numbers of cases without denominators can be deceiving. The cumulative incidence (or risk) of upper respiratory tract infections in the shelter was highest in the winter months and lowest in the summer months much to the surprise of shelter staff (Figure 6.5). They believed that the summer and early fall months were the months of highest risk for upper respiratory tract infections in their cats because they saw more cases during those months. However, they also saw many more cats at risk in those months. Impressions are often not borne out when data are examined. The staff in this shelter realized that they needed to be equally attentive to their protocols (including

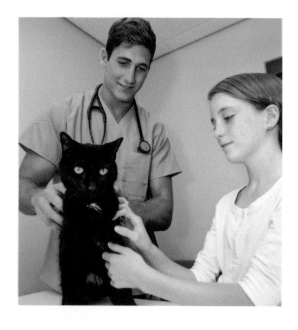

minimizing the average length of stay) to reduce the risk of URI throughout the year, not just during the summer months when they assumed that the incidence of URI was the highest.

**DATA NEEDED** The number of new cases and those susceptible during each season (or month if monthly incidence is tracked) of the year must be known to calculate and graph the seasonal cumulative incidence estimates. These calculations can be done as described previously, designating each season as the period of interest.

---

**6** *Have changes in protocol (e.g., shortening the average length of stay) lowered the incidence of disease over time?*

---

**WHAT AND WHY?** The effectiveness of a change in protocol designed to minimize disease is *best demonstrated* by showing a decline in the incidence of disease after implementation of the protocol. Demonstration of a decline in the incidence indicates that the change was effective. It also helps to motivate staff to continue their efforts, and can assist in acquiring funds to support future disease reduction efforts. The shelter in Figure 6.6 had the goal of reducing their average length of stay (ALOS) for cats with the goal of improving flow within the shelter and reducing the cumulative incidence of feline upper respiratory tract infections. After instituting daily rounds and other strategies to reduce their ALOS, not only did the ALOS decrease (data not shown), but the cumulative incidence of URI also fell from 2013 to 2014.

---

**7** *What is the overall mortality rate and how does disease impact euthanasia and other deaths within your shelter?*

---

**WHAT AND WHY?** Medically-related euthanasias usually are performed for two reasons: (1) to end non-remediable suffering and (2) as a result of having insufficient resources (e.g., monetary, personnel, space) to treat animals (that could be saved if those resources became available). In order to distinguish between these reasons, we recommend that shelters track them separately.

Tracking euthanasias of animals with "treatable and manageable" diseases enables shelters (with the goal of saving a growing percentage of these animals) to assess their progress. These numbers can also assist shelters in anticipating treatment costs needed to save similar animals in the future. The data can be used to bolster grant applications or target fund-raising efforts to cover these costs. Monitoring euthanasias of animals with treatable diseases may identify changes in the health of entering animals that could reflect the inability of pet owners to afford veterinary care. Such data might prompt community programs to assist these owners and save lives. Alternatively, an increase in the number of euthanasias due to untreatable or severe diseases may represent changes in the health of animals entering the shelter, be the consequence of outbreaks of severe disease, or reflect declining adherence to disease prevention/control protocols within the shelter.

Monitoring the frequency of non-euthanasia deaths can be a measure of the propriety of medical decision-making in your shelter or a reflection of the health (often age-related) of the animals brought to the shelter. The mortality rate or percentage of dogs (and cats) dying within the shelter (i.e., non-euthanasia deaths) is calculated by dividing the number of dogs (or cats) dying (not euthanized) by all animals residing in the shelter during the period of interest. This metric represents the probability of dying (other than from euthanasia) in the shelter. The probability of a cat dying in the shelter in Table 6.2 was 1.7% in 2014 (See Mortality all causes).

Rarely, mortality rates can provide insight into possible problems with care provided by the shelter. For example, it has been reported that a few shelters have avoided euthanasia (and allowed animals to die) in order to keep the percentage of animals euthanized low (to impress donors). Fortunately, in most shelters, the mortality rate is naturally very low, principally occurring in un-weaned kittens or among injured animals that die before euthanasia can be performed. The goal should be to minimize medically-related deaths either due to euthanasia or natural causes, while remaining consistent with your shelter's humane mission. We believe that shelters should not perpetuate suffering.

**DATA NEEDED AND INTERPRETATION** In our experience most shelters track reasons for euthanasia, including those that are medically related. Many do not distinguish between those that might be treated (if resources existed) and those that could not be saved under any circumstances.

To calculate the metrics in the row entitled "Euthanasias for medical reasons" in the Annual Medical Profile in Table 6.2, the number of cats (or dogs) euthanized for medical reasons was divided by all cats (or dogs) that resided in the shelter during the time frame of interest. This denominator included all animals present on the first day of the time period plus the number of incoming animals during the period. These statistics are based on the number of euthanasias for medical reasons *among all animals that could have been euthanized* (i.e., all animals in the shelter during 2014). For example, the 6.2% in Table 6.2 (row entitled "Euthanasias for medical reasons") represents the probability that a cat in this shelter in 2014 would be euthanized for a medical reason. This same approach can be used for the treatable and non-treatable categories.

Many shelters report the proportion of medically-related euthanasias *among those animals euthanized*. In the shelter in Table 6.2, 128 total cats were euthanized in 2014. Of these, 76% (97/128) were euthanized for medical reasons. The approach used depends on the question that your shelter is seeking to answer and convey to its constituents. We prefer reporting the actual probability that entering animals will be euthanized for a medical reason because this metric directly reflects the risk of being euthanized for a medical issue in this shelter.

**HELPFUL HINTS** Non-euthanasia deaths can be due to a variety of reasons including congenital abnor-

malities, severe injuries or disease. Therefore, the overall mortality rate is not necessarily a reflection of disease severity or the rate of animals that might have survived with treatment. Ideally, shelters should track non-euthanasia deaths by their causes, but practically speaking, if mortality is usually very low, further subdivision may be unhelpful.

# RECOMMENDED QUESTIONS

> **8** What is the difference between the general health status of entering and exiting animals?

**WHAT AND WHY?** Whether a shelter uses Asilomar categories or develops its own method of monitoring the general health status of incoming and outgoing animals, we believe tracking this type of information is helpful. As discussed in the Intake and Outcome chapters, tracking the general health status of incoming and outgoing animals separately provides important insights. Comparing them to each other can also be revealing. For example, if the general health status of incoming animals was better than it was at final disposition, the situation would raise the question "why?" This scenario could be a red flag for poor care within the shelter, or it might just reflect the occurrence of a recent outbreak of severe disease. Similarly, an improvement in general health status between intake and final disposition can reflect positively on the shelter's medical management of their animals (something to emphasize to donors).

**DATA NEEDED AND INTERPRETATION** An assessment of the general health of each animal at entry and again at final disposition within a specified time frame is needed.

By monitoring the health status of animals at the time of intake and final disposition, the shelter

# FIGURE 6.7 ASILOMAR STATUS OF DOGS AT INTAKE AND AT FINAL OUTCOME (2010 – 2012)

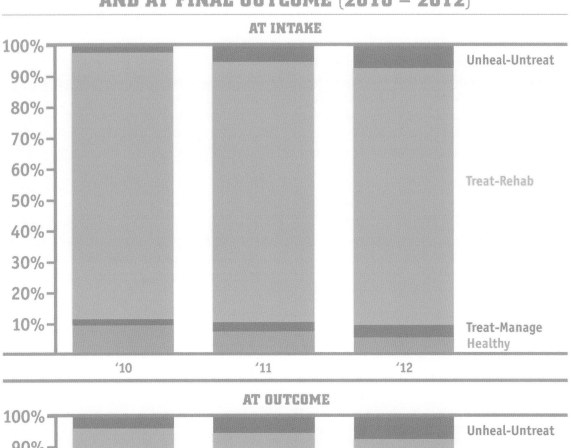

AT INTAKE

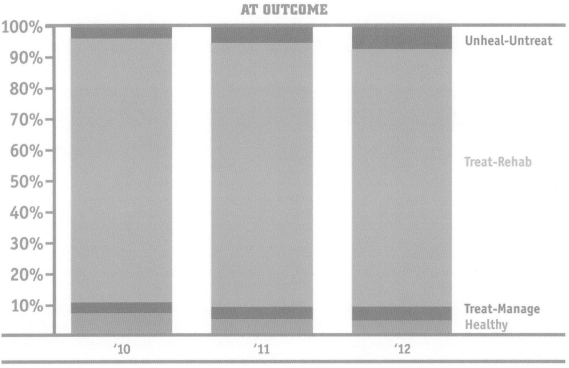

AT OUTCOME

in Figure 6.7 realized that as the percentage of unhealthy/untreatable animals at entry rose, so did the percentage in this category leaving the shelter during the same time frame. Had they looked only at the Asilomar status at outcome, the staff might have worried that the percentage of animals becoming unhealthy/untreatable and treatable-manageable was increasing in their care over time. Shelter funds were reallocated to cover the costs of care for the increasing number of sick animals. Plans were also made to develop programs to assist community members needing veterinary services.

**HELPFUL HINTS** The percentage of animals whose health declines while in the shelter should be small. Also, note that tracking general health status at intake or outcome requires: good definitions of the health categories of interest; training of staff; consistent usage of categories; and complete recording of this information.

# QUESTIONS FOR YOUR CONSIDERATION

**9** *What percentage of animals has a particular disease or condition at a given point in time?*

**WHAT AND WHY?** The **prevalence** (or **prevalence proportion**) of a disease is the proportion of animals in a population that has that particular condition. Be careful not to confuse prevalence with incidence. Incidence measures are a risk of developing disease (or getting sick), whereas prevalence can be thought of as the amount of a "disease" that exists or the proportion of animals that have that disease in a population. Disease prevalence can be measured at a point in time (**point prevalence**) or over a period (**period prevalence**), although the latter is less often used (Rothman, 2012; Gordis, 2014; Fletcher et al, 2014).

POINT PREVALENCE IS DEFINED BELOW.

(NUMBER OF ANIMALS WITH A PARTICULAR DISEASE) ÷ (NUMBER OF ANIMALS IN THE POPULATION AT RISK OF DISEASE) AT A PARTICULAR POINT IN TIME

It is often expressed as a percentage. Prevalence is useful in shelters to measure the frequency of diseases such as feline leukemia, feline immunodeficiency virus infection and canine heartworm disease among animals at their point of entry into the shelter. Knowing the point prevalence of these diseases at entry provides insight into trends in the community. They can also inform the need for space and resources to treat disease or house affected animals. For example, if your shelter treats heartworm-infected dogs, knowing the point prevalence among entering dogs can facilitate planning for medications, further diagnostics, and potential foster homes. Knowing the frequency of cats entering with FeLV or FIV enables a shelter to plan for housing of these animals if it chooses to make them available for adoption. Point prevalence estimates are also used to estimate the predictive values (positive and negative) associated with the interpretation of various diagnostic and screening tests (Fletcher et al, 2014).

Prevalence estimates are often used to plan for medical resources to have on hand. For example, a shelter might track the period prevalence of conditions such as feline hyperthyroidism, canine hypothyroidism or diabetes mellitus in order to have medications on hand to treat them (in shelters that treat these conditions).

**DATA NEEDED** Determining the point prevalence of a disease in your population requires knowing the number of animals diagnosed with that disease and dividing that number by the population at risk. For example, if you are interested in knowing the prevalence of FeLV or FIV among cats entering your shelter, the "population at risk" would be the number of animals tested at their point of entry (point in time) over a given time period. Notice, this might not include all entering cats, as some may be euthanized or returned to owners quickly, making testing unnecessary. When discussing prevalence, always specify the population (e.g., cats tested, all animals residing in the shelter) that was used in the denominator. As you may have noticed in the Medical Profile in Table 6.2, the "% affected" value was accompanied by a fraction. This was done to identify the actual number of animals that were evaluated for that condition.

**INTERPRETATION** The number and prevalence of FeLV and FIV cases among entering cats in the shelter in the Profile (Table 6.2) were assessed in order to plan for housing these cats while they awaited adoption.

**HELPFUL HINTS** In the veterinary literature, the terminology "prevalence rate" is commonly used to refer to point prevalence. For the same reason that epidemiologists only use the term incidence rate when referring to the calculation of incidence density, most do not favor the terminology "prevalence rate." (See Appendix 1)

## 10 How long does it take on average for animals with a specific disease to recover from disease?

**WHAT AND WHY?** For many shelters, diseases that may have meant euthanasia in the past are now routinely treated. Treating disease has associated costs, and knowing those costs will enable shelters to better plan for care. The most significant costs associated with treating disease are usually those associated with the number of medical care staff, their time commitment, and the time affected animals spend in the shelter. Monitoring the length of time between diagnosis and recovery from disease

can help define the staff-time and care-related costs associated with disease treatment, as well as assess the efficacy of medical protocols.

**DATA NEEDED** In Chapter 5 we discussed lengths of stay in specific areas of the shelter and the concept of "time to event." Monitoring the time to recovery from a disease (e.g., respiratory infections) is essentially the same. The time to recovery is first calculated for each affected animal by subtracting the date of diagnosis from the date of recovery and adding 1 day. Then times to recovery are summed over all affected animals and divided by the number of animals treated (or affected if not treated) to calculate the average time to recovery. Unfortunately, we are not currently working with shelters that record recovery times for any disease so no graph is included. Examining recovery times for some diseases (e.g., feline and canine upper respiratory tract infections) may be useful in working towards shortening them for various age and other subgroups in shelters, as well as ascertaining costs of care.

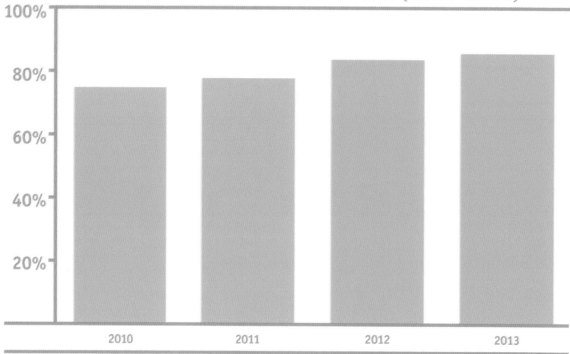

## FIGURE 6.8 THE PERCENTAGE OF DOGS STERILIZED IN THE SHELTER BEFORE ADOPTION (2010-2013)

**HELPFUL HINTS** The primary challenge to accomplishing this calculation is training staff to accurately and consistently record dates of diagnosis and recovery for all animals affected by the diseases being monitored. Entering disease-related data (including diagnosis and recovery dates) should be incorporated into your treatment protocols. Restricting these analyses, at least initially, to one or two diseases can enhance compliance with entering the appropriate dates.

In some shelters, the primary diseases represented in their cat and dog isolation areas are feline and canine upper respiratory tract infections, respectively. If this is true in your shelter and your shelter is diligent about recording the movement of animals into and out of isolation wards, you could calculate time-to-recovery for upper respiratory tract infections using times spent in Isolation.

## 11 How many animals underwent a particular treatment or procedure in a particular time period?

**WHAT AND WHY?** The number of animals undergoing spay / neuter surgery or treatment for heartworm infection, for example, is useful to many shelters. Funding agencies may request such numbers as part of grant proposals, or your shelter may be interested in tracking its progress towards goals associated with these procedures (e.g., increasing the number of spay/neuter surgeries performed by your shelter prior to adoption – Figure 6.8). Similarly, your shelter may be interested in monitoring its needs (e.g., foster homes, funds) associated with treating particular diseases.

**DATA NEEDED** Recording procedures and treatments in electronic medical records or on paper will facilitate summarizing these data if they are standardly defined and recorded. Sometimes procedures are recorded in "notes" sections (where details can be freely typed), but these note areas are not easily "searchable" either in paper records or using software. They can be, therefore, very difficult to summarize.

**HELPFUL HINTS** Shelter management software providers increasingly offer shelters the option to customize the list of procedures and treatments that are entered into animals' records, usually via drop-down menus. Rather than having a drop down list containing dozens of procedures, consider including only the procedures that your shelter commonly performs and wants to quantify. A streamlined list will likely facilitate data entry.

## SUMMARY

Quality care for individuals and good medical records provide the basis for providing optimal care for shelter populations. The incidence of disease in populations is the primary indicator of population health. High frequencies of disease cause suffer-

ing; often lead to euthanasia or death; increase the average length of stay; limit a shelter's capacity for care; and increase costs. For these reasons, it is incumbent on shelters to minimize the frequency of disease in their facilities. If shelters don't quantify disease frequency, at least for their most common infectious diseases, they cannot track their progress towards minimizing them. Without goals to limit the frequency of disease, shelters frequently perpetuate the status quo - too much disease. *Allocating a large proportion of the medical budget for treatment-associated costs (or worse, euthanizing animals for disease) at the expense of preventive measures is not compatible with the humane mission of shelters.*

We recognize that entering and retrieving the data necessary for disease surveillance and the calculation of the metrics in this chapter can be frustratingly difficult with current software programs. We also realize that many small animal veterinarians are unfamiliar with using metrics for population care. In order to practice true preventive, population-oriented medicine in shelters, however, these impediments must be removed. Shelters must insist that the data needed be easily accessible to them from their software. Shelter veterinarians must access and monitor disease frequency (e.g., incidence, prevalence) to optimize the population care that they provide. **The potential payoffs are huge: suffering from disease can be reduced; time in residence can be shortened; more animals can be saved; the numbers of euthanasias can be reduced; and resources can be diverted from treatment to prevention.**

# CLOSING COMMENTS

Our primary objective for writing this book was to encourage shelters to make greater use of the data they collect to improve the welfare of their animals and shelter operations. With regular review of metrics, shelters can succinctly characterize their animal populations and management, evaluate the effectiveness of their programs, set goals, and communicate progress to constituencies. The book suggests metrics relating to common shelter goals regarding intake, outcomes, and management of animals within the shelter. Ultimately, however, decisions as to which metrics are monitored should re-

flect what makes sense for the needs of each shelter.

We hope that at least some of the examples suggest ways that your shelter can use its data more extensively. Timely analysis and review of relevant data should be an essential component of decision-making and program evaluation. Granting agencies are increasingly asking that shelters evaluate the impact of their funded programs. One means to achieve this is through monitoring metrics associated with program success. Similarly, the effectiveness of internally funded programs should be evaluated to assess whether monies are being spent wisely; and successful programs can be tweaked to increase their effectiveness as a consequence of regular evaluation of data.

Appropriately analyzed and thoughtfully presented metrics enhance communication with staff, volunteers, members of Board of Directors, and the community. Most shelters communicate numbers of incoming animals and lives saved in their annual reports, but could summarize the breadth of their many other activities more thoroughly. Presenting additional summary metrics judiciously and thoughtfully can raise awareness in the community and stimulate greater interest.

Staff and volunteers work hard to care for animals in their charge and to implement programs and initiatives that improve the welfare of those animals. It is often difficult for these care givers to grasp the full impact of their efforts. When discussions of the importance of staff/volunteer contributions are augmented with metrics documenting improvements over time, these can be powerful motivators for continued diligence; they can also validate the daily importance of staff and volunteer contributions.

Shelters collect data daily, most using some type of computer software. Many shelter resources (particularly staff time) are devoted to that collection. Yet, many shelters use only a fraction of the data they collect, and some of the information is of suspect quality. If shelters start using their data broadly, motivation to improve quality and completeness will increase, justifying the investment in data collection.

One impediment to achieving greater use of shelter data is the difficulty of retrieval associated with many software programs. It is imperative that shelters demand easy and flexible retrieval, including data visualization from shelter software companies. It makes little sense to collect data that cannot be retrieved in an easy and useful format.

In summary, we believe strongly that animal shelters can improve the welfare of their animals and their operations by regularly reviewing influential metrics. We hope that this guide stimulates the shelter community to embrace the expanded use of metrics as a key

component of its life-saving mission. As the use of metrics evolves, we hope that discussions and examples of their use will expand. We are developing a website as a resource and clearinghouse to facilitate discussion, collect ideas, provide examples, and further encourage the use of metrics in animal shelters. We look forward to your comments regarding the book, and ideas for stimulating interest in using metrics more extensively.

# APPENDIX 1

# THE MATH OF IT

## INTRODUCTION

Some readers of this Guide will have some epidemiological and/or statistical training in their background and others will not. Some readers, particularly the veterinarians, will have learned how disease is measured in populations of animals, but it may have been years ago. Regardless of your background, however, the materials in this Appendix are provided to increase (or refresh) your understanding of some basic statistical and epidemiologic concepts used in this book. For additional information, references to several statistics and epidemiology texts are provided (see References section) (Dawson & Trapp, 2004, Rothman, 2012, Fletcher et al, 2014, Gordis, L, 2014, Petrie & Watson, 2006), and many others have been published.

Comprehending large numbers of observations is facilitated by condensing and summarizing them. For example, if a shelter was interested in understanding how many of the dogs entering the shelter in June were already neutered, studying a list of 200 entering dogs and their neuter status would be difficult (if not impossible) without summarizing the information. It is much easier to understand (and share with others) that 80/200 (40%) were neutered and 120/200 (60%) were sexually intact at admission. Thus, data regarding shelter animal populations are almost always most useful and interpretable when summarized with a few metrics (or statistics) that capture the key information and enable we humans to interpret them.

Some of these summary metrics (e.g., mean, minimum, maximum) are provided by shelter software providers today. Other summary metrics are not. If the basic metrics explained in this Appendix are not provided in your software, they can be calculated using spreadsheet programs, dedicated statistical packages or by hand. As shelters begin to make more extensive use of their data, means to obtain appropriate summary metrics will undoubtedly become easier.

Animals and other entities (e.g., shelters) have characteristics by which we describe them. For example, animals can be characterized by their age, gender, breed or weight. Shelters can also be characterized using numerous descriptors (e.g., the number of animals they admit, the species that they accept). Each characteristic or descriptor is called a **variable** in statistical parlance.

# SUMMARIZING DATA

The statistics or metrics that best summarize data depend on the type of observations in a variable and the scale on which those observations are measured (Dawson & Trapp, 2004). Data take two general forms: categorical (qualitative) or continuous (quantitative).

## CATEGORICAL (QUALITATIVE) DATA

Some characteristics or variables describing things (e.g., animals, disease) fall naturally into categories or groups. For example, the gender of animals is "male or female"; animals are "alive or dead" or "healthy, mildly, moderately, or severely ill." As a consequence, information regarding these characteristics is considered categorical data. Other examples of categorical data include source (e.g., stray, owner-surrendered), species (e.g., canine, feline) and jurisdiction (e.g., Town X, Town Y). Data that are partitioned into groups are categorical.

**Nominal** and **ordinal** scales of measurement are used for categorical data. Data are **nominal** if they can be categorized or classified into mutually exclusive and exhaustive categories that have no inherent order. For example, data regarding gender are nominal. The categories are male and female and all animals can be classified as only one or the other. Status (alive or dead), source of animal (e.g., stray, owner-surrendered), outcome (e.g., adopted, euthanized, transferred) are examples of nominal data.

**Ordinal** data also have mutually exclusive categories, but the categories have an inherent order. For example, disease is often categorized as to whether it is mild, moderate or severe in nature. Numerical values may be assigned to represent the various levels and analyzed as ordinal data. For example, body condition might be scored 1=cachectic, 2=thin, 3=optimal, or 4=overweight, 5=obese. Notice, however, that one cannot measure, in a mean-

ingful quantitative sense, the distance between the different categories. Other examples of ordinal data include stages of cancer, or frequency of events (e.g., never, rarely, sometimes, often, frequently).

## CONTINUOUS (QUANTITATIVE) DATA

Observations of other variables are continuous in nature. Observations for which the differences between numbers can be measured on a numerical scale are continuous (e.g., age, intake numbers, weight). For example, age is a continuous variable because the difference between being 2 and 5 years of age is 3 years, and the difference between being 7 and 10 years of age is 3 years. If you were measuring the number of animals entering the shelter, the difference between the intake of 213 cats in June and 269 cats in July is 56 cats. In contrast, the difference between being "male and female" or "mildly and moderately ill" is not measurable on a numerical scale. There are formally two types of continuous data (interval and discrete).

**Discrete continuous data** are usually counts of things (e.g., number of animals, cages or red blood cells). For example, shelters count the number of cats and dogs they impound each year or the number of owner-surrendered, stray, transferred-in, returned or seized animals they accepted in the month of September. Each animal, red blood cell, or cage is unique from other animals, red blood cells or cages, respectively. These counts have many uses including for grant requests, annual reports, and strategic planning. Other examples of continuous data collected in shelters include the number of cats euthanized each year, number of spays performed last year, etc.

**Interval continuous data** are measurements of things (e.g., age, weight, length), the value of which depends on the precision of the instrument used to measure it. For example, if your scale only measures to the nearest kg, a dog might weigh 4 kg. If, however, the scale weighs to the nearest tenth of a kg, the same dog could weigh 4.4 kg; if the scale weighs to the nearest one hundredth of a kg, the same dog could weigh 4.37 kg and so forth. Theoretically, a dog could have an infinite number of weights, depending on the precision of the scale.

## TABLE A1.1 GENDER AND NEUTER STATUS OF 80 CATS PRESENTING TO A RABIES VACCINATION CLINIC

| GENDER AND NEUTER STATUS | NUMBER | PERCENTAGE |
|---|---|---|
| Female, neuter | 35 | 44 |
| Female, intact | 27 | 34 |
| Male, neuter | 10 | 12 |
| Male, intact | 8 | 10 |
| **TOTAL** | **80** | **100** |

# SUMMARIZING CATEGORICAL AND CONTINUOUS DATA

**Categorical data** (nominal or ordinal) are commonly summarized by reporting the number and percentage of values in each category (called a frequency distribution). When using percentages, all possible categories describing that variable must be represented. For example, if source of animal is summarized, then all possible sources must be represented in the summary. If there are many sources, an "other" category is also allowable, so long as the percentages sum to 100% of all possibilities. When calculating percentages the numerator is the number of animals in one possible category and the denominator is the sum of animals in all possible categories.

For example, data regarding gender and neuter status among 80 cats from a rabies clinic are summarized in Table A1.1. Among the 80 cats in the table above, 44% are neutered females, 34% are intact females, 12% are neutered males and 10% are intact males. Notice that the percentages must add up to 100% over these 4 mutually exclusive categories.

Ordinal data regarding severity of disease for 61 transport dogs with kennel cough are summarized below (Table A1.2).The majority of the dogs with kennel cough experienced mild signs (65%), but 25% had moderate disease and 10% were severely ill.

If an ordinal variable has many levels (e.g., a cleanliness measure ranging from 1=filthy to 10=immaculate), data from this ordinal variable could be analyzed as if it were continuous (discussed next).

## TABLE A1.2 SEVERITY OF ILLNESS AMONG 61 TRANSPORT DOGS WITH KENNEL COUGH

| SEVERITY OF DISEASE | NUMBER | PERCENTAGE |
|---|---|---|
| Mild | 40 | 65 |
| Moderate | 15 | 25 |
| Severe | 6 | 10 |
| **TOTAL** | **61** | **100** |

# FIGURE A1.1 FREQUENCY DISTRIBUTION (OR HISTOGRAM) OF THE AGES OF THE FIRST 10 CATS ENTERING A SHELTER ON JUNE 1*

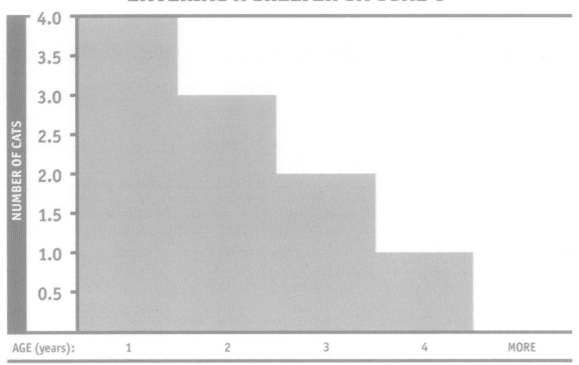

*Notice that 4 cats that entered were 1 year of age, 3 cats were 2, 2 were 3 and 1 was 4 years old.

**Continuous data** are summarized depending on the pattern of their frequency distribution (or histogram).

**WHAT IS A FREQUENCY DISTRIBUTION?** A **frequency distribution** shows all of the possible observations made for a variable and the number of times each value was observed. When generating a frequency distribution of continuous data, all of the observations are ordered from lowest to highest and the number of each possible value is counted and plotted. In Figure A1.1 above, the ages of the first 10 cats entering a shelter on June 1st have been ordered from youngest to oldest and the frequency of each age observed has been plotted. This plot is also called a **histogram**. [A frequency distribution/histogram can also be generated using the percentage of times each possible value was observed among all of the observations].

If there are large numbers of observations with many possible values, some of the values may be combined to form ranges of values and any observations falling in that range are counted and plotted. For example, the weights of all adult cats presenting to a shelter in the month of June and July are plotted in Figure A1.2. All cats with weights 2.2 - 2.49 kg were counted in the first bar, all cats with weights 2.5 - 2.79 kg were counted in the second bar, etc.

If a frequency distribution has a bell shape to it (similar to the one for weight above) it is said to have a **Gaussian distribution** and is described as having a "**bell-shaped curve**".

Continuous data that have a Gaussian distribution (or a bell-shaped distribution) are said to be **"Normally distributed."** Note that the word **"Nor-**

# FIGURE A1.2 THE DISTRIBUTION OF WEIGHTS OF CATS ENTERING A SHELTER IN JUNE - JULY

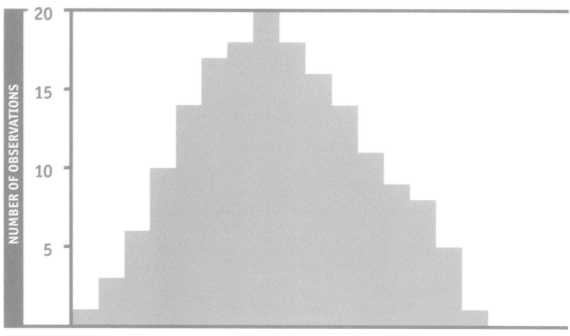

NUMBER OF OBSERVATIONS

WEIGHT (kg):  2.2  2.5  2.8  3.1  3.4  3.7  4.0  4.3  4.6  4.9  5.2  5.5  5.8  6.1  6.4  6.7  7.0  7.3  more

mal" used in this context does NOT mean usual or healthy. Rather it refers to a pattern or type of distribution of data that has a "bell shape" to it. Data that do not have a Gaussian distribution, such as those shown in Figure A1.3 regarding Length of Stay of cats in a shelter, are called **non Gaussian** (or **non Normally distributed**). Non Normally distributed data can have an infinite number of distribution patterns. That is, they can be skewed, have multiple peaks, etc.

**The shape of the frequency distribution that continuous data assume determines how that data should "best" be summarized.** If the data are Gaussian, they are usually summarized using means and standard deviations, and if they are non Gaussian (or non Normal), they are usually summarized using medians and percentiles, medians and the minimum and maximum numbers, or medians and a range.

## MEASURES OF THE MIDDLE OF A SET OF CONTINUOUS NUMBERS

Means and medians are called **"measures of central tendency"** because they are intended to convey where the middle of the frequency distribution of data (or observations) lies.

**Mean** is also known as the *arithmetic mean* or *average*. It is the sum of all the numbers observed divided by the number of observations. For Normally distributed data, the mean (or average) represents that number above which approximately ½ of the values lie and below which approximately ½ of the values lie. Also, the values above and below the mean mirror one another; that is, they are distributed above and below the mean as a mirror image. The mean is intended to convey the value that is at the center of all of the data values that were used to calculate it. It is best used when the distribution

# FIGURE A1.3 DISTRIBUTION OF THE TOTAL NUMBER OF DAYS CATS RESIDED IN A SHELTER IN 2014

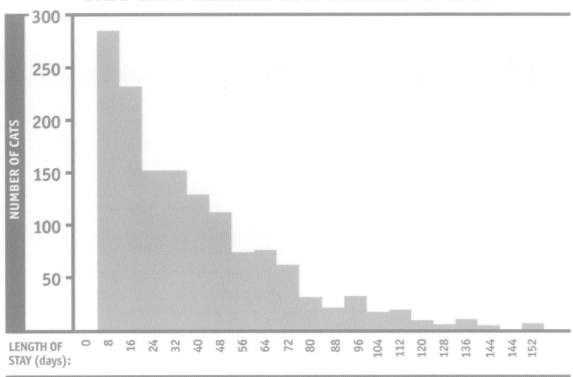

LENGTH OF STAY (days):

of the data has a bell-shape or Gaussian curve. So, when a shelter reports that its average length of stay (ALOS) for cats is 20 days for the month of June, this *implies* (but does not guarantee) that roughly half of the cats stayed more than 20 days and half stayed less than 20 days. If data that are not Normally distributed are summarized using a mean, that mean is unlikely to represent the middle of the data. Another of the limitations of using means to summarize data is that a few extreme values in non Normal data can have a large influence on where the mean actually lies with regards to other values.

**Median** is, <u>by definition</u>, the middle-most value in a set of observations. It lies at the 50th percentile and divides the observations into two equally sized groups - ½ above the median and ½ below. Medians are calculated by ordering all the observations from smallest to largest and then identifying the middle-most value.

## MEASURES OF THE VARIABILITY OF THE DATA

Statistics such as means and medians convey where the middle-most observation of a group of observations lie, but distributions can have the same mean (or median) and look very different. For example, the two distributions of the ages of cats residing in two shelters in April have identical means (8.5 years), but their overall distributions of values are different (Figures A1.4 and A1.5). The ages of cats from Shelter A (Figure A1.4) are spread around the mean more widely (4.6 to 13 years) than the ages of the cats from Shelter B (6.9 to 10.4 years) with the same mean (Figure A1.5).

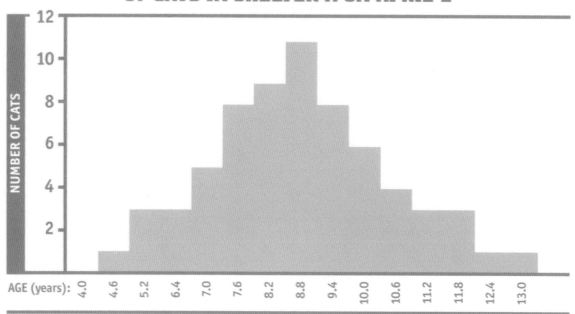

# FIGURE A1.4 DISTRIBUTION OF AGES OF 67 CATS IN SHELTER A ON APRIL 2

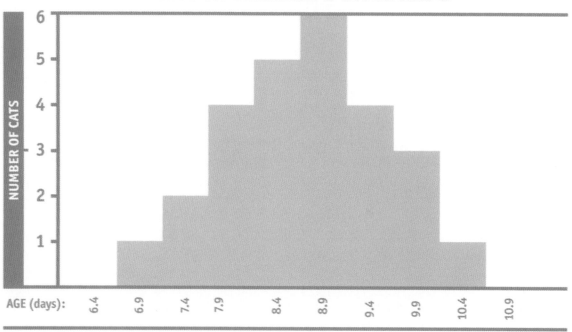

# FIGURE A1.5 DISTRIBUTION OF AGES OF 26 CATS IN SHELTER B ON APRIL 2

For this reason, continuous numbers are also described by using a measurement of the variability (or spread) of the data around the mean (or median). Not surprisingly, the "best" measures of the variability of continuous data also depend on **whether or not the frequency distribution of the data has a bell-shaped curve.**

## STANDARD DEVIATION MEASURES THE VARIABILITY OF NORMALLY DISTRIBUTED DATA

A standard deviation measures the average variability of the observations around the mean of *Normally* distributed data. The properties of the Gaussian or Normal Distribution have been studied extensively and knowledge of the standard deviation of a set of data can be used to define and convey how the data are distributed about the mean. For example, the interval bounded by the mean plus one standard deviation and the mean minus one standard deviation encompasses approximately 68% of the observations of a *Normally* distributed variable. Similarly, the mean ± 2 standard deviations includes approximately 95% of the observations of a variable with a bell-shaped distribution. See a statistics text for a more complete discussion of the Gaussian distribution (Dawson & Trapp, 2004, Petrie & Watson, 2006).

In the examples above for Shelter A and Shelter B, the variability of the ages of cats from Shelter A is larger around the mean of 8.5 years compared to the ages of cats from Shelter B. The ages of 67 cats from Shelter A have a standard deviation of 1.9 years, whereas the ages of the 27 cats from Shelter B are much closer (i.e., don't vary as much) to the mean of 8.5 years, with a standard deviation of only 1.0 year. Computer programs (e.g., spreadsheet programs or dedicated statistical packages) run algorithms today to calculate standard deviations for users.

## PERCENTILES, QUARTILES AND RANGE

If observations are not Normally distributed as illustrated in Figure A1.3, then a standard deviation does not describe the variability well. That is, ~68% of the data (i.e., observations) will not fall within plus or minus 1 standard deviation of the mean. The Length of Stay data in Figure A1.3 are said to be skewed to the right, but Non Gaussian data can be skewed to the left, have two peaks, be flat, or have any of an infinite number of shapes that are *not* bell-shaped.

Since standard deviations do not describe the variability of non Gaussian data well, the variability of such data is described in other ways. The most common approach is to use percentiles, and among the percentiles that could be calculated, quartiles are commonly reported. Percentiles (including the quartiles) are calculated first by putting all of the values in numerical order starting with the smallest and ending with the largest. Then the values corresponding to the particular percentiles are identified.

---

**LOOKING AT THE LENGTH OF STAY DATA IN FIGURE A1.3, THE QUARTILES ARE:**

**1ST QUARTILE:   10 DAYS**
**2ND QUARTILE:   27 DAYS**
**3RD QUARTILE:   50 DAYS**

The first quartile tells you the number below which ¼ of the observations lie or above which 3/4s of the data lie. The second quartile is the median and tells you the number below (and above) which ½ of the data lie; and the third quartile tells you the number below which 3/4s of the data values lie, and above which ¼ of the observations lie.

---

In the Length of Stay data, ¼ of the cats stayed in the shelter less than 10 days; 3/4s more than 10 days; ½ stayed less than 27 days and ½ more than 27 days; and 3/4s stayed less than 50 days and ¼ stayed more than 50 days.

## RANGE, MINIMUM, MAXIMUM

The variability of non Normally distributed data can also be described using their range, defined as the difference between the largest observation in the data and the smallest. Since the range does not provide information about the smallest and the largest numbers (only the difference), the minimum (or smallest) observation and the maximum (or largest) observation are often preferred to the range. If the minimum and maximum numbers are reported, the range is easily calculated. The range for the Length of Stay data for the 1429 cats in Figure A1.3 is 158 days whereas the minimum stay is 1 day and the maximum is 159 days.

**HELPFUL HINTS** The shelters with which we have worked have skewed Length of Stay data like that in Figure A1.3. If the mean length of stay is calculated for these data (or data skewed to the right as this distribution is), the mean will *not* be at the center of the data. Rather it will be above the median, pulled upwards by values for the cats with the longest lengths of stay. In these data, the mean was 35 which overestimates the value above which ½ of the cats had longer lengths of stay. Similarly, if a standard deviation is calculated to represent the variability in these skewed data, it will not convey the true variability to the consumer. For these reasons, we use median and quartiles to summarize Length of Stay data that are not Normally distributed.

That said, we are not aware at this time that any of the current software providers have reports with medians and percentiles. Ideally, the distribution of your Length of Stay information should be evaluated (i.e., graphed) in order to select the best approach to summarizing it. Since this is not practical for most shelters at this time, the mean Length of Stay (if used consistently) can be used to monitor progress towards lowering this metric in your populations (even if your data are not Normally distributed). It is important, however, to recognize its limitations and interpret its meaning correctly.

Continuous data can be made categorical by forming categories. For example, age of entering animals can be categorized into groups: < 4-week olds, 4-8 week olds, 9-14 week olds, etc. **When converting continuous data into categories, <u>always</u> form mutually exclusive categories.** If the age categories had been < 4-week olds, 4-8 week olds, 8-14 week olds, and so forth, the category into which a 4-week old kitten should be put in this example is unclear. Does it go in the first or second age category? If you allow animals to be recorded in more than one category, staff collecting the data cannot be sure where to put particular animals and the entry will be inconsistent. Also, your shelter may not be able to distinguish whether the age of animals entering the shelter is changing over time, or staff members are entering data differently. Grouping of continuous data is often done to enhance understanding of the data.

**SUMMARY** Categorical data are usually summarized with the numbers and percentages of animals that fall within mutually exclusive categories. Continuous data are usually summarized according to the pattern of the frequency distribution of their observations (i.e., numbers): if the data have a bell-shaped pattern, then a mean and standard deviation should be calculated; if the data are shaped in any configuration other than a bell-shaped one, then a median (and percentiles, minimum and maximum, or range) should be used. As mentioned earlier, **summary statistics are intended to enhance understanding of data. If they are calculated and used incorrectly, they will mislead your shelter and other consumers of your shelter's information.**

# MEASUREMENT OF THE FREQUENCY OF DISEASE AND DEATH IN SHELTER POPULATIONS

Measures of disease frequency are necessary to: monitor the health of a population; assess the effectiveness of disease control/prevention programs; identify and characterize an outbreak in your shelter; enhance understanding of what is happening; and communicate with shelter colleagues in a meaningful way.

**A note about the definition of "disease"** Epidemiologists prefer to monitor the occurrence of *di-*

agnosed disease in lieu of signs of disease because most signs are associated with many diseases. This approach is preferred because different diseases have different etiologies and may require different approaches to prevention and control. In shelters (where resources are often limited), definitive diagnoses may not always be possible, however. In these instances, the frequency of signs (e.g., diarrhea or vomiting) can be used judiciously in place of diagnoses. For example, monitoring the incidence rate of diarrhea in young kittens can be helpful in identifying the beginning of an outbreak and trigger further diagnostic workups to identify a specific cause(s). Also, when diagnoses (such as upper respiratory tract infections) are made, the specific agent(s) responsible is usually not known. Fortunately, since control strategies are essentially the same regardless of the URI agent(s) involved, further diagnostic workups are not necessary for the implementation of effective control measures and disease monitoring. For these reasons we define the word "disease" broadly in the following pages.

## MEASUREMENTS OF MORBIDITY: INCIDENCE OF DISEASE

The most useful measurement of disease frequency or morbidity in shelters is **incidence**. Unfortunately, different terms have been used to describe incidence measurements in different Epidemiology texts (Rothman, 2012, Fletcher et al, 2014, Gordis, 2014). In this Guide, we use the terms "cumulative incidence" and "incidence density" to describe the two common incidence measurements. Cumulative incidence is also called "incidence proportion" and incidence density is also called "incidence rate". Both calculations are measures of the frequency of illness (morbidity) occurring in populations.

**Cumulative incidence (or incidence proportion)** Cumulative incidence (CI) is calculated by counting the number of *newly diagnosed* cases of "disease" (e.g., parvovirus) in a specified interval of time (e.g., one year, one month) and dividing that count by the number of animals that were eligible (or at risk) to develop that disease during the same time interval.

NUMBER OF NEW CASES OF A PARTICULAR DISEASE DIAGNOSED *DURING A SPECIFIED INTERVAL*

÷

NUMBER OF ANIMALS *IN THE POPULATION AT RISK* OF THAT DISEASE DURING THE INTERVAL

Notice that individuals in the population "at risk" do NOT have the disease when the interval begins and are susceptible (to the best of our knowledge) to develop that disease during the interval. Cumulative incidence measures the fraction of susceptible animals that developed disease during an interval of time, and represents the probability (or risk) of animals developing the disease during that interval. Cumulative incidence estimates range between 0 and 1 (e.g., 0.3, 0.67) and have no units. Cumulative incidence is often expressed as a percentage by multiplying the fraction by 100 (e.g., 0.67 X 100 = 67%).

**See examples of calculations at the end of this Appendix.**

*In stable populations* where new animals do not arrive and leave frequently, only the average size of the population at risk is often known, not the exact number of animals that were at risk at the beginning of the interval. In these instances, **cumulative incidence** is measured by counting new cases occurring in the interval divided by the average number of animals present (and at risk) during the interval (usually determined on the middle-most day of the interval). This is how many incidence estimates quoted in the veterinary literature have been calculated. They are good measures of the risk (or probability) of developing disease when the population is relatively stable during a time frame. Many epidemiologists do not call estimates of cumulative incidence, "rates," but most of the veterinary literature does refer to them as such. We have used the word "rate" to describe cumulative frequency measures (e.g., mortality rate) in some places in the book.

**Attack rate** is another term for cumulative incidence used in the context of an outbreak or epidemic (where disease has occurred in a defined group of animals during a relatively short time frame). The population at risk (or the population susceptible to developing the disease) is defined as the number of susceptible animals at the outset of the outbreak (where "susceptible to developing" is defined with the best information available).

In most animal shelters, the population that could develop a particular event (e.g., an upper respiratory tract infection, death) changes day-by-day as animals enter and leave the organization. Therefore, **the population at risk is unstable** because it has a different group of animals at risk each day. When animals enter and leave the shelter frequently and stay for varying lengths of time, they don't all have an equal opportunity to be exposed to or develop most infectious diseases (e.g., upper respiratory infections, parvovirus). For example, a cat that is reclaimed 1 day after entering the shelter has a low probability of being exposed to an agent causing upper respiratory tract disease compared to a cat staying 10 days.

Despite the fact that most shelter populations have animals with varying periods of observation, we recommend using cumulative incidence estimates of disease in your disease surveillance system to monitor disease incidence in your shelter. **We recommend counting the number of new cases of a particular disease occurring in a specified interval (e.g., Spring) and dividing that number by the number of animals entering during that interval plus those still at risk and in the shelter at the beginning of the interval.** We believe that if shelters use this approach consistently over time and for other comparisons (e.g., incidence of males compared to females), it will be adequate for disease surveillance and facilitate evaluation of disease-related goals.

The other common measure of incidence used by epidemiologists (primarily in research studies) is **incidence density or incidence rate** as defined by epidemiologists (Rothman, 2012, Fletcher et al, 2014,

Gordis, 2014). **This calculation is designed to help handle populations where individuals have varying lengths of observation, and it can be relatively difficult to calculate and understand.** We refer readers who intend to conduct research in shelters and who need to estimate the incidence of disease in their studies to epidemiology resources describing the calculation of incidence density (as this metric should be used in the research context). **We do not recommend incidence density metrics for routine use in shelters.**

**USEFULNESS OF CUMULATIVE INCIDENCE**  Since CI measures the risk of developing disease (e.g., parvovirus, panleukopenia), it is the basic metric of disease surveillance, control and prevention programs. Some of its specific uses are described in Table A1.3. This list is not exhaustive, but presents several applications in use.

## PREVALENCE OF DISEASE

**Prevalence** is another measure of morbidity, but differs from incidence in that **existing** cases of disease are counted (regardless of when they first developed) and divided by all animals at risk in the population. Notice that incident cases (i.e., new cases) are counted and added to all cases that may exist at a point in time (or during a period of time) and the sum of these is the total number of prevalent cases. Prevalence measures are commonly called prevalence rates.

The most common measurement of prevalence is called **point prevalence**. It is defined as the number of existing cases (or the number of animals that *have* the disease) at **one** point in time divided by the number of animals in the population at risk at that point in time.

NUMBER OF ANIMALS
THAT HAVE A
PARTICULAR DISEASE

÷

NUMBER OF ANIMALS
(AT RISK) OF THAT DISEASE
IN THE POPULATION
AT A GIVEN POINT IN TIME

## TABLE A1.3 USES OF CUMULATIVE INCIDENCE (CI) IN ANIMAL SHELTERS

| |
|---|
| **To establish baseline incidence rates of common infectious diseases\* by species** |
| By time (monthly, seasonally, annually) |
| Age groups (e.g., < 8 weeks, 8 – 16 weeks, 17 weeks – 11 months, 1-7 years, > 8 years) |
| Source (e.g., owner-surrendered, stray, feral, seized) |
| **To monitor the effectiveness of control efforts to reduce the incidence rates of common infectious diseases** |
| For the population overall |
| By any high-risk groups identified in the assessment of baseline |
| **To examine associations of disease with possible factors that may enhance (or diminish) disease frequency (e.g., length of stay in the shelter)** |
| **To identify or confirm outbreaks** |

\*Common infectious diseases should be dictated by what occurs frequently in your shelter. See Chapter 6, Table 6.3

This fraction is often expressed as a percentage by multiplying by 100. The most common uses of prevalence data are for planning for health services (e.g., ordering drugs), monitoring the frequency of chronic conditions or calculating the predictive values of diagnostic and screening tests. Therefore, it is often unnecessary to define the population at risk as rigorously as in the calculation of an incidence rate (where the intent is to measure the risk of developing some event).

The other measure of prevalence (used less frequently) is **period prevalence**. It differs from point prevalence in that disease is not measured at just one point in time, but rather all existing cases of disease are measured during a specified *interval of time* and then divided by the average population present during that interval in stable populations.

**USES OF PREVALENCE IN SHELTER** Prevalence measures are used to assess the frequency of diseases (e.g., FeLV, heartworm infestation) that may require identifying special adopters or needs for treatment. These are also used in calculating the predictive values of diagnostic and screening tests.

## MEASUREMENTS OF MORTALITY

The risk of death is measured in several ways. All measures are characterized by the number of deaths in the numerator that occurred in a particular period of time. Notice that the estimation of the risk of dying is synonymous with measuring the incidence of death.

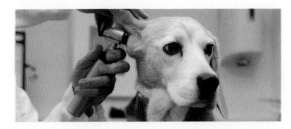

**Mortality rate (i.e., cumulative mortality or mortality proportion)** The risk of dying is measured by dividing the number of animals that died in a specified interval by the number of animals at risk of dying in that interval. (Almost always, all of the animals are at risk of dying in a specified interval).

$$\frac{\text{NUMBER OF ANIMALS THAT DIE IN THE INTERVAL}}{\text{NUMBER OF ANIMALS AT RISK OF DYING IN THE INTERVAL}}$$

Sometimes **cause-specific mortality measures** are calculated and presented. For example, a shelter might calculate the mortality due to canine influenza in their shelter annually.

$$\frac{\text{NUMBER OF ANIMALS DYING OF THE CAUSE OF INTEREST (E.G., INFLUENZA) IN A SPECIFIC INTERVAL}}{\text{NUMBER OF ANIMALS AT RISK OF DYING IN THE POPULATION DURING THAT SPECIFIED INTERVAL}}$$

Since mortality rates are estimates of the incidence of death, mortality density rates can also be calculated, but will not be discussed here.

## CASE-FATALITY RATE

Another frequently calculated measurement of mortality is the **case-fatality rate**. It is often calculated in outbreaks to indicate the severity of the disease involved, and is estimated by dividing the number of animals dying of a particular disease

by the number of cases of that disease that were at risk of dying.

$$\frac{\text{NUMBER OF ANIMALS DYING OF THE DISEASE}}{\text{NUMBER OF CASES OF THE DISEASE DURING A SPECIFIED INTERVAL (USUALLY DURING AN OUTBREAK)}}$$

Each of these measures of mortality is often expressed as a percentage. The mortality statistics described above may not always be true rates in the epidemiologic sense, but we will call them rates because the terminology is widely used and understood in veterinary medicine. Other measures of mortality and morbidity exist, and we refer interested readers to the References section of the book for more information.

**Uses of mortality measurements in shelters** The overall mortality rates by species help shelters understand the risk of animals dying in their care during specific intervals (e.g., year, during an outbreak). Cause-specific mortality rates by species enable shelters to understand the risk of dying of specific causes. Case-fatality rates underscore the severity of outbreaks due to various causes.

Most shelters have low mortality rates because animals that are suffering from severe illness are euthanized before they die naturally. Therefore, the comments above can also apply to euthanasia rates if the reasons for euthanasia are carefully tracked and separated from other reasons for euthanasia (e.g., lack of space).

**Morbidity and mortality measurements in subgroups** In general, disease frequency and mortality measures are often calculated for subgroups where disease risk may vary. For example, age group is an important and common modifier of the risk of disease and death in populations. Comparing overall mortality or morbidity rates between populations without accounting for differences in their age distributions

## TABLE A1.1 (repeated)
## GENDER AND NEUTER STATUS OF 80* CATS
## PRESENTING TO A RABIES VACCINATION CLINIC

| GENDER AND NEUTER STATUS | NUMBER | PERCENTAGE |
| --- | --- | --- |
| Female, neuter | 35 | 44 |
| Female, intact | 27 | 34 |
| Male, neuter | 10 | 12 |
| Male, intact | 8 | 10 |
| **TOTAL** | **80** | **100** |

*5/85 or 6% of cats had no information regarding their gender/neuter status.

can lead to inaccurate conclusions (Rothman, 2012). Differences in disease frequency associated with other factors (e.g., source, length of stay) should also be considered when overall rates between populations are compared for the same reason. Also, calculating the risk of disease or death in various subgroups of animals can identify high-risk groups and direct control and prevention efforts to increase their effectiveness.

**WHAT TO DO ABOUT MISSING DATA?** Shelters should strive to have staff enter *accurate* and *complete* data regarding every variable of interest to the shelter. That said, sometimes data are not recorded or are obviously incorrect (e.g., the dog's age is 40 years). The handling of missing data is a complex subject, and readers interested in research are encouraged to consult other resources (Howell, n.d.). One of the easiest approaches to managing missing data is to omit them from summary calculations, but report the percentage of missing data separately from the summarized data. For example, if a shelter had missing data regarding the gender/neuter status of 6% of its cats, the data would be summarized using only the data for the 94% of cats with information. See Table A1.1 repeated above. Notice that there is not an additional category of cats missing this information in the table, but the consumer is aware that 6% of cats attending the rabies clinic had no data regarding their gender/neuter status. The data in Table A1.1 would be inter-

preted "Among those cats presenting to a rabies vaccination clinic *with information regarding their gender/neuter status*, 44% were neutered females, 34 % were sexually intact females . . ." Overall, 6% (5/85) of the cats attending were missing this information.

When reporting summary information regarding a variable with continuous data, missing information is also omitted, but reported separately. For example, one might report that "The median length of stay of kittens in a shelter was 10 days among the 96% of kittens who had LOS data recorded."

Reporting the number and percentage of animals missing information is important because if a large percentage of data for a variable is missing, this diminishes confidence in the validity of the data. Similarly, it begs the question of whether those that lacked information for a variable had a similar distribution as those with it.

# EXAMPLES OF CALCULATIONS

We provide some data below for you to practice calculating various morbidity and mortality calculations.

**EXAMPLE 1:** Data in Table A1.4 pertain to an outbreak of parvovirus in dogs at a shelter during July – August 2014.

# TABLE A1.4 DATA REGARDING THE OCCURANCE OF PARVOVIRUS IN DOGS IN AN ANIMAL SHELTER DURING AN OUTBREAK

| DESCRIPTIVE STATISTICS FOR DOGS DURING JULY - AUGUST 2014 | PUPPIES | ADULTS |
|---|---|---|
| Died (all causes) | 12 | 3 |
| Died of parvovirus | 7 | 0 |
| Developed parvovirus | 52 | 4 |

# TABLE A1.5 MORBIDITY AND MORTALITY RATES ASSOCIATED WITH A PARVOVIRUS OUTBREAK

| CALCULATIONS FOR ALL DOGS IN THE SHELTER | RATE (%) | PROPORTION |
|---|---|---|
| Overall mortality rate | | |
| Mortality rate from parvovirus (cause-specific mortality rate) | | |
| Cumulative incidence of parvovirus | | |
| Case fatality rate for parvovirus | | |
| **DISEASE MEASURES AMONG PUPPIES** | **RATE (%)** | **PROPORTION** |
| Overall mortality rate | | |
| Mortality rate from parvovirus | | |
| Cumulative incidence of parvovirus | | |
| Case-fatality rate for parvovirus | | |
| **DISEASE MEASURES AMONG ADULTS** | **RATE (%)** | **PROPORTION** |
| Overall mortality rate | | |
| Mortality rate from parvovirus | | |
| Cumulative incidence of parvovirus | | |
| Case-fatality rate for parvovirus | | |

There were 25 healthy puppies and 6 healthy adult dogs in residence on July 1 in this shelter and no dogs with parvovirus. Over the next two months, 325 puppies and 44 adult dogs entered the facility. The dogs that died of any cause, died of parvovirus, and that developed parvovirus during the interval are listed in Table A1.4.

Use the data to calculate the cumulative incidence and mortality rates experienced during the outbreak. Record your answers in Table A1.5.

Calculating population metrics are only one step towards better managing population health. Interpreting the meaning of the metrics, explaining them to others in the shelter, and using that information to implement new protocols or reaffirm old ones is the ultimate goal.

**QUESTION:** Looking at the data entered in Table A1.5, answer the following questions. Justify your answers.

**What do the data suggest about the susceptibility of puppies to parvovirus disease compared to adult dogs in this shelter?** (Assume that these rates are statistically significantly different).

**What do the data suggest about the severity of parvovirus infections in puppies compared to adults? Are your answers consistent with what you understand about the biology of parvovirus in dogs?**

Answers are on pages 155.

**EXAMPLE 2** Looking at the data in Table A1.6 calculate the prevalence rates for each year for FeLV and FIV and record your answers in the table.

**QUESTION** How would you explain these prevalence rates to a shelter staff member unfamiliar with prevalence metrics? *Answer is on page 155.*

## TABLE A1.6 PREVALENCE OF FELV AND FIV INFECTIONS AMONG CATS AT ENTRY INTO SOMEWHERE SHELTER (2011-2014)

| YEAR | NUMBER POSITIVE FOR FeLV | NUMBER OF CATS TESTED FOR FeLV | PREVALENCE OF FeLV | NUMBER POSITIVE FOR FIV | NUMBER OF CATS TESTED FOR FIV | PREVALENCE OF FIV |
|------|------|------|------|------|------|------|
| 2011 | 42 | 1408 | | 20 | 1408 | |
| 2012 | 39 | 1377 | | 15 | 1377 | |
| 2013 | 33 | 1170 | | 13 | 1170 | |
| 2014 | 41 | 1193 | | 17 | 1193 | |

# TABLE A1.4 (repeated)
## ANSWERS TO QUESTIONS REGARDING EXAMPLE 1

| DESCRIPTIVE STATISTICS FOR 400 DOGS IN SOMEWHERE SHELTER DURING (JULY – AUGUST 2014) | PUPPIES N=350* | ADULTS N=50* |
|---|---|---|
| Died (all causes) | 12 | 3 |
| Died of parvovirus | 7 | 0 |
| Developed parvovirus | 52 | 4 |

* These are the puppies/dogs that were potentially susceptible. They include the 25 puppies in residence on July 1 plus the 325 puppies that entered the facility: July 1 - August 31. Similarly, there was a total of 50 adult dogs at risk during the interval (6 in residence on July 1 plus 44 that entered the facility).

## TABLE A1.7 MORBIDITY AND MORTALITY RATES ASSOCIATED WITH A PARVOVIRUS OUTBREAK

| CALCULATIONS FOR ALL DOGS IN THE SHELTER | RATE (%) | PROPORTION |
|---|---|---|
| Overall mortality rate | 4% | (15/400) |
| Mortality rate from parvovirus (cause-specific mortality rate) | 2% | (7/400) |
| Cumulative incidence of parvovirus | 14% | (56/400) |
| Case-fatality rate for parvovirus | 13% | (7/56) |
| **DISEASE MEASURES AMONG PUPPIES** | **RATE (%)** | **PROPORTION** |
| Overall mortality rate | 3% | (12/350) |
| Mortality rate from parvovirus | 2% | (7/350) |
| Cumulative incidence of parvovirus | 15% | (52/350) |
| Case-fatality rate for parvovirus | 13% | (7/52) |
| **DISEASE MEASURES AMONG ADULTS** | **RATE (%)** | **PROPORTION** |
| Overall mortality rate | 6% | (3/50) |
| Mortality rate from parvovirus | 0% | (0/50) |
| Cumulative incidence of parvovirus | 8 % | (4/50) |
| Case-fatality rate for parvovirus | 0% | (0/4) |

## What do the data suggest about the susceptibility of puppies to parvovirus disease compared to adult dogs in this shelter? (Assume that these rates are statistically significantly different).

ANSWER: Puppies (with a cumulative incidence of 15%) appear to be more susceptible to developing parvovirus than adults (with an incidence of 8%). This conclusion assumes that both the adults and puppies had roughly equal opportunity to be exposed to the virus. The difference in risk might also be explained by differences in prior immunity.

## What do the data suggest about the severity of parvovirus infections in puppies compared to adults?

ANSWER: Since the case-fatality rate in puppies was 13% compared to 0% in adults, the data suggest that puppies experience more severe parvovirus disease than adult dogs.

## Are your answers consistent with what you understand about the biology of parvovirus in dogs?

ANSWER: Yes.

ANSWERS TO QUESTIONS FOR EXAMPLE 2:

### TABLE A1.6 (repeated) PREVALENCE OF FELV AND FIV INFECTIONS AMONG CATS AT ENTRY INTO SOMEWHERE SHELTER (2011-2014)

| YEAR | NUMBER POSITIVE FOR FeLV | NUMBER OF CATS TESTED FOR FeLV | PREVALENCE OF FeLV | NUMBER POSITIVE FOR FIV | NUMBER OF CATS TESTED FOR FIV | PREVALENCE OF FeLV |
|------|------|------|------|------|------|------|
| 2011 | 42 | 1408 | 3% | 20 | 1408 | 1% |
| 2012 | 39 | 1377 | 3% | 15 | 1377 | 1% |
| 2013 | 33 | 1170 | 3% | 13 | 1170 | 1% |
| 2014 | 41 | 1193 | 3% | 17 | 1193 | 1% |

## How would you explain these prevalence rates of FeLV or FIV to a shelter staff member unfamiliar with prevalence metrics?

ANSWER: Among cats entering the shelter each year the prevalence describes the percentage of cats that were positive for FIV (or FeLV). The cats may have developed their infection a month, a year, two years, etc before entering, but at the point in time that they entered, they were infected.

# DISPLAYING METRICS MEANINGFULLY

*The goal of displaying metrics is to facilitate your understanding and enlighten your audience with the clarity of your presentation.*

Your shelter has set appropriate measurable goals, and metrics have been calculated to monitor progress towards their achievement. The next challenge is to display the metrics (summarized data) in a manner that facilitates understanding of what is truly happening. Data presentations can either inform or mislead. In this discussion we make the assumption that shelters wish to present their data as truthfully as possible.

Shelters can choose from numerous options to present their metrics. Information can be displayed in tables, graphs or with pictograms, and much has been published about data display. In this Appendix we summarize briefly some of the principles of data presentation using shelter examples. There is no one method to display data, but all presentations should emphasize clarity first, and aesthetics or artistic creativity second. Feel free to experiment with multiple data presentations, keeping the principles discussed below in mind. We provide references at the end of this Appendix to encourage readers to seek additional guidance.

creased for owner-surrendered, stray, returned-adoption and transferred-in cats combined?" Notice that this process requires carefully framing the questions you want to ask of, and illustrate with, the data.

**Note** If your shelter routinely monitors many of the same questions (as they relate to shelter goals), then the process of framing these basic questions need only take place once. Then the data regarding these routine surveillance questions can be monitored at regular intervals without repeating the framing step. Once data are pulled to answer your question, the type of display can be selected to maximize clarity of the answer.

# DECIDING ON HOW TO DISPLAY DATA

**You have a myriad of choices as to how to display your data. Pick the presentation that clearly and succinctly conveys the message you seek to understand (or present).**

For simple questions such as "How many owner-surrendered cats entered the shelter in 2014?" a sentence can easily summarize the answer. "In the calendar year 2014, the shelter accepted 1,232 owner-surrendered cats." For other data, you can consider tables or graphs. We have excluded pictograms from the options because most shelters don't employ a graphic artist, and for basic data presentation, tables and graphs should suffice.

## TABLES

Graphing is not always superior to presenting data in tabular form. In general, tables are a good choice when you want to display: precise numbers; information regarding several distinct questions; a summary of many events; or several types of data with different units of measurement. Two examples of the use of tabular display are provided in Tables A2.1 and A2.2. The Profiles presented at the beginning of each chapter in this book are a good example of data that would be difficult to display in one graph.

# BEGIN WITH THE QUESTION OF INTEREST

As discussed in the Chapter 2, goals should be sufficiently specific that they lead to: clearly described steps to achieve them; and specific means to evaluate or measure progress towards reaching them. Similarly, when seeking to decide how best to display data, the message you wish to convey must be specific and clear. Many data-display gurus suggest describing what you hope to convey (i.e., the purpose of the display) in one or two sentences before attempting to create your data presentation. This sounds easy, right? Well, it is often easier said than done.

For example, consider the question "is the shelter's live release rate increasing?" Before you can pull and display data relating to this question, you must first clarify your inquiry. For which species? For which intake groups? For which time frame? The purpose of the visual display can be defined by clearly specifying the answer to these questions. For example, "Over the past 3 years (2012-2014), has our live release rate in-

# TABLE A2.1 OUTCOME PROFILE FOR DOGS AND CATS FROM SOMEWHERE SHELTER (2014)

**TIME FRAME: 2014**
**SHELTER DESCRIPTION: Open Admission**
**ANIMAL CONTROL CONTRACT: Yes**
**CRUELTY INVESTIGATION: Yes**

| | 🐕 TOTAL = 545* | | 🐈 TOTAL = 1587* | |
|---|---|---|---|---|
| | # | % Outcome Elligible | # | % Outcome Elligible |
| **Released Alive** | **464** | **85.1** | **1,348** | **84.9** |
| Adoptions | 265 | 48.6 | 1,301 | 82.0 |
| Transfers-out | 9 | 1.7 | 0 | — |
| Returned to Owner | 190 | 65.7† | 47 | 8.3† |
| **Not released alive or lost** | **59** | **10.8** | **165** | **10.4** |
| Euthanized | 58 | 10.6 | 136 | 8.6 |
| Died in shelter | 1 | 0.2 | 28 | 1.9 |
| "Lost" | 0 | — | 1 | 0.0 |
| **\*\*Still in Shelter** | **22** | **4.0** | **74** | **4.7** |

\* Excludes seized animals, but includes animal intakes in 2014 plus animals Still-in-Shelter at the beginning of the day on 1/1/14

\*\* Includes animals Still-in-Shelter system on 12/31/14

† Rates calculated among stray animals only

The numbers of dog impoundments over time by Jurisdiction for Somewhere Shelter are provided in Table A2.2. Graphing data for many categories (e.g., towns) over time is difficult as many numbers are involved. A tabular display, however, shows the precise numbers for each town, and large differences among the towns are evident. Small differences and trends in the data are more difficult to discern, and two displays, a table and a line graph might enhance understanding, depending on the goal(s).

# TABLE A2.2 NUMBER OF DOG IMPOUNDMENTS FOR TOWNS WITH ANIMAL CONTROL CONTRACTS WITH SOMEWHERE SHELTER (2009-2013)

| JURISDICTION | 2009 | 2010 | 2011 | 2012 | 2013 |
|---|---|---|---|---|---|
| Town A | 84 | 74 | 75 | 76 | 53 |
| Town B | 19 | 19 | 35 | 33 | 14 |
| Town C | 137 | 140 | 139 | 145 | 144 |
| Town D | 47 | 43 | 36 | 24 | 19 |
| Town E | 51 | 35 | 35 | 34 | 18 |
| Town F | 46 | 42 | 60 | 67 | 46 |

## Characteristics of good tables

Five general guidelines for producing useful tables are listed below.

### 1 TITLE

The title should concisely convey to the reader the "what, where and when" of the message contained in the data. For example, review the two titles below for Table A2.1.

**OUTCOME PROFILE**

**VS.**

**OUTCOME PROFILE FOR DOGS AND CATS FROM SOMEWHERE SHELTER: 2014.**

The second title is preferred because it conveys to the reader that this is an Outcome Profile for dogs and cats for Somewhere Shelter for the period 2014. If this table was to be shared with people not working with the shelter, it might also include the location (Somewhere, NY).

### 2 COLUMN HEADINGS

The headings of each column should clearly identify the data presented in it, including any essential de-

scriptors such as the units of measurement or time period. Often the label for a column describes the group to which the data pertain (e.g., 🐕) (Table A2.1) and the second heading identifies the format of the data (% or #). If percentages are presented, it is often important to indicate the total number to which the percentages pertain (i.e., the denominator). For example, 85.1% of 545 dogs were released alive in Table A2.1.

## ③ ROW DESCRIPTORS

The label for each row should describe the nature of the data in that row. In Table A2.1, the row entitled "Released Alive" informs the reader that the data in that row pertain to animals released alive in 2014.

## ④ FOOTNOTES

Footnotes are encouraged if they provide information that clarifies the data and enhances the consumer's ability to use the information in the table. For example, one of the footnotes in Table A2.1 makes clear that the Table excludes data pertaining to seized animals, but includes animal intakes in 2014 plus animals "Still-in-Shelter" at the beginning of the day on 1/1/14.

## ⑤ SOURCE OF INFORMATION LINE

The source line describes where the data were obtained. For most tables or graphs generated for a particular shelter, this line is irrelevant, as the source (e.g., the shelter) is obvious. If, however, data from several distinct organizations are combined or data from other sources (e.g., U.S. Census) are incorporated into a table, then indicating the source of these data is important.

Key pieces of information should be "highlighted" for the consumer such that it is extracted easily. This can be done with bolding (as in Table A2.1) or with shading. Spacing can also enhance or detract from understanding.

### WITHOUT GOING INTO DETAIL, SEVERAL ADDITIONAL TIPS ARE PROVIDED BELOW

*Keep your use of words to a minimum.*

*Minimize the number of decimal places for your data. Most shelter data are not measured even to the tenths of a unit, so presenting data measured to two or more decimal places is almost always unwarranted.*

*When placing data in a column, align the data such that each piece of information shares the same location in relation to the decimal point.*

*Use a common symbol for missing data. For example, NA (not available or not applicable), or M (missing) or a dash "-" to indicate that the data were missing or not applicable, not just overlooked.*

*Use appropriate separators for the data such as a comma after the thousands column (1,232 instead of 1232).*

*Be consistent in your presentation of the data throughout the table. If you are assembling a presentation for an audience, and several tables are included, keep the formatting of data and style across tables as similar as possible.*

To reiterate, the goal of presenting of data is not to impress the audience with your creativity in pre-

Photo Credit: Meredith Robinson

sentation (despite technology making it relatively easy), but **rather to impress them with the clarity of your presentation.**

## VISUAL DISPLAYS OF DATA: CHARTS/GRAPHS

Some people distinguish between graphs and charts, but we make no such distinction.

The visual presentation of data is a powerful strategy for enhancing understanding and conveying their meaning. The types of charts we find most useful for addressing basic shelter questions (and easy to generate in spread sheet or other programs that graph) are **bar, stacked bar, line, and pie charts.** If one of these fails to meet your needs, choose another chart type that better displays data addressing your particular question. Regardless of the format you choose, remember that the objective is to clearly display the data such that the answer to the question of interest (or purpose of the chart) is clear. **A graph embellished with all manner of creative additions (e.g., pictures, exotic fonts) is often less clear than a straightforward, no-frills graph.**

You should answer three general questions before choosing the type of graph you wish to use to summarize your data.

**1** *Who is your audience?*

**2** *What specifically do you want to learn (or what message do you want to convey)?*

**3** *What do you want to do with the data – describe, compare, show trends or analyze relationships?*

Charts are particularly helpful when you want to display:

*Comparisons*

*Trends (i.e., changes over time)*

*Distributions of the data over several categories*

*Component parts of a whole (e.g., % distribution of all intake types)*

*Associations between two variables (e.g., time in shelter and weight of animals)*

# FIGURE A2.1 COMPARISON OF THE FREQUENCY OF INTAKE TYPES FOR DOGS (N=591) AND CATS (N=1845)*: (2014)

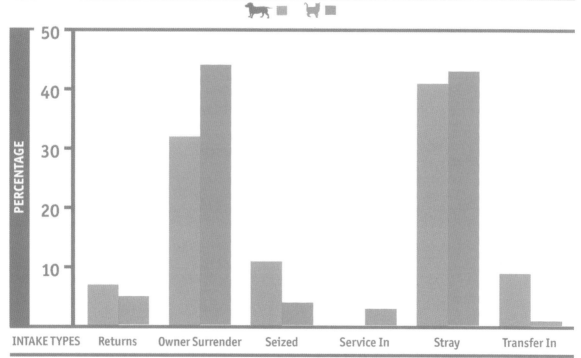

* Service-in category: housed temporarily at the shelter while their owners looked for alternative housing arrangements.

* Percentages on the vertical axis are restricted to 0-50%.

Characteristics of a useful chart:

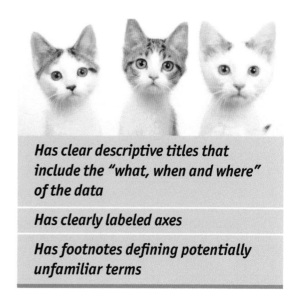

| |
|---|
| **Captures peoples' attention** |
| **Presents information clearly, simply and accurately** |
| **Usually addresses one question at a time** |
| **Summarizes data succinctly** |
| **Does not mislead** |
| **Clarifies comparisons and illustrates trends and differences** |

**Has clear descriptive titles that include the "what, when and where" of the data**

**Has clearly labeled axes**

**Has footnotes defining potentially unfamiliar terms**

Photo Credit: Penny Adams

# FIGURE A2.2 FREQUENCY OF OUTCOMES AMONG DOGS INCLUDING AND EXCLUDING THOSE SEIZED (2014)

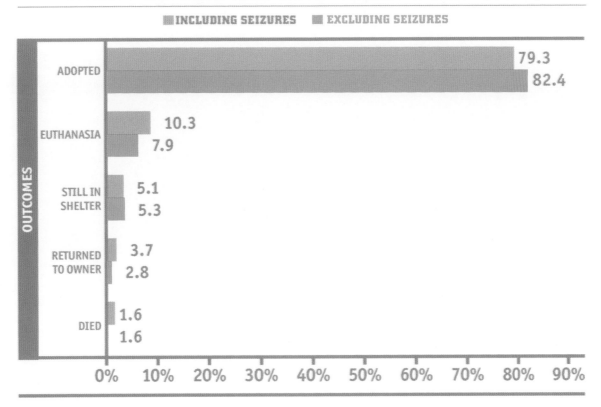

## Choose the type of chart to use

### SIMPLE BAR CHARTS

We often use two types of bar charts (simple and stacked) for shelter data. They are relatively easy to create and to read. They work particularly well for comparing numbers or percentages in various groups or categories. Several examples are provided.

From the vertical bar graph in Figure A2.1, it is clear that a higher percentage of cats than dogs entered as owner-surrendered and as strays, but a higher percentage of dogs compared to cats were returned, seized or transferred-in to this shelter in 2014.

Figure A2.2 is also a bar chart, but showing the bars presented horizontally. It is easier to compare the values in each category if they are ordered by size (largest to smallest or vice versa). In order to

clarify the actual percentage associated with each bar, the explicit percentages are presented on the graph. The specific percentages could have been shown in Figure A2.1 as well if it was important to know them precisely.

In Figure A2.3, the trend in the adoption rate for cats over time is illustrated. Since the primary intent of this display is to evaluate trends, the exact percentages adopted each year are not presented.

**HELPFUL HINTS** When a scale of numbers or percentages does not begin at 0 (on the vertical axis of Figure A2.3 in this graph), that should be clearly noted on the graph. The relative changes in the adoption rate over time look very different when the vertical scale includes (Figure A2.4) or excludes 0 (Figure A2.3).

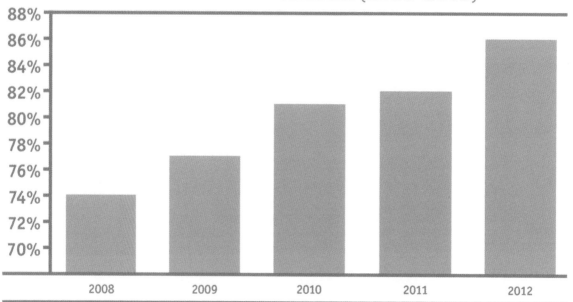

# FIGURE A2.3 ANNUAL ADOPTION RATE* OF CATS FROM SOMEWHERE SHELTER (2008-2012)**

\* The adoption rate is defined as the percentage of cats adopted among owner-surrendered, stray, transferred-in and returned cats entering this shelter annually, plus cats in those categories on January 1 of each year.

\*\* The scale of this graph begins at 68%, not 0. There has been a 16% increase in the adoption rate of cats between 2008 and 2012.

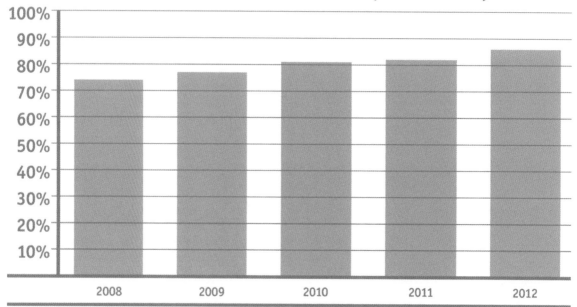

# FIGURE A2.4 ANNUAL ADOPTION RATE* OF CATS FROM SOMEWHERE SHELTER (2008-2012)

\* The adoption rate is defined as the percentage of cats adopted among owner-surrendered, stray, transferred-in and returned cats entering each shelter annually plus cats in those categories on January 1 of each year.

Spreadsheet and other graphing programs enable you to either "fix" the limits of the axes or to have the program do it automatically.

## STACKED BAR CHARTS

Stacked bar charts are helpful to illustrate and compare components of totals and can be used to visualize trends over time in several categories simultaneously. In Figure A2.5, the shelter was interested in tracking the health status of its cats at entry (using its Asilomar matrix) over a time period when the economy worsened in the region. Since the total number of cats entering this shelter was decreasing over time, comparing the numbers of cats admitted does not clearly capture the relative changes occurring in the Asilomar status. The relative changes are better illustrated using percentages of cats in each health category as in Figure A2.6. This figure displays an increase in the proportion of cats unhealthy/untreatable and treatable-rehabilitatable and a corresponding decrease in healthy cats at entry over time. The number of cats admitted each year by their health category was also important to note, however, as the numbers highlighted the animals for which the shelter now needed to provide care.

The graph in Figure A2.7 could be used to monitor whether the overall average length of stay was decreasing over time, and if so, the relative contribution of each segment of time contributing to that overall average length of stay.

Progress was made shortening the overall average length of stay between 2008 and 2012, primarily by shortening the time cats spent in holding and time to spay/neuter surgery. The graph suggests that additional progress could be made by shortening the time cats spend on the adoption floor (e.g., "fast tracking" some) to further diminish the ALOS.

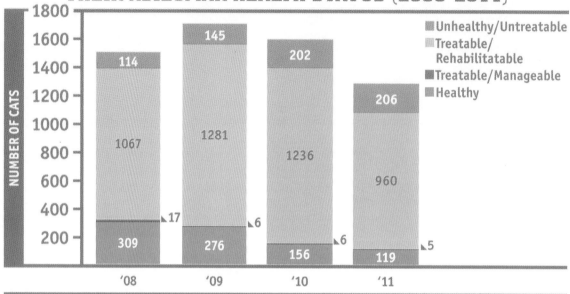

# FIGURE A2.5 DISTRIBUTION OF THE NUMBERS OF CATS ENTERING SAVING ANIMALS SHELTER BY THEIR ASILOMAR HEALTH STATUS (2008-2011)

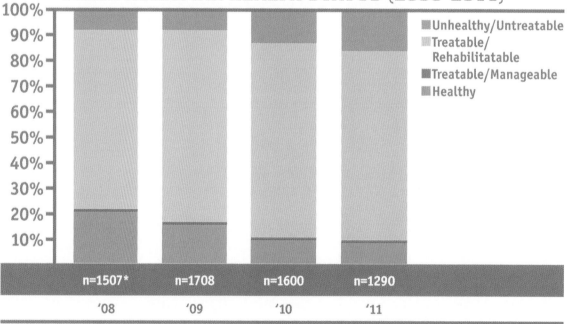

# FIGURE A2.6 PERCENTAGE OF CATS ENTERING SAVING ANIMALS SHELTER BY THEIR ASILOMAR HEALTH STATUS (2008-2011)

* Total cat intake each year.

# FIGURE A2.7 OVERALL AVERAGE LENGTH OF STAY* (ALOS) AND AVERAGE TIME TO VARIOUS "EVENTS" FOR CATS ADOPTED FROM SAVING ANIMALS SHELTER (2008 – 2012)

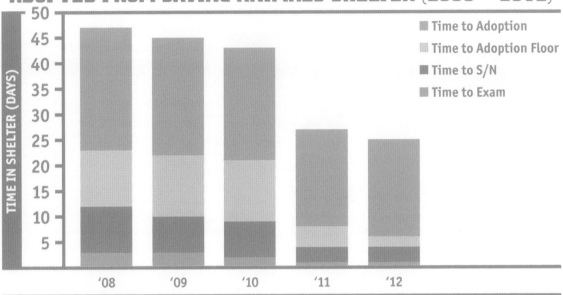

# FIGURE A2.8 DISTRIBUTION OF SOURCES FOR
# 582 DOGS ENTERING SAVING ANIMALS SHELTER (2013)

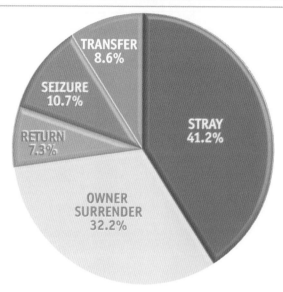

## PIE CHARTS

Pie charts are particularly helpful when the intent is to show the relative distribution of the component parts (or categories) of a whole. The relative frequency of each category is proportional to the size of the slices of the pie. For example, the shelter in Figure A2.8 was interested in showing members of its Board of Directors the relative distribution of the sources for entering dogs in 2013.

## LINE CHARTS

Line charts often work well to visualize trends over time. For example, the intake of dogs and cats are displayed using a line chart from 1997–2011 in Figure A2.9. Displaying a minimal number of horizontal grid lines to help the reader read the magnitude of the points (by moving their eyes from a point to the vertical axis) is often helpful.

As was true for bar charts, pay attention to the scale used on the vertical axis. The intent of Figure A2.10 was to illustrate the changes in intake of dogs over time in two shelters.

Notice that these shelters vary widely in the total number of dogs that they admit. To accommodate this wide variation in intake, the minimum value on the vertical axis could not be higher than ~700 (for Shelter A) or less than ~ 20,000 (for Shelter B). The relative changes in intake from 2006 to 2013 in each shelter are difficult to discern from this graph because the scale is so broad. You could compensate for this by providing the percentage change for each shelter from 2006 to 2013 below the chart, but the visual pattern of change within each shelter is still obscured.

Data for these shelters are probably best displayed using two charts (Figures A2.11 – A2.12). The percentage changes across shelters can then be compared. Dog intake declined 10% in Shelter A and 2.7% in Shelter B.

The examples used thus far have pertained to data and trends on an annual basis. Data and trends should also be evaluated at monthly and seasonal levels. The information in Figure A2.13 illustrates seasonal and monthly trends in intake by age of cats (kittens vs adults).

# FIGURE A2.9 TRENDS IN THE ANNUAL INTAKE OF DOGS AND CATS AT SAVING ANIMALS SHELTER (1997-2011)

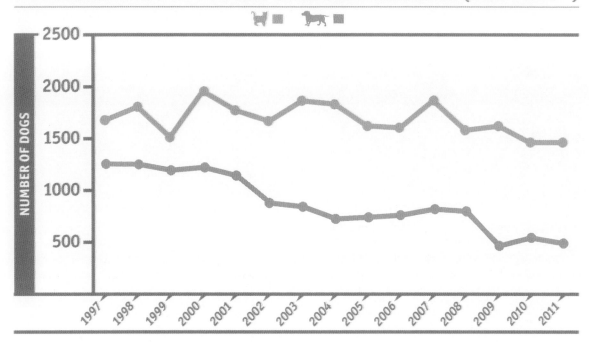

# FIGURE A2.10 COMPARISON OF ANNUAL INTAKE NUMBERS OF DOGS TO 2 SHELTERS (2006 - 2013)*

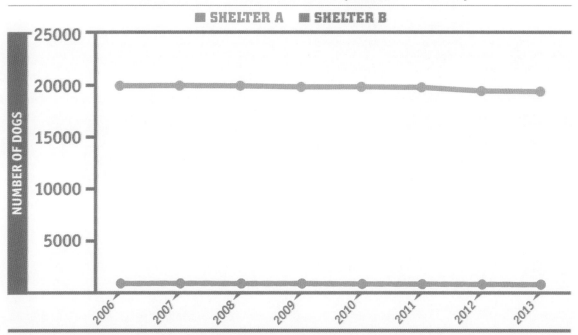

* Shelter A had a 10% decline and Shelter B had a 2.7% decline in dog intake.

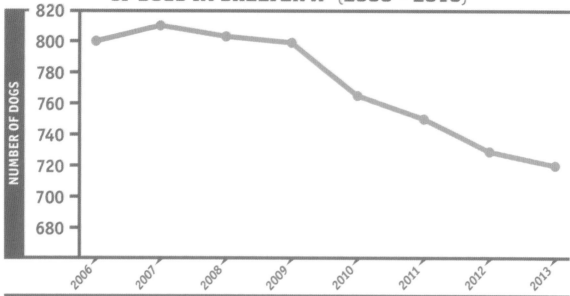

# FIGURES A2.11 TREND IN ANNUAL INTAKE NUMBERS OF DOGS IN SHELTER A* (2006 - 2013)

* The scale of the graph begins at 660, not 0. There has been a 10% decrease in the intake of dogs from 2006 – 2013.

# FIGURES A2.12 TREND IN ANNUAL INTAKE NUMBERS OF DOGS IN SHELTER B* (2006 - 2013)

* The scale of the graph begins at 19,100, not 0. There has been a 2.7% decrease in the intake of dogs from 2006 – 2013.

# FIGURE A2.13 MONTHLY INTAKE OF KITTENS** AND ADULT CATS AT SOMEWHERE SHELTER (JANUARY 2008 – DECEMBER 2010)

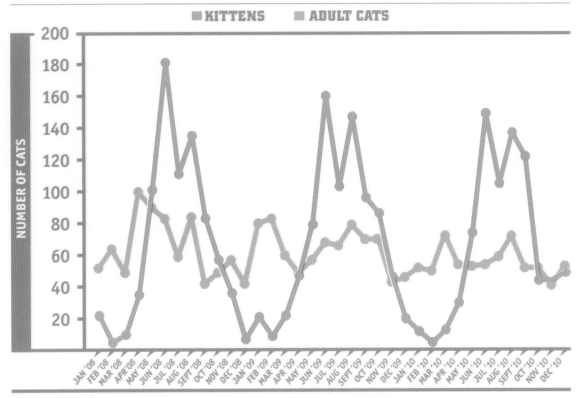

\* Kittens are defined as those < 6 months of age and adults as cats ≥ 6 months of age.

Figure A2.14 illustrates dog impoundments by town using a linear graph. Notice that it is difficult to read precise numbers and to interpret absolute differences between towns. It is easier, however, to see the trends and to discern relative differences among the towns.

## VARIATIONS ON THESE APPROACHES

Figure A2.15 is a combination bar and line graph illustrating the numbers of dogs entering Somewhere Shelter (1990 – 2011) compared to the intake per thousand human population in the community served by the shelter. When using a graph with two vertical axes it will be very important to explain to the audience what they are seeing – either verbally or in writing – as these charts are often difficult to understand at first viewing.

Photo Credit: MACC Nashville, TN

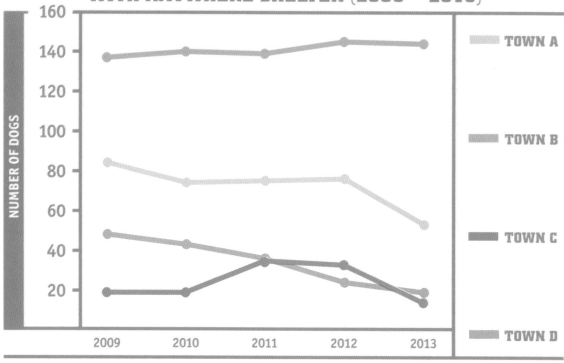

**FIGURE A2.14 ANNUAL DOG IMPOUNDMENTS FOR TOWNS WITH ANIMAL CONTROL CONTRACTS WITH ANYWHERE SHELTER (2009 – 2013)**

# SUMMARY

If you are not sure which data presentation format to use, experiment with several methods. Today's spreadsheets and graphing programs facilitate making different types of charts. Similarly, word processors make "playing" with table construction relatively easy. "Simple" and "unembellished" are key words that should describe your charts and tables. The intent is to explain and clarify, not to impress with fancy presentation. If you are planning to share your metrics with a broader audience (e.g., Board of Directors or the public), have several people not involved with the data analysis or construction of the presentation look at the display first. If they find it easy to understand then your planned audience probably will as well. Have fun and learn from your data!

Photo Credit: MACC Nashville, TN

# FIGURES A2.15 DOG INTAKE PER THOUSAND PEOPLE VERSUS ABSOLUTE DOG INTAKE NUMBERS FOR SOMEWHERE SHELTER (1990 - 2011)

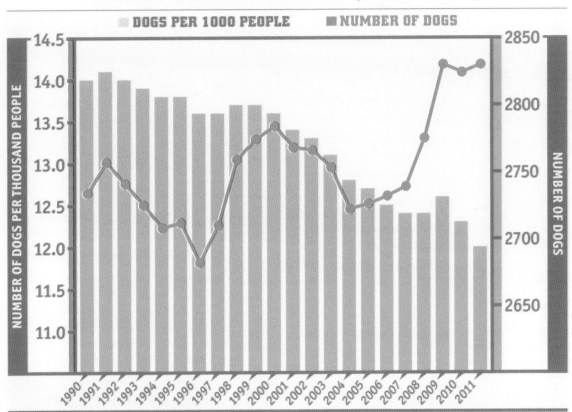

* Source for human census data: www.census.gov

# TIMING OF ANALYSES

## INTRODUCTION

For shelters that have not been evaluating their data regularly, the question of when and how frequently they should examine their metrics arises frequently. There is no one answer to this question as the nature and frequency of monitoring metrics depend heavily on your shelter's goals. That said, an extensive review of your shelter's metrics should take place at least annually. For many metrics (e.g., disease rates, ALOS), however, only monitoring once yearly is likely to miss information that could improve your operations in a timely manner.

## COMPARISONS OF DATA FROM THE YEAR(S) BEFORE

Many of the metrics suggested in this Guide can be run retrospectively – that is, for past time periods if the data are accessible. For example, if you want to monitor your shelter's Risk Live Release Rate (RLRR) by month, then examining the RLRR by month for the last several years will provide a context within which to interpret your current data. We recommend looking back at data from previous years in order to enhance understanding of recent information.

*Suggestions* for the frequency of monitoring various summary metrics are presented in Table 1. We suggest subsetting your data into at least two age groups: juveniles (specifically defined) and adults. A third age group, unweaned animals is im-

portant for shelters planning to place these animals in foster care and to monitor their health. For metrics monitored monthly, it is easy to look at seasonal trends as well by combining data across the months in a season. Those metrics that we find helpful to monitor quarterly/seasonally have an "X" in Table A3.1 in the quarterly column.

# MONITORING DISEASE DURING AN OUTBREAK

Depending on the cause of a disease outbreak, at least daily monitoring of the incidence of that disease is important. Diseases with explosive incidence or incubation periods measured in hours may require even more frequent assessment. Monitoring frequently will enable the construction of an informative **epidemic curve**.

## DAILY MONITORING

Daily inventories or counts of animals at a set time by location in the shelter system (including offsite venues and foster care) are probably the most important metrics to monitor daily. These can also be reported by source (e.g., owner-surrender, stray) and age group. Assessing the shelter's census in relation to housing capacity maximizes the shelter's ability to take timely actions to remedy overcrowding, and to design and evaluate the success of scheduled admissions programs. Various other reports can also be helpful to the daily management of animals. These might include reports listing animals requiring vaccinations, treatments, preparation for transfer, and so forth for each day.

## WEEKLY MONITORING

Recording and plotting the numbers of animals still in the shelter (SIS) at the end of each week over time

# TABLE A3.1 SUGGESTED FREQUENCY FOR MONITORING VARIOUS METRICS IN YOUR SHELTER

| All reports are done separately for dogs and cats | Annually | Quarterly | Monthly | Weekly |
|---|---|---|---|---|
| **INTAKE** | | | | |
| Annual Intake Profile | ✔ | | | |
| Intake by day of the week by source | | | ✔ | ✔ |
| Trends in intake | ✔ | ✔ | ✔ | |
|     By age group, source | ✔ | ✔ | ✔ | |
| Returned adoptions | ✔ | | ✔ | |
| Intake by jurisdiction | ✔ | | | |
| Intake by health status | ✔ | ✔ | | |
| Intake by breed | ✔ | | | |
| Intake by spay/neuter status | ✔ | | | |
| Intake by reasons for surrender | ✔ | | | |
| Intake by human population | ✔ | | | |
| Intake by geographic location (GIS) in the community | ✔ | | | |
| **OUTCOMES** | | | | |
| Annual Outcome Profile | ✔ | | | |
| Rate-Based Live Release Rate | ✔ | | ✔ | |
|     By source, age group | ✔ | | ✔ | |
| Adoption rate | ✔ | | ✔ | |
| Return-to-owner rate | ✔ | ✔ | ✔ | |
| Transferred-out rate | ✔ | ✔ | ✔ | |
| Returned to community rate | ✔ | | ✔ | |
| Still-in-shelter rate | | | ✔ | ✔ |
| Euthanasia rate | ✔ | | ✔ | |
| Mortality rate | ✔ | | ✔ | |
| Lost/Other rate | ✔ | | | |
| Reasons for euthanasia | ✔ | | | |
| Outcomes by health status | ✔ | | | |
| Adoptions by day of week | | | ✔ | ✔ |

| All reports are done separately for dogs and cats | Annually | Quarterly | Monthly | Weekly |
|---|:---:|:---:|:---:|:---:|
| **CAPACITY** | | | | |
| Staff Capacity Profile | ✔ | | ✔ | |
| Average daily inventory* | | | ✔ | ✔ |
|    By location | | | ✔ | ✔ |

*Inventory: number of animals present at a specific time of day (e.g., midnight) each day.

| All reports are done separately for dogs and cats | Annually | Quarterly | Monthly | Weekly |
|---|:---:|:---:|:---:|:---:|
| **AVERAGE LENGTH OF STAY (ALOS)** | | | | |
| Annual ALOS Profile | ✔ | | | |
| ALOS | ✔ | | ✔ | |
|    By breed, source, age | ✔ | | ✔ | |
| Average time to adoption | ✔ | | ✔ | |
| Average time to euthanasia | ✔ | | ✔ | |
| Average time in foster care | ✔ | | ✔ | |
| Average time on the adoption floor | ✔ | | ✔ | |
| Average time to spay/neuter | ✔ | | ✔ | |
| **MEDICAL DATA** | | | | |
| Annual Medical Profile | ✔ | | | |
| * Trends in incidence of URI in cats | ✔ | | ✔ | |
|    By age group | ✔ | | ✔ | |
| * Trends in incidence of canine respiratory complex | ✔ | | ✔ | |
| * Trends in incidence of other disease(s)/signs | ✔ | | | |
| Euthanasia due to disease | ✔ | | ✔ | |
| Mortality due to disease | ✔ | | ✔ | |
| Prevalence of FeLV, FIV, heartworm disease | ✔ | | | |
| Number of S/N surgeries performed: | | | | |
|    On shelter-owned animals | ✔ | | ✔ | |
|    On privately owned animals | ✔ | | ✔ | |
| Percentage of shelter animals sterilized at final disposition | ✔ | | ✔ | |
| General health status at entry and exit | ✔ | | ✔ | |

*If these diseases are of interest to your shelter. The frequency of monitoring will depend on the magnitude of the problem.

can quickly alert the shelter to delays in animal flow that it might not otherwise recognize. If the numbers of animals SIS begin to increase beyond the shelter's capacity for care, reasons for the problem must be researched and remedies enacted.

## MONTHLY MONITORING

Many metrics should be monitored and plotted by month throughout the year (Figure A3.1). For example, a line graph of intake data for stray cats could be updated monthly to illustrate monthly trends. Ideally, similar data from the previous 1-2 years would also be presented on the same graph to look for changes over time and to assess the usual variability in these counts.

## QUARTERLY MONITORING

Many metrics may vary seasonally. Either the monthly data (divided into quarters) can be monitored or all of the data for a quarter can be summarized and plotted. Health status information for entering and exiting animals are probably best reviewed on a quarterly or annual basis to allow sufficient time for changes to be expressed (if they occur).

# FIGURE A3.1 INTAKE OF STRAY CATS BY MONTH: 1/2011–8/2013

**2011** **2012** **2013**

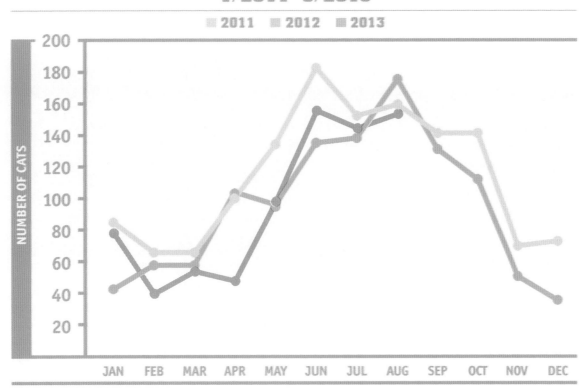

## ANNUAL MONITORING

Depending on the budget cycle of a shelter, a month or two before the budget is decided for the next year is an ideal time to collate and review metrics from the previous year for members of the Board of Directors and staff. The metrics can help with setting goals and budgets. If data have been monitored monthly throughout the year, surprises will be minimized and the shelter can focus on planning. Most shelters also produce an annual report for the public that should contain some of the metrics suggested above.

## SUMMARY

This appendix contains suggestions only, and monitoring of data should be tailored to a shelter's specific needs and resources.

# GLOSSARY

*The definitions of terms in this Glossary are a key to interpreting their meaning in this book and may differ from those used in other sources.*

**ACTION PLANS** describe in detail how a goal will be achieved. Such plans are most effective if they include a prioritized checklist of steps that serves as a roadmap to the achievement of the goal.

**ASILOMAR ACCORDS** were written in 2004 by a group of animal welfare industry leaders from throughout the U.S. at the Asilomar Conference Grounds in Pacific Grove, CA. They were written to build bridges across various sheltering philosophies and encourage the development of strategies for reducing the euthanasia of healthy and treatable shelter animals. Four categories describing the general health status of shelter animals were created: healthy, treatable-rehabilitatable, treatable-manageable, and unhealthy-untreatable (shelteranimalscount.org). These categories were defined in the Accords in broad and general terms. Shelters were instructed to define the specific diseases, conditions and behavioral issues that would be associated with each category in their shelter based on how reasonable, caring owners might provide care for animals with these conditions in *their* community.

**AVERAGE DAILY INVENTORY** see Daily Inventory

**AVERAGE LENGTH OF STAY (ALOS)** see Length of Stay

**CARE-DAY (OR CAGE-DAY)** is a day or fraction of a day that an animal spends in the shelter and requires care and housing space.

**CARE–DAYS (ALSO CALLED CAGE-DAYS)** of housing space are the number of humane housing spaces available for housing animals during a specified period of time. They are calculated by multiplying the number of Humane Housing Units (HHUs) by the number of days in the time period of interest. These calculations are frequently done by age group (e.g., kittens vs adult cats) and size of adults since humane housing needs often vary by these subgroups.

**CASE-FATALITY RATE** is the number of animals dying of a particular disease divided by the number of cases of that disease in a defined time period. It is often calculated in outbreaks to indicate the severity of the disease involved and is usually expressed as a percentage.

**CATEGORICAL DATA** see Variable

**COMMUNITY ANIMALS** have been defined in various ways. Most often we use this terminology to refer to animals that reside in the shelter from your community. The most common categories of these animals are owner-surrendered, stray, returned adoptions and seized animals originating in the shelter's service area. We distinguish these animals from those originating outside of your community that do not reflect the effects of your shelter's programs (e.g., educational, S/N, TNR).

**COMMUNITY CATS** This terminology has come to refer to cats that enter a shelter as strays, and are apparently unowned. They may be feral (un-socialized to humans), previously owned (lost or abandoned), or owned, but without identifying information.

**CONTINUOUS DATA** see Variable

**CUMULATIVE INCIDENCE** or **INCIDENCE PROPORTION** is the number of newly diagnosed cases of "disease" (e.g., parvovirus) divided by the number of animals that were eligible (or at risk) to develop that disease in a specified interval of time (e.g., one year, one month). This metric is usually expressed as a percentage. Many in veterinary medicine refer to this metric as an *incidence rate*. It measures the risk of animals developing "disease" in a specified period of time. Technically it requires that all animals "at risk" be followed for the entire period which is not true in many shelters. Despite this, we recommend its use in shelters for disease surveillance because it is easy to understand and is adequate for routine monitoring of disease frequency.

**DAILY INVENTORY** is the number of animals in a shelter (or area) each day. The words "census" and "inventory" may have different definitions in various software programs. Consult your software provider to clarify the definitions used in your software.

> **AVERAGE DAILY INVENTORY** is the sum of the daily inventory numbers divided by the number of days in a specified period of time.

**DISEASE** is defined very broadly in this book. The metrics we discuss relate not just to disease as traditionally defined but also to a broad range of factors that relate to animal welfare (e.g., outcome, movement through the shelter).

**DISEASE SURVEILLANCE** is 1) the ongoing sys-

tematic collection, orderly consolidation, analysis and interpretation of health-related data in populations, and 2) the prompt dissemination of this information to the people who are in a position to act on that data.

**DYNAMIC HOUSING CAPACITY** see Housing Capacity.

**FAST-TRACKED ANIMALS** are highly adoptable shelter residents (often puppies, kittens, small or purebred dogs) that can have very short lengths of stay if offered for adoption as soon as possible, even ahead of less adoptable animals.

**GEOGRAPHIC INFORMATION SYSTEMS (GIS)** is computer software that enables data to be gathered, analyzed and mapped geographically (http //www.esri.com/what-is-gis). In shelters, for example, it can be used to map the origin of various intake groups such as kittens, stray cats or other groups in order to identify high intake areas and target preventive measures to them. Many other uses are possible.

**GOALS** are very specific, actionable steps tied to an objective that are designed to be intermediate steps towards achievement of that objective. For example, a goal related to the objective of reducing shelter intake of cats might be "the shelter will double the number of owned cat S/N surgeries in Trailer park A and B over the next 6 months."

> Goals should be **S.M.A.R.T** - **S**pecific, have a **M**easureable marker of achievement, **A**ttainable (achievable), **R**elevant and **T**ime-bound (have an explicit time when the goal should be completed).

**GRAPHS** (or **CHARTS**) Numerous types of graphs or charts can be used to visually display data.

> **BAR GRAPH** consists of vertical or horizontal bars whose lengths are proportional to amounts or quantities of data

or things being displayed. Bar graphs are used to facilitate comparisons between categories of animals, costs, and other categorical variables.

**STACKED BAR GRAPH** is used to compare the parts to a whole. The bars in a stacked bar graph are divided into categories of the whole and the number (or percentage) of animals in each category are placed adjacent to one another in the same bar.

**PIE CHART** is a graphic representation of categorical data where each category of a variable is represented by a "slice" in a circle resembling a pie. The relative sizes of the slices correspond to the relative sizes or percentages of the various categories (e.g., each slice might contain the number (or percentage) of animals that are < 6 months, 6-24 months, and > 24 months of the variable age).

**LINE GRAPH** is a graph that uses points connected by lines to show how something changes in value, often as time progresses.

**HOST FACTORS** This terminology is used by epidemiologists and veterinarians to describe characteristics of animals that can profoundly affect their susceptibility and response to disease; they are important to preventive and disease control strategies. In a broader sense these same characteristics often affect how animals are managed in an animal shelter. The most common host factors include species, age, gender, neuter status, and breed.

## HOUSING CAPACITY

**STATIC HOUSING CAPACITY** is the number of animals that can be humanely housed at any one point in time. This could be within the entire shelter system, the shelter building(s), in an area of the shelter or in foster care.

**DYNAMIC HOUSING CAPACITY** is the number of animals that can be humanely housed during any period of time. This also could be within the entire shelter system, the shelter building(s), in an area of the shelter or in foster care. The dynamic housing capacity can also be thought of as "animal flow-through" or "throughput" of animals during a period of time.

**STAFF CAPACITY FOR ANIMAL CARE** is the number of staff necessary to provide humane care to animals of all types in a shelter. Guidelines exist for calculating the minimum staff needed to clean and feed shelter animals, but not yet for other types of care.

**HUMANE HOUSING UNIT (HHU)** is defined in this book as an animal housing space that meets or exceeds current guidelines for housing an animal (ASV, 2010). It may be a cage, run, space in a room or some other form of housing. The definition of an HHU often varies by the characteristics of the animal (e.g., age, size).

**INCIDENCE RATE** (or **INCIDENCE DENSITY**) is another measure of the incidence of disease used in epidemiologic research to quantify the rate of disease occurrence in populations where animals in the "at risk" population enter and leave the population frequently during the period of interest. It is expressed as the number of new cases per a measure of animal-time (e.g., cat-days, dog-months).

**INTAKE** of animals to a shelter (broadly defined) can include owner-surrendered animals, strays, returned adoptions, transfers-in, animals born in the shelter's care, legally held animals (e.g., seized and health department holds for rabies observation), animals boarding, in special programs (e.g., domestic violence housing for pets), dead on arrival (DOA), privately owned animals entering to be sterilized, cats trapped for sterilization and returned to the community or to a colony, or animals euthanized at the owner's request. Which groups of animals are

Photo Credit: Adrian Budnick Puptography

counted in the overall intake metrics of a shelter is determined by each shelter.

**LENGTH OF STAY (LOS)** is the total number of days an animal spends in the care of a welfare organization/shelter. It is commonly calculated as follows **(Date of exit – Date of entry) + 1 day**. A complete or fraction of a day of residence is usually counted as 1 day.

> **AVERAGE LENGTH OF STAY (ALOS)** is the sum of the LOS values for all animals in the organization/shelter divided by the number of animals in a defined period of time.
>
> Computer programs can calculate ALOS more precisely using the actual time of day an animal enters and leaves the shelter. We prefer attributing a full day to animals that spend even partial days in residence. This is because animals in residence for less than a day still require housing, food, and staff care.

**LIVE RELEASE RATE (LRR)** has been defined in several ways. All calculations are usually converted to percentages by multiplying the fractions by 100.

> **INTAKE-BASED LRR** divides all animals released alive in a given period of time by the number of animal entering the shelter in that same time period.
>
> **ASILOMAR LRR** is the number of animals released alive divided by those released alive, plus those euthanized, plus healthy and treatable animals surrendered by their owners for euthanasia in the same time period.
>
> **FINAL DISPOSITION-BASED LRR** is the number of animals released alive divided by the number of animals that have had a final disposition in the same time period.
>
> **RATE-BASED LIVE RELEASE RATE (RLRR)** is the number of animals that were released alive divided by all those that were "eligible" in a given period of time to be released. "Eligible" animals usually include all animals entering the shelter during the period plus those that were already present at the beginning of the first day of the interval. We recommend that the RLRRs of seized animals, on rabies hold, and in special programs be analyzed separately.
>
> **Other outcome metrics** (e.g., adoption rate) can be calculated using the same denominator as the live release rate - but with the number of animals adopted, lost, euthanized, died, returned-to-the community or transferred-out in the numerator. These fractions are also usually multiplied by 100 to create percentages. The return-to-owner rate is calculated by dividing the number of animals returned to their owners by the number of stray animals in the shelter during the same time frame.

**MEAN** is the sum of all numbers observed divided by the number of observations. For *Normally* distributed data, the mean represents that number above which approximately ½ of the observations lie and below which approximately ½ of the observations lie. Synonyms include arithmetic mean or average.

**MEDIAN** is the middle-most value in a set of observations that has been ordered from the smallest to the largest value. It lies at the 50th percentile and divides the observations into two equally sized groups - ½ above the median and ½ below.

**METRICS** are summary data that shelters use to measure how they are doing. The word metrics is also used to refer to a standard of measurement or a benchmark. In this book, our use of the terminology will sometimes refer only to data as a measure of what a shelter is doing (e.g., the shelter is accepting 32% of cats that have already been neutered), and at other times as a measure of how a shelter is progressing (e.g., benchmarking its progress over time towards meeting its goals).

**MORTALITY RATE (SYNONYMS: CUMULATIVE MORTALITY OR MORTALITY PROPORTION)** is the number of animals dying of natural causes divided by the number of animals at risk of dying in a specified interval of time. The rate is often expressed as a percentage.

**NORMALLY DISTRIBUTED DATA (SYNONYM: GAUSSIAN)** describe the distribution of a set of observations where the middle of the data is the mean and other observations are distributed symmetrically around the mean giving the entire distribution a "bell-shape."

**OBJECTIVES** usually flow from an organization's Mission statement and state in broad terms what a shelter wishes to accomplish with regards to its Mission. Objectives generally are lofty aspirations that may take many years to accomplish or may never be completely achieved. For example, a shelter might have an objective of eliminating animal intake from the community, realizing that this might take years or never be achieved. Many shelters develop a few broad objectives accompanied by many sub-objectives.

**OUTCOME RATES** see Live Release Rate

**OUTCOME STATUS** describes the final disposition of an animal at the end of a time period of interest (e.g., annually, seasonally, monthly). Outcomes can include adoptions, returns-to-owners, transfers to other organizations, euthanasias, died-in-shelter, lost-in-shelter, returned-to-the community, placed-in-a-barn and other categories used by a shelter. We also include the category, "still-in-shelter" which refers to animals that remain in the shelter's care at the end of the period of interest so that all possible outcomes at the end of a period are represented.

**OUTCOME-ELIGIBLE ANIMALS** are those that can experience (or are at risk of experiencing) specific outcomes during a specified period of time. The precise nature of these animals depends on the question a shelter is asking.

**PERCENTILES OF A SET OF NUMBERS** in a distribution of numbers are calculated first by putting all of the values in numerical order starting with the smallest and ending with the largest.

The 25th percentile (or 1st quartile) is that number above which 3/4s of the data in a set of numbers lies. The 50th percentile (or second quartile) is the median and tells you the number below (and above) which ½ of the data lie; and the 75th percentile (or third quartile) tells you the number above which ¼ of the observations lie.

Other percentiles in a distribution can also be calculated. For example, the 95th percentile would tell you the number above which 5% of the data lie.

**PERIOD PREVALENCE** is a measure of prevalence in which the number of existing cases during a specified period of time is divided by the number of animals at risk during that period of time.

**POINT PREVALENCE** is a measure of the frequency of disease in a population; it is the number of existing cases of a particular disease (or the number of animals that have the disease) divided by the number of animals in the population at risk of that disease at a particular point in time. Many in veterinary medicine call this metric a "point prevalence rate."

**RANGE** is the difference between the highest and lowest number in a distribution of numbers. This difference does not tell you the value of the highest or lowest number. The **minimum** and **maximum** numbers in a set of number are used as another measure of the variability of data. The range can be calculated knowing these numbers (e.g., maximum value – minimum value).

**SLOW-TRACKED ANIMALS** are shelter residents for which no special attempts are made to expedite their flow through the shelter.

**STANDARD DEVIATION** is a measure of the average

variability of observations around the mean of Normally distributed data.

**STILL-IN-SHELTER (SIS)** are animals that remain in the shelter's care at the end of a specified time interval.

**STRATEGIES** describe in general terms how the objectives of a shelter will be achieved. For example, strategies for reducing shelter intake from the community might include a spay/neuter program for low-income residents, a TNR program for free-roaming cats, and a behavior hotline to assist residents with behavioral issues that might lead to relinquishment. Multiple strategies are usually associated with any objective.

**VARIABLE** is any characteristic, number, or quantity that can be measured or counted. Age group, gender, final disposition, and type of shelter are examples of variables. Variables are often defined by the type of data that they contain.

**CATEGORICAL VARIABLES** contain data that are collected in mutually exclusive categories such as gender (male or female), and outcome (alive, dead, or still-in-shelter).

**CONTINUOUS VARIABLES** contain data for which the differences between numbers can be measured on a numerical scale (e.g., age, intake numbers, weight). Continuous data can be broken down into categories to make them categorical variables.

# REFERENCE LIST

ASPCApro. (2013a) The X Maps Spot GIS Program [Information on a page]. Retrieved from http://www.aspw=capro.org/gis. Accessed April 13, 2014.

ASPCApro. (2013b) NFHS Basic matrix aspca.pro/sites/default/files/nfhs-basic-matrix-fillable.pdf.

ASPCApro. (2013c) ASPCA research: Less is more on the adoption floor [Information on a page]. http://www.aspcapro.org/resource/saving-lives-adoption-marketing-research-data/aspca-research-less-more-adoption-floor, Accessed, March 12, 2014.

ASPCApro. (2014a) Live release rate and animals at risk [Information on a page]. http://aspcapro.org/live-release-rate-and-animals-risk, Accessed March 10, 2015.

ASPCApro. (2014b) Turning visitors into adopters [Information on a page]. Retrieved from http://www.aspcapro.org/resource/saving-lives-research-data/turning-visitors-adopters, Accessed, March 12, 2014.

ASPCApro. (2015a) What's the deal about data? [Information on a page]. Retrieved from http://www.aspcapro.org/resource/saving-lives-research-data/whats-deal-about-data), Accessed April 11, 2014.

ASPCApro. (2015b) Video introduction to GIS mapping [Information on a page]. Retrieved from http://www.aspcapro.org/resource/saving-lives-research-data/video-introduction-gis-mapping, Accessed, March 12, 2014.

Association of Shelter Veterinarians (2010) Guidelines for Standards of Care in Animal Shelters"(http://www.sheltervet.org/about/shelter-standards/), Accessed June 4, 2013.

Cannas da Silva, J., Noordhuizen, J. P., Vagneur, M., Bexiga, R., Gelfert, C. C., & Baumgartner, W. (2006). Veterinary dairy herd health management in Europe: constraints and perspectives. *Veterinary Quarterly*, 28, 23-32.

Caribbean Animal Health Network (n.d.) Presentation of Data http://www.caribvet.net/en/system/files/presentation20of20data_word.pdf, Accessed July 8, 2014.

Clancy, E.A., Rowan, A.N. (2003). Companion animal demographics in the United States: A historical perspective. In (Salem, D.J., Rowan, A.N., eds) The State of the Animals II, Humane Society Press, pgs. 9-26.

Conrad, S. (in Burkus, D.) (2012) Setting effective organizational goals. [Guest post] http://www.davidburkus/2012/04/setting-effective-organizational-goals/, Accessed Nov 5, 2014.

Cothran, H.M., Wysocki, A.F., Farnsworth, D., Clark, D.L. (2015) Developing SMART goals for your organization. University of Florida, IFAS Extension, http://edis.ifas.ufl.edu/fe577, Accessed, Dec 8, 2016.

Davis, Jeffery (1996) Chapter 1, Managing and Achieving Organization Goals. American Management Association, New York, NY. Retrieved from http://www.flexstudy.com/catalog/index.cfm?location=sch&coursenum=95086, Accessed Nov 27, 2014.

Dawson, B., Trapp, R.G. (2004). Basic and Clinical Biostatistics, New York: Lange Medical Books/McGraw-Hill, pgs. 26-27, 76-78.

DiGiacomo, N., Arluke, A., & Patronek, G. J. (1999). Surrendering pets to shelters: The relinquishers' perspective. *Anthrozoos* 11: 41-51.

Dinnage, J., Scarlett, J.M. (2009) Descriptive epidemiology of feline upper respiratory tract disease in an animal shelter *Journal of Feline Medicine & Surgery* 11: 817-825.

Dwyer, D., Groves, C., Blythe, D. (2014) in Infectious Disease Epidemiology (Nelson, KE, Masters Williams, C (eds). Burlington, MA: Jones & Barlett Learning, LLC, an Ascend Learning Co., pgs. 106-107.

Edinboro, C.H., M.P. Ward, and L.T. Glickman. (2004) A placebo-controlled trial of two intranasal vaccines to prevent tracheobronchitis (kennel cough) in dogs entering a humane shelter. *Preventive Veterinary Medicine*. 62: 89-99.

Farm Animal Welfare Council. (n.d.) Five Freedoms. http://webarchive.nationalarchives.gov.uk/20121007104210/http://www.fawc.org.uk/freedoms.htm, Accessed April 17, 2015.

Fletcher, R.H., Fletcher, S.W., Fletcher, G.S. (2014). Clinical Epidemiology: The Essentials. Philadelphia: Wolters Kluwer/Lippincott Williams & Wilkins, pgs. 18-22; 111-120

Frank, J. M. & Carlisle-Frank, P. L. (2007). Analysis of programs to reduce overpopulation of companion animals: Do adoption and low-cost spay/neuter programs merely cause substitution of sources? *Ecological Economics*. 62: 740-746.

Gavin, Ed (1989) In the name of mercy. http://doggymomblog.files.wordpress.com/2012/05/ed-duvin-article-1989.pdf, Accessed July 31, 2014.

Gordis, L. (2014) Epidemiology. Philadelphia: Elsevier/Saunders, pgs. 41-49.

Griffin, B. and Hume, K.R. (2006) Recognition and management of stress in housed cats, in Consultations in Feline Internal Medicine, Vol. 5 (ed: J. August), W.B. Saunders Company, St. Louis, Missouri, pgs. 717-734.

Haston, R.(2015) Beyond labels: understanding the true impact of live release rates and intake policies. https://www.youtube.com/watch?v=quWrG7YAjkw&feature=youtu.be, Accessed March 24, 2015.

Haughey, D. (2014) SMART goals. http://www.projectsmart.co.uk/smart-goals.php, Accessed Nov. 18, 2014.

Howell, D.C. (2015) Treatment of missing data – Part 1. http://www.uvm.edu/~dhowell/StatPages/Missing_Data/Missing.html, Accessed November 12, 2016.

Humane Society of the United States (HSUS). (2010) General staffing recommendations for kennel caretaking. http://www.animalsheltering.org/resource_library/policies_and_guidelines/kennel_caretaking_staffing.html.

Hurley, K. F. (2004). Implementing a population health plan in an animal shelter: Goal Setting, data collection and monitoring, and policy development. In L. Miller & S. Zawistowski (Eds.), Shelter Medicine for Veterinarians and Staff. Ames, Iowa: Blackwell Publishing, pgs. 211-234.

Kessler, M. and Turner, D. (1999) Socialization and stress in cats (Felis silverstris catus) housed singly and in groups in animal shelters. *Animal Welfare*, 8: 15-26.

Knafflic, Cole Nussbaumer (2015) Storytelling with Data: *A Visual Guide for Business Professionals*. Hoboken, NJ: John Wiley and Sons, Inc., pgs. 35-69.

Koret Shelter Medicine Program (2015a) Length of stay. http://www.sheltermedicine.com/library/length-of-stay-los, Accessed, July 4, 2016.

Koret Shelter Medicine Program (2015b) Fast track/slow track flow-through planning. http://www.sheltermedicine.com/library/resources/fast-track-slow-track-flow-through-planning, Accessed Dec 6, 2016.

Koret Shelter Medicine Program (2015c) http://www.sheltermedicine.com/library/adoption-driven-capacity-calculator-your-shelter-s-key-to-saving-lives-and-providing-great-care, Accessed July 5, 2016.

Lawler, D.F. (1998) Prevention and management of infection in catteries. In Infectious Diseases of the Dog and Cat, (C.E. Greene, Ed.), Philadelphia: WB Saunders Co., pgs. 701-706.

Lyons, R. (n.d.) Best practices in graphical data presentation. Library Assessment Conference, (http://libraryassessment.org/bm~doc/workshop_lyons_ray.pdf, Accessed July 8, 2014.

Locke, E.A., Latham, G.P., Smith, K.J., Wood, R.E. (1990) A Theory of Goal Setting & Task Performance. Prentice Hall College Div.

Maddie's Fund, (2015) Shelter and rescue statistics [Information on a page]. Retrieved from http://www.maddiesfund.org/shelter-and-rescue-data.htm, Accessed September 26, 2016.

Marsh, P. (2010) Replacing Myth with Math. Concord, New Hampshire: Town and Country Reprographics. www.shelteroverpopulation.org/SOS_Chapter-1.pdf, Accessed May 12, 2014.

McMillan, F.D. (2000) Quality of life in animals. Journal of the American Veterinary Medical Association 216:1904-1910.

McMillan, F.D. (2013) Quality of life, stress, and emotional pain in shelter animals. In: Shelter Medicine for Veterinarians and Staff. 2nd edition. (eds. L. Miller & S. Zawistowski). pp. 83-92. Wiley-Blackwell, Iowa, pgs. 83-92.

National Animal Care and Control Association (NACA) (2009) Determining Kennel Staffing needs. http://www.nacanet.org/?page=kennelstaffing, Accessed December 8, 2016

New, J. C. J., Salman, M. D., Scarlett, J. M., Kass, P. H., Vaughn, J. A., Scherr, S. et al. (1999). Moving: Characteristics of dogs and cats and those relinquishing them to 12 U.S. animal shelters. Journal of Applied Animal Welfare Science, 2: 83-96.

Newbury, S., Hurley, K. (2013) Population management. In: Shelter Medicine for Veterinarians and Staff. 2nd edition. (eds. L. Miller & S. Zawistowski) Wiley-Blackwell, Iowa, pgs. 93-113.

Patronek, G. J., Glickman, L. T., Beck, A. M., McCabe, G. P., & Ecker, C. (1996a). Risk factors for relinquishment of cats to an animal shelter. Journal of the American Veterinary Medical Association, 209: 582-588.

Patronek, G. J., Glickman, L. T., Beck, A. M., McCabe, G. P., & Ecker, C. (1996b). Risk factors for relinquishment of dogs to an animal shelter. Journal of the American Veterinary Medical Association, 209: 572-581.

Pedersen, N.C. (1991) Common infectious diseases of multiple cat environments. In Feline Husbandry, (eds. N. Pederesen, Goleta, CA): American Veterinary Publications, pgs. 163-176.

Petrie, A., Watson, P. (2006) Statistics for Veterinary and Animal Science. Oxford: Blackwell Publishing, pgs. 33-41.

Rochlitz, I. ( 2005) A review of the housing requirement of domestic cats (Felis silverstris catus) kept in a home. Applied Animal Behavior Science, 93: 97-109.

Rothman, K.J. (2012). Epidemiology: An Introduction. Oxford: Oxford University Press, pgs. 38-47; 53-57.

Rowan, A. N. & Williams, J. (1987). The success of companion animal management programs: a review. Anthrozoos, 1:110-122.

Rowan, A. N. (1992). Shelters and Pet Overpopulation: A statistical black and white. *Anthrozoös*, 5: 140-143.

Salman, M. D., Hutchison, J., Ruch-Gallie, R., Kogan, L., New, J. C., Kass, P. H. et al. (2000). Behavioral reasons for relinquishment of dogs and cats to 12 shelters. *Journal of Applied Animal Welfare Science*, 3:93-106.

Salman, M. (2003) Surveillance and Monitoring Systems for Animal Health Programs and Disease Surveys. In: Animal Disease Surveillance and Survey Systems: Methods and Applications (Salman, M, ed.) Iowa: Iowa State Press and Blackwell Publishing Co.

Scarlett, J. M., Salman, M. D., New, J. G. J., & Kass, P. H. (1999). Reasons for relinquishment of companion animals in U.S. animal shelters: Selected health and personal issues. *Journal of Applied Animal Welfare Science*, 2:41-57.

Scarlett, J. & Johnston, N. (2012a). Impact of a subsidized spay neuter clinic on impoundments and euthanasia in a community shelter and on service and complaint calls to animal control. *Journal of Applied Animal Welfare Science*, 15:53-69.

Scarlett, J.M. . (2012b, March). Magical Metrics and Dazzling Data: How Medical Fact-Finding Guides Shelters to Improved Animal Health. Podcast http://www.maddiesfund.org/Maddies_Institute/ Webcasts/Magical_Metrics_and_Dazzling_Data. html, Accessed May 13, 2014.

Schwartz, B., Ward, A. (2004) The paradox of choice. In Positive Psychology in Practice, (Linley, P.A., Joseph, S., eds), pgs. 86-103.

Shelter Animals Count (n.d.) Asilomar Accords http://www.shelteranimalscount.org/who-we-are-/history, Accessed, December 8, 2016.

Shelter Animals Count (2016) Basic Animal Data Matrix http://shelteranimalscount.org/docs/default-source/DataResources/sac_basicdatamatrix.pdf?sfvrsn=2, Accessed November 22, 2016,

Tufte, E.D. (2001) The Visual Display of Quantitative Information. Cheshire, CT: Graphics Press.

United Nations Economic Commission for Europe. (2009) Making Data Meaningful Part 2. A Guide to Presenting Statistics. Geneva: United Nations. http://www.unece.org/stats/documents/writing. html, Accessed July 8, 2014.

Weiss, E., Slater, M., Garrison, L., Drain, N., Dolan, E., Scarlett, J.M., Zawistowski, S.L. (2014) Large dog relinquishment to two municipal facilities in New York City and Washington, D.C.: Identifying targets for intervention. *Animals* 4(3):409-433. Doi:10.3390/ani4030409.

Wenstrup, J. & Dowidchuk, A. (1999). Pet overpopulation: data and measurement issues in shelters. *Journal of Applied Animal Welfare Science*, 2:303-319.

White, S. C., Jefferson, E., & Levy, J. K. (2010). Impact of publicly sponsored neutering programs on animal population dynamics at animal shelters: The New Hampshire and Austin Experiences. *Journal of Applied Animal Welfare Science*, 13:191-212.

Zawistowski, S., Morris, J., Salman, M. D., & Ruch-Gallie, R. (1998). Population dynamics, overpopulation, and the welfare of companion animals: New insights on old and new data. *Journal of Applied Animal Welfare Science*, 1:193-206.

Printed in Great Britain
by Amazon

21549430R00114